Acknowledgements

Academic books come to fruition for a variety of reasons. Some are planned out years in advance and represent a labour of intellectual love. Others are the findings of discrete research projects. Some come to pass with the aim of filling a particular gap in the market. All three of those reasons contributed in part to the development of this book, but the real catalyst was a chance discussion with Agenda Publishing's Alison Howson in the Spring of 2016. Alison's interest in corruption analysis and my frustration at not having a text around which I could shape my teaching led to this book being born. Without her enthusiasm both during that original conversation and thereafter, this book would not exist.

The aim of the book is simple: it looks to analyse what corruption is, why it happens and what options there are for tackling it. Clearly, none of these three questions are as easy to answer as they are to ask, and any and every conceivable answer will find someone out there who disagrees with it. Corruption is that type of beast. This book nonetheless aims to offer undergraduates and postgraduates, policy-makers and interested members of the public the opportunity to think through what they know about corruption and why they (think they) know it. While, unfortunately, it cannot tell anyone for sure what they need to do to eradicate corruption, it can hopefully make readers pause to think before accepting many of the "common-sense" solutions that are often peddled.

Even if the details of this book only came together thanks to that conversation with Alison, the book itself has been in the making for a much longer period of time. A decade and a half or so of teaching corruption analysis to undergraduates at the University of Sussex has made me well aware that most research sticks rigidly to a particular disciplinary approach. Economists, political scientists, historians, psychologists and anthropologists all regularly write on different parts of the corruption mosaic. But they often write for others in their own discipline. Rarely do they write with the intention of crossing disciplinary boundaries and talking to those who might think and work differently. This book tries to use the best of all these approaches to offer a fuller picture of the corruption challenge.

The University of Sussex deserves particular thanks for allowing me the time and space to go on research leave to get that writing done. Just about all the book was written in my wife's hometown of Liuzhou, Guangxi Province, southern China. Indeed, I often wonder what the ever-affable and patient staff of the Starbucks in the Wanda Centre in Liuzhou thought of the "lǎowài" who turned up day in, day out to drink his Americano and tap away on his MacBook. Come what may, the (no doubt inadvertent) support that 柯康弘, 刘鋆, 蒙娜, 熊伟, 陈思伶, 叶静旋, 梁润, 李晓彤, 裴开秋 and 莫榕燕 offered was very much appreciated.

Others also helped in small and not so small ways that really meant a lot. Liz Dávid-Barrett, Dave Bevan and Dominic Corley very generously read chapters and gave useful feedback, while 王海宇, arguably the keenest footballer the world has ever known, was ever-willing to get me involved in football games in Liuzhou. The scores of what soon became familiar faces on the running track at the Guangxi University of Science and Technology were also a welcome part of the writing routine. That even includes those who insisted on running the wrong way round the track (although I draw the line at the backward walkers; you guys really do need help). 林微, Nassar Abaalkhail, Tom Guy, Grace and Pete Hough, Michael Koβ, Sam Power, Andrew Sanders, Paul Taggart and Dan Taylor also all, in their different ways, made contributions that meant a lot.

The reason, however, that this book was indeed written so far away from home was not just because my wife, Ying Lin, a master of juggling things so that I could get the time and space to write, fancied spending a bit of time back in China. It was to introduce our twins, Stan and Vince, to the Chinese part of their family and, with that, to a part of who they are. They were, of course, too young to really take too much of it in, but no matter. They were also obviously blissfully unaware that while they were having fun in the soft play centre their dad was also trying to write a book. No matter again. This book is dedicated both to Ying and to them.

Analysing corruption

Analysing corruption

Dan Hough

First published in 2017 by Agenda Publishing

Agenda Publishing Limited
The Core
Science Central
Bath Lane
Newcastle upon Tyne
NE4 5TF
www.agendapub.com

ISBN 978-1-911116-54-7 (hardcover)
ISBN 978-1-911116-55-4 (paperback)

British Library Cataloguing-in-Publication Data
A catalogue record for this book is available from the British Library

Typeset by T&T Productions Ltd, London
Printed and bound in the UK by CPI Group (UK) Ltd, Croydon, CRO 4YY

Contents

Abbreviations

ACA	Anti-corruption agency
APSR	*American Political Science Review*
ASEAN	Association of Southeast Asian Nations
BASF	Badische Anilin und Soda Fabrik
BEEPS	Business Environment and Enterprise Survey
BFIU	Financial Intelligence Unit (Bangladesh)
BPI	Bribe Payers Index
CCDI	Central Commission for Discipline Inspection (China)
CFM	Citizen Feedback Model (Pakistan)
CoC	Control of Corruption (Worldwide Governance Indicator)
CoE	Council of Europe
CPC	Communist Party of China
CPI	Corruption Perceptions Index
CPIB	Corrupt Practices Investigation Bureau (Singapore)
CSPL	Committee on Standards in Public Life (UK)
DCO	District coordination officer (Pakistan)
DPA	Deferred prosecution agreement
ECHR	European Convention on Human Rights
EITI	Extractive Industries Transparency Initiative
FATF	Financial Action Task Force
FBI	Federal Bureau of Investigation (US)
FCPA	Foreign Corrupt Practices Act (US)
FIFA	Federation Internationale de Football Association
GCB	Global Corruption Barometer
GCR	Global Competitiveness Report
GDP	Gross domestic product
GRECO	Group of States against Corruption (within the Council of Europe)
ICAC	Independent Commission against Corruption (Hong Kong)
ICRG	International Country Risk Guide

IDA	International Development Association (of the World Bank)
IMF	International Monetary Fund
IfG	Institute for Government (UK)
IPAB	www.ipaidabribe.com
IRM	Implementation Review Mechanism (of the UNCAC)
IPSA	Independent Parliamentary Standards Authority (UK)
JMI	Jeunesses Musicales International
LIBOR	London Interbank Offered Rate
MACN	Maritime Anti-Corruption Network
NATO	North Atlantic Treaty Organization
NGO	Non-governmental organization
OCP	Open Contracting Partnership
OECD	Organisation for Economic Co-operation and Development
OGP	Open Government Partnership
OLAF	European Anti-Fraud Office
PETS	Public Expenditure Tracking Surveys
PIDA	Public Interest Disclosure Act (UK)
SFO	Serious Fraud Office (UK)
TI	Transparency International
TWFY	www.theyworkforyou.com (UK)
UKBA	UK's Bribery Act (2010)
UNCAC	United Nations Convention against Corruption
USAID	United States Agency for International Development
WGI	Worldwide Governance Indicators

1.

The corruption challenge

Corruption, so it seems, is everywhere. One indicator of this is the amount of coverage that it gets in the popular press. In 2015, for example, the word "corruption" appeared 1,240 times in UK newspaper article headlines. "Fraud" was even more prevalent, appearing on 4,177 occasions. The word "bribery", meanwhile, came up a mere 264 times.[1] The types of cases covered were wide, varied and often bewildering. On one day alone in the UK (24 November 2015), *The Independent* was analysing how the Vatican was putting reporters on trial who had previously uncovered corruption cases in its midst, while *The Times* was reporting a story about an apprentice jockey who was facing a ban from horse racing on account of deliberately riding to lose.[2] At the same time, *The Herald* was discussing Kenyan President Uhuru Kenyatta's anti-corruption reforms, while *The Guardian* was analysing FIFA's alleged corruption problems.[3]

The world of academia is also covering issues of corruption in ever more depth and breadth; a search in mid-2016 for the term "corruption" on JSTOR, the digital library of academic publications, revealed no less than 169,941 journal articles in which corruption was mentioned. "Fraud", meanwhile, appeared in 105,144 articles, and "bribery" came up on 22,971 occasions. While not all of those articles will have been on corruption as it

---

1. Data collected via Nexis.com. The data do not include duplicate articles circulated by news groups. Newswires and websites were also excluded. Data correct as at 19 August 2016.
2. Day (2015), "Vatican to put on trial reporters who exposed shameful corruption", *The Independent*, 24 November, p. 24; Wright (2015), "Apprentice jockey Egan faces corruption ban", *The Times*, 24 November, p. 70.
3. Smith (2015), "Kenyatta vows to act on corruption", *The Herald*, 24 November, p. 12; Gibson (2015), "Sepp Blatter facing life ban from football for Platini payment", *The Guardian*, 24 November.

is understood in the social sciences, it is still clear that the term, and concepts that are closely linked to it, are on a lot of people's minds.

There are plenty of good reasons for that. In 2014, the World Economic Forum estimated that $2.6 trillion was being lost yearly to corruption, while the World Bank has claimed that $1 trillion is paid out every year in bribes (OECD 2014: 1). In 2015, Global Financial Integrity, a Washington-based non-governmental organization (NGO), bemoaned the fact that between 2004 and 2013 developing and emerging economies lost $7.8 trillon in illicit financial flows (Kar & Spankers 2015). Furthermore, it is not just in the most impoverished parts of the world that corruption takes place; as the Organisation for Economic Co-operation and Development (OECD) has noted, it has been estimated that between 5 and 10 per cent of the budgets of Medicare and Medicaid, the American health care programmes, go missing on account of corruption (OECD 2014: 3). In Europe, meanwhile, one report has claimed corruption could be costing EU members upwards of €179 billion (Hafner *et al.*, 2016). The nature and extent of corruption might vary from place to place, but nowhere is exempt. The numbers are by definition rough and ready, and they should in many ways be treated with a significant degree of caution, but they are still an indication of the costs that pervasive corruption brings with it.[4] It is no wonder that corruption has become one of the key public policy challenges of our times.

Widely discussed though corruption now is, we still know surprisingly little about what works in the fight against it. Indeed, the concept itself remains hugely contested. However, that has not prevented scholars and practitioners from creating a wide array of anti-corruption tools. In the international arena, for example, there are conventions, treaties and multilateral agreements (see Table 1.1). A total of 140 states and territories have signed the United Nations Convention against Corruption (UNCAC), while 41 countries are signatories to the OECD's anti-bribery treaty. International organizations such as the Council of Europe (CoE), the Arab League and the African Union have all created tools for helping (and at times compelling) their member states to take the fight against corruption forwards.

Furthermore, national governments, business representatives and civil society organizations have come together to create thematically focused

---

4. There is a real need to be careful when trying to quantify how much corruption exists (see Chapter 4), or indeed how much it costs. Estimates really are just that: guesses. Some go as far as claiming that corruption analysis is plagued by what are in effect made-up statistics. See, for example, Stephenson (2015) and Walton (2016).

Table 1.1 The main international conventions and agreements that aim to tackle corruption.

Agreement	Date constituted/came into force	Aims	No. of signatories/members	Further information
UNCAC	2005	The only legally binding universal anti-corruption instrument. Potentially far-reaching approach; many (although not all) provisions are mandatory. Five main areas covered: prevention, criminalization and law enforcement, international cooperation, asset recovery, and technical assistance and information exchange.	140	http://bit.ly/2Img3rG
OECD anti-bribery treaty	1999	Peer-driven process. Countries monitor each other to ensure that the treaty's obligations have been met. Ongoing process.	41	http://bit.ly/1YYZ2BN
CoE's Civil Law Convention	2003	To coordinate attempts to define common international rules pertaining to civil law and corruption. Convention is monitored by GRECO.	35	http://bit.ly/2kOVWVm
CoE's Criminal Law Convention	2002	To coordinate attempts to criminalize corruption practices. Convention is monitored by GRECO.	46	http://bit.ly/2ccj4as
Arab League's Convention on Corruption	2010	Particular emphasis on increasing international cooperation, particularly with regard to the extradition of offenders, the provision of mutual judicial assistance and the restitution of assets.	21	http://bit.ly/2IgFvSY
African Union Convention on Preventing and Combating Corruption	2003	Covers a wide range of offences in both the public and the private sectors. All provisions are mandatory. Impressive set of aims, regional cooperation, mutual legal assistance and help to recover stolen assets.	35	http://bit.ly/2kOVu9y
Inter-American Convention against Corruption	1996	The main anti-corruption initiative of the Organization of American States. Represents the regional consensus on what to do about a wide range of corruption issues. Focus on public sector corruption.	28	http://bit.ly/2kiKZgw

All information correct at time of writing.

international anti-corruption initiatives. To give just three examples, the Extractive Industries Transparency Initiative (EITI) looks to try to bring greater transparency and openness to the notoriously opaque business of natural resource extraction; the Maritime Anti-Corruption Network (MACN) seeks to bring businesses together, with a view to eliminating corruption from the maritime industry; and the Financial Action Task Force (FATF) tries to coordinate international anti-money laundering efforts.[5] Such agreements are broad-ranging in scope and substance, and – unsurprisingly – have had mixed results. At the domestic level, too, there have been a plethora of initiatives that cater for specific sets of national and local challenges. We see much-vaunted domestic anti-corruption plans launched in places such as the UK, along with global open data and transparency initiatives. We have even seen game shows such as *Integrity Idol* develop in places like Nepal.[6] The world is not suffering from a lack of anti-corruption initiatives.

This book can neither outline all of these different approaches in detail nor claim to come up with remedies that undoubtedly work everywhere. Tackling corruption is clearly not that simple. What this book can do is analyse what might work as well as what certainly will not and why. It can also explain how anti-corruption thinkers can learn from the (many) mistakes of the past. To misquote Albert Einstein, making a mistake is not the issue: the skill is in not making the same mistake twice. This book, in other words, analyses why so many anti-corruption policies fail, with a view to drawing lessons as to which ones might plausibly work in the future.

While the aim is to keep the analysis of corruption focused on the real world, this book also has a theoretical focus. Over the past 20 years, there has been considerable debate about not only how best to conceptualize corruption, but also what causes it, what its effects are and ultimately what (if indeed anything) should be done to counteract it. There have been interesting and thoughtful contributions from scholars coming from a wide range of theoretical and disciplinary traditions, and this book tries to do justice to at least some of that diversity. Lawyers and legal scholars, for example, instinctively start with legal frameworks and legal

---

5. For more details on the EITI, see https://eiti.org/. For more details on the MACN, see www.maritime-acn.org, and for more on the FATF, see www.fatf-gafi.org, all last viewed on 16 August 2016.

6. For more on the UK's anti-corruption plan, see UK Government (2014). For more on Nepal's *Integrity Idol* game show, see www.integrityidol.org/countries/nepal, viewed on 17 August 2016.

processes. Their focus on issues of legal best practice, the impact of anti-corruption laws on company and individual behaviour and the challenges of law enforcement have helped governments trying to craft appropriate anti-corruption legislation. Economists, meanwhile, have tended to place a more obvious stress on the incentives that lead to corrupt behaviour. They have subsequently been vocal in suggesting policies and institutional frameworks that might conceivably prevent corruption from occurring, but they are less keen to get involved in complex debates about what corruption actually is. Anthropologists have faced the very opposite problem. Their work remains heavily context specific and rich in detail, but they have traditionally remained suspicious of anything that looks like a generalized theory of corrupt action. All of these approaches, despite their relative weaknesses, contribute something to the debate.

In a practical sense, this book looks at the corruption challenges in both the developed and the developing world. It will analyse international attempts to tackle the problem (see Chapter 7) and unpack and scrutinize the most prominent national (and, indeed, subnational and local) anti-corruption initiatives (see Chapters 8 and 9). A wide range of real-world examples are also used to illustrate the main arguments made.

ANALYSING CORRUPTION

The book centres around three simple questions: what is corruption, what causes corruption and what works in the fight against corruption? The analysis presented in the substantive chapters covers plenty of ground, but these three questions remain at the core of the book. Chapter 2 starts by illustrating that the analysis of corruption has come a long way since it was first discussed in earnest by the likes of Plato and Aristotle. For those thinkers, corruption was more about moral decay than it was about abusing public power for private gain. Indeed, corruption was often understood as being about aberrations that took a polity away from a non-corrupt state of being. The emphasis was much less on the behaviour of individuals fulfilling their daily duties, and much more on bigger questions of community and statehood.

Over time, that focus changed. The international consensus now places individual behaviour at the centre of much corruption thinking. Corruption (in the Western world, at least) has come to be seen as a process via which errant individuals behave inappropriately to enrich themselves. In the mid- to latter part of the twentieth century, this also led to corruption, often indirectly but sometimes quite explicitly, being rather patronizingly understood as a developing-world problem. The West had systems, so the often-unspoken argument went, which stressed a neutral, meritocratic bureaucracy that put a premium on fairness, equality before the law, efficiency and competence. This ensured that when corruption appeared it was nipped quickly in the bud. Developing countries did not enjoy the merits of a Weberian bureaucracy and subsequently had to deal with corruption on a much larger scale. A neat and tidy argument to make in an era of colonial thinking; not such an effective one if you really want to understand the nuances of corruption across different polities. Time has moved on.

It was the stream (which soon became something of a torrent) of corruption scandals that engulfed many Western states through the 1970s, 1980s and 1990s that really brought corruption to the forefront of people's minds. Scandals such as Watergate in the US, the Flick Affair in Germany, Back to Basics in the UK and Tangentopoli in Italy indicated that the West itself might have corruption problems that needed dealing with.[7] In the 1990s, the international policy community also "discovered" corruption as a policy problem, and began talking about how to counteract it. Furthermore, groups of economists, anthropologists, psychologists and political scientists also began to confront the serious methodological challenges that have traditionally plagued corruption analysis. The quality of data available to analysts of corruption improved (see Chapter 4), and approaches to the subject subsequently became more rigorous.

All of these developments aside, the moral focus that occupied much of the early work on corruption has not vanished. Working out what is morally and ethically acceptable remains important in helping us understand precisely what corruption is. The fact that moral standards differ ensures that these definitional debates can at times appear to be never-ending, but that cannot be an excuse for hastily glossing over them. When trying to pin down the notion of corruption, one is inevitably drawn into philosophical discussions that do not easily lend themselves to empirical answers. This also affects how (and, indeed, whether) we go about tackling corruption (see Chapters 7–9). While it is therefore tempting to view corruption as something that is always "wrong" or "bad", Chapter 2 illustrates

---

7. For more on the rise of scandals in the Western world, see Garrard & Newell (2006). For more on the relationship between scandals and politics, see Thompson (2000).

that there are still a number of moral and ethical challenges that bring this one-dimensional understanding of corruption into question.

DEFINITIONS AND MEASUREMENTS

Chapter 3 brings the discussion of what corruption is right up to date. As noted in the previous paragraph, defining corruption can be both difficult and frustrating, yet it is something that has to be done. To use an analogy, a patient cannot simply walk into a doctor's consulting room and ask for some drugs to make herself better. For starters, the doctor would not have any idea what drugs to give her; the remedy for breathing problems is going to be altogether different to that for tennis elbow. The doctor needs to ask the patient to explain what is wrong, to outline her symptoms, to define the problem. Only then can the doctor understand the nature of the problem and begin to think about the ailment's particular causes. Corruption and anti-corruption need to follow the same logic, and a fundamental part of that logic is defining right at the beginning what exactly the problem is.

Chapter 3 argues that, in essence, there are four contemporary types of definition: (a) those that are based around legal understandings of corruption, (b) those that centre around an abuse of entrusted power, (c) those that involve business transactions and, finally, (d) what has recently come to be understood as "legal corruption". Approaches that take the law as their starting point begin, unsurprisingly, with a given state's legal framework. This has the advantage of giving the corruption analyst clear markers as to what is and what is not corrupt. It brings much-needed clarity to what can become a confusing debate. However, public servants are usually well aware of what the law says. They also know that breaking it normally leads to trouble, so they generally do not do it. Rather, they may well find ways of bending the law, or skillfully circumventing it, to get what they want while legitimately claiming they have done nothing wrong. Furthermore, laws differ across both time and space; what might be considered corrupt in contemporary politics may not have been seen as that a relatively short time ago. Plus, what the law considers corrupt in one country may not be seen as any such thing in other (ostensibly similar) polities. There is, therefore, a danger that using the law as your benchmark can cause as many problems as it solves.

Many analysts subsequently look to bring context back into the discussion. They do so by understanding corruption as the abuse of entrusted power for private gain. Elected politicians and appointed public servants are expected to use discretion in acting impartially. If they deliberately act in a way that is in line with their own interests, or, indeed, the interests of friends, family or other vested parties, rather than the state's, then they are perceived to be acting corruptly. The advantage of this approach is that it is more flexible: duties in given settings may differ, but so will understandings of what is corrupt. In some places, however, elected politicians are expected to abuse their public roles to enrich their family and friends. The notion of public office being exclusively about public service can still sometimes have a very Western feel to it.

Latterly, there has been an increasing focus on the role that business plays in corrupt practices. For many, the instinct is still to believe that business reacts to the selfish demands of corrupt public officials, but there has been some interesting work done recently on how transactions that ostensibly have nothing to do with the public sector can and should be understood as corrupt. The case of bankers rigging the London Interbank Offered Rate (LIBOR) in London in 2012 is a case in point. This involved a series of fraudulent actions that were undertaken by bankers to influence interbank lending rates. The LIBOR is, among other things, used to influence interest rates in the UK as a whole, so bankers were effectively defrauding UK mortgage payers to enrich themselves. Finally, of late there has been increasing discussion of what can best be termed "legal corruption".[8] Legal corruption concerns situations in which economic and political elites shape rules, regulations and ultimately policies from within the system for their own benefit. This generates huge rents, is legal and comes about on account of an ability to dictate what is and what is not acceptable practice.

Once we understand what corruption is (or, indeed, which parts of the corruption challenge we are interested in), we can begin to think about how much of it exists. We do this in Chapter 4. When policy-makers claim that they want to tackle corruption, they are by definition making a statement that they want to see levels of it go down. However, knowing how much corruption exists in the first place is a task fraught with difficulty. Chapter 4 outlines the most well-known ways of approaching such a task, illustrating what these approaches do well and where they fall down before moving on to analysing how their findings should and (perhaps most importantly) should not be used.

---

8. See, for example, Kaufmann & Gillies (2016) and Kaufmann & Vicente (2005).

The measurement story starts off with Transparency International (TI), arguably the most well-known anti-corruption non-profit organization. In 1995, TI published the first of the composite indices of corruption, the Corruption Perceptions Index (CPI). The CPI reveals how much corruption is perceived to exist in the public sector across (in 2016) 176 countries. It is widely known and widely cited, and has been instrumental in getting more people talking about the challenge of corruption. Other attempts to measure corruption at a broad level have followed, with the more nuanced and sophisticated "control of corruption" indicator of the Worldwide Governance Indicators (WGI) leading the way.

Yet these indicators have to deal with some severe methodological challenges; they are more or less complex polls of polls, and they boil each country's score down to one simple number. Furthermore, these data are perception based, and perceptions can be considerably different from reality. These indices also concentrate on public sector corruption, deliberately ignoring corruption that emanates from the private sector: a legacy of the assumptions that have traditionally been made about what corruption is (see Chapter 3).

Chapter 4 also explains how criticisms of these indices have led to a number of more focused, and arguably more innovative, attempts to measure corruption; these range from the Global Corruption Barometer (GCB), effectively a glorified survey of individuals around the world, to entities such as the Bribe Payers Index (BPI). Most interestingly, ever more sophisticated and focused proxy indicators are being developed, a number of which reveal fascinating patterns of corrupt behaviour. Chapter 4 concludes by acknowledging that the multitude of attempts to measure corruption – via perceptions, experience and proxies – has helped to raise the profile of corruption analysis. There is nevertheless a danger in taking these data too literally. Corruption is complex, multifaceted and riddled with nuance, and this makes reducing it to one number very difficult indeed. The very best of these measurements can be used to shed light on problems and challenges, but many of the others should be used, at best, with caution.

CAUSES OF CORRUPTION

Chapter 5 moves on to outline the key drivers of corrupt practice. The majority of corruption analysis adopts what can broadly be understood as a principal–agent approach. This is – as the field has been, and arguably continues to be – dominated by political economists, and the assumptions that they generally bring with them fit nicely into this analytical framework. To the political economist, the key driver of corruption is self-interest. Corruption takes place because, at their core, people are rational actors, adept at assessing the costs and benefits of future behaviour. If the costs of corruption are low and the benefits are high(er), then we should expect to see corruption occur. Even when actions do not bring obvious material benefits, there will be less tangible reasons (i.e. personal feelings of satisfaction and happiness) that motivate behaviour. People are therefore always corruptible, and whether they actually act in a corrupt fashion will depend on the cost/benefit framework within which their decisions are being made.

Much of this analysis starts from a position that embraces a set of behavioural assumptions that fundamentally distrust both people in general and politicians in particular. This has led some analysts to be crystal clear that government intervention in the economy is the real problem, and that if one wants to make progress in weeding out corruption, then reducing the size and scope of the state's activities is a very good starting point. Chapter 5 highlights how analysts in other disciplines have criticized that position as well as how they (anthropologists, political scientists, sociologists, psychologists) have broadened our understanding of what drives people to act corruptly. Much of the criticism comes from those who reject the notion that people are rational actors per se: people are not born, so critics argue, with a particular nature; everything that we do is learnt through conditioning. It is this conditioning that, so opponents argue, shapes whether someone does or does not choose to act in a corrupt fashion.

There is also a discussion of a newer, third approach that views corruption as a response to a given problem or challenge. In post-conflict states, corruption can help maintain a stability that simply would not be possible otherwise; on a more mundane level, it can help people cope with the everyday challenges of dealing with poor public services. Corruption in this scenario is not actually the problem. On the contrary, it is the solution to a problem (that of there being, say, far too few good schools or hospitals). Corruption in contexts like this helps you get things done. This does not make corruption "good" or "right", but in circumstances like these we need to think about corruption as one part of a larger process.

Chapter 5 illustrates that we need to think about what the particular drivers of corruption are before we can move on to thinking about how to mitigate or, ideally, eliminate them. This applies not just to the world of politics but also to the economy, as Chapter 6 illustrates. This chapter begins by explaining that the effects of corruption on economic development are overwhelmingly negative. Indeed, commentators across the ideological and theoretical spectrum believe that corruption skews the allocation of resources, frequently has a detrimental effect on economic growth, undermines both the rule of law and property rights and impacts negatively on standards of living.

However, Chapter 6 illustrates two further things. First, the economic impact of corruption will not be the same everywhere. Indeed, context is important in explaining why corruption can be so utterly corrosive in some places but appears to be much less so in others. Corruption may in some contexts plausibly help to generate a stability that helps to – in the short and medium term, at least – generate positive economic benefits. This section of the chapter finishes by illustrating that even where authors have argued that corruption can have positive economic effects, they nevertheless come at the cost of hardwiring in problems that future generations will ultimately have to deal with.

Second, Chapter 6 looks at how legal corruption contributes significantly to the economies of many states in the Western world (Kaufmann & Gillies 2016). As noted above, activities that fall into this category can range from the system of offshore finance that was laid bare thanks to the Panama Papers to the problem of state capture and actors legally shaping systems in their own interest. These processes can help foster economic growth, but they can also help "generate huge rents for the elite, increase their power, and exacerbate a country's political and economic inequality" (ibid.). Chapter 6 argues that it is not just resource-rich and transition countries where this is evident: the tax systems in many industrialized countries are excellent examples of precisely this problem. Companies are frequently able to game their tax payments in ways that are perfectly legal but which throw up a whole series of moral and ethical questions. In 2013, for example, Starbucks paid corporation tax in the UK for the first time in five years, having skilfully arranged its financial affairs during that period in order to pay nothing at all.[9] By 2015, the company was paying £8.1 million in corporation tax, a sum that nearly matches the total cumulative amount that it paid in 14 years previously (Davies 2015). While Starbucks' tax management strategy clearly is not corruption in the classical sense,

---

9. For more on this, see Macalister (2013).

it does give rise to questions about how powerful players like these are allowed to get into a position where their tax liability is so negligible. Critics subsequently argue that it is a corruption of the system, even if legally these actors are doing nothing wrong.

We also see a plethora of enablers of corruption earning their living by providing services to those looking to reinvest dirty money. Indeed, in financial centres such as London, accountants, estate agents, lawyers and a range of other service providers often find themselves under little to no obligation to ask where money comes from as large transactions take place. They simply provide the services required without the need to ask any questions about where the funds to buy property, cars, places in expensive schools and the like come from. These providers generally act very much within the law, but this is either because lawmakers choose to turn a blind eye to the loopholes in place (often fearing economic consequences if they act against them), or because they simply have not got the tools available to turn the screws on the enablers' industry.

TACKLING CORRUPTION

Only once we have covered all of this territory can we begin to think about how we might tackle corruption. Chapters 7–9 subsequently introduce the options available. Chapter 7 looks at international attempts to coordinate anti-corruption activity. While the US initially led the way with its Foreign Corrupt Practices Act (1977) (see Chapter 8), the OECD soon took over in trying to persuade the international community to adopt similar anti-corruption practices. This resulted in the OECD's anti-bribery treaty, signed in 1997, in force since 1999 and now ratified by 41 countries (see Table 1.1). The major international instrument for coordinating anti-corruption activity nonetheless remains the UNCAC. This convention is not short on high-minded ideas, but its actual impact remains questionable.

The analysis then moves on to both the World Bank and International Monetary Fund (IMF), two institutions that, in their different ways, have tried to push anti-corruption agendas. Chapter 7 also looks briefly at other approaches to tackling corruption in the international arena. While the performance of many of these initiatives will never be as impressive as critics want it to be, they do nonetheless have focused roles to play in helping keep anti-corruption discourse at the forefront of policy-makers' minds and in slowly making corrupt practices more difficult to get away with.

While corruption is very frequently a transnational phenomenon, many of the attempts to tackle it start, and indeed remain, at the national level. This disconnect between the international nature of corruption and the generally national responses to it is a serious problem. Chapter 8 analyses the main tools that national governments have at their disposal and highlights the lessons that can be learnt from both the successes and failures of these tools. Rather than go through a succession of possible anti-corruption options, this analysis begins by outlining the challenges that governments with relatively strong institutions of governance and relatively low levels of corruption face.[10] Petty corruption is rarely a significant problem in what Michael Johnston has called "influence markets", the focus is more on an anti-corruption agenda built around transparency initiatives, accountability drives and nuanced efforts to tackle particular national variants of legal corruption (Johnston 2013).

In countries with patchy institutions of governance and significant corruption challenges, the options are in many ways more varied and even more in need of translation into a national context. They also include a number of high-profile anti-corruption mechanisms that patently have not worked. These range from anti-corruption commissions (implemented in over 50 states, little more than a handful of which have seen the commissions make a genuine impact) to ever more intricate sets of laws and regulations (which have often been found lacking in terms of implementation). This section illustrates the importance of understanding the nature of the problem that you are trying to solve before undertaking reform. Finally, Chapter 8 discusses anti-corruption mechanisms in states with serious, widespread corruption problems. In these states, the best anti-corruption tools often have surprisingly little to do with corruption at all. In a state where the rule of law is patchy or non-existent, anti-corruption laws (or, indeed, laws more generally) mean very little. The challenge here is to improve the basic tools of governance, in the knowledge that then and only then can the issue of corruption be brought on to the agenda.

The final substantive chapter (Chapter 9) looks at one of the fastest-growing areas of anti-corruption thinking: the role that civil society more broadly and individual citizens in particular can play in fighting corruption. Again, the nature of the state within which these groups and individuals are active will affect the way that they do their work, but it remains

---

10. For a much more detailed analysis of governance regimes and anti-corruption, see Hough (2013).

clear that, across the board, in democracies and authoritarian states alike, they have a role to play. Chapter 9 also analyses the rise of professional anti-corruption actors and NGOs that have become skilled at influencing both national governments and international organizations. The sector as a whole still has its critics; indeed, the chapter will outline why some anthropologists in particular view this "anti-corruption industry" with a fair amount of scepticism.

Box 1.1. The many faces of corruption

Corruption comes in all shapes and sizes, and can potentially be found in all situations and settings. Here are just five examples.

- In 2008, Siemens settled corruption allegations to the tune of $800 million. It remains (at time of writing) the largest settlement ever under the US's Foreign Corrupt Practices Act (FCPA), just ahead of French company Alstom's $772 million settlement in 2014.
- In 2013, a Chinese student at the University of Bath in the UK, Yang Li, was found guilty of trying to bribe his lecturer into giving him a better grade. He was sentenced to 12 months imprisonment.
- In 1995, Mona Sahlin, then Deputy Prime Minister of Sweden, repaid over 50,000 Swedish krona (about $5,500 at today's exchange rate) on account of the so-called Toblerone Affair. Sahlin admitted claiming personal expenses (including a Toblerone chocolate bar, hence the scandal's name) on a credit card issued to help cover working costs.
- In 2016, 45 of Chinese province Liaoning's 102 representatives in China's National People's Congress were dismissed for securing their seats via vote-buying. A total of 523 of the 619 representatives in Liaoning's provincial congress were dismissed for the same offence at the same time.
- In 2008, English professional footballer Andy Mangan was banned from playing for five months for betting on the outcome of a match between Accrington Stanley and his then club, Bury.

The analysis is also taken one step further by analysing how citizens can sidestep the mediatory role that NGOs often play and become anti-corruption activists themselves. The rise of "armchair auditing" in the West is one example of this.[11] It is nonetheless in the developing

---

11. In the UK, for example, the UK's anti-corruption champion, Eric Pickles, has called for an army of armchair auditors to keep government in check (see UK Government 2010).

world where anti-corruption strategies that put the citizen at the centre of affairs have the most potential. Chapter 9 outlines how, for example, participatory budgeting has grown in prominence (originally in parts of Brazil, but latterly elsewhere), while web- and phone-based anti-corruption initiatives have developed in an array of places. It will also unpack how left-field anti-corruption tools such as television shows and anti-corruption songs have tried to heighten awareness of the damage that corruption does.

Chapter 9 concludes by arguing that there are plenty of reasons to be hopeful that these new and innovative ideas have a contribution to make. However, at the same time, we should not expect too much of them. Indeed, the actual outputs are, as yet, only very limited in scope. In states where corruption is the norm, it is also asking a lot of people to act in a way that could well lead to negative consequences for themselves. A citizen may not want to pay a bribe to a doctor, but it is likely that they will do so if not paying leaves them unable to access the treatment they need. These approaches nonetheless have potential, and they are likely to be where we see some of the most innovative new anti-corruption ideas.

In short, this book should offer the reader the opportunity to think a little more about why corruption has proven to be so hard to tackle as well as what (at least some of) the anti-corruption options are moving forwards. As was noted on page 1, corruption is now very much a hot topic. We have no way of knowing whether there is more or less corruption now than there was in the past, but we certainly do know that it is a topic that garners plenty of attention. Yet, the apparent ubiquity of corrupt practices has also, at times, led to the term being used very loosely. This brings with it real dangers. The recent elections in the US and parts of Europe have illustrated that corruption can simply become a description of what your political opponent does (or stands for), or a way of delegitimizing a process or set of behaviours that you do not like. In those contexts, the term borders on the meaningless.

Worse still, those who peddle corruption in such vague terms may help drive disaffection with politics more broadly. Dissatisfaction with the outputs of a political system does not automatically mean that the system itself is corrupt, yet that is what many politicians of a populist ilk are happy to claim. It is easy to describe something as corrupt when what one is really saying is that one is unhappy with the way politics is currently functioning. That may be, as corruption is indeed distorting political life, but it may not. Politics is, after all, a process of engineering compromise solutions without having those involved resort to violence. There are winners and losers. The process is messy. There are never enough resources to go round. But in successful states, that process has a legitimacy born out of a faith that those who have lost this time round may not do so next time. When allegations of corruption are bandied about without sufficient explanation as to what is being described, and why it is seen as corrupt, then politics is in danger of failing. It is with that in mind that the remaining chapters of this book try to throw light on why we need to understand more about what corruption is, and what causes it, before we can begin to think about how to tackle it. A good place to start doing that is by looking at the history of the term itself, and that is precisely what we do in Chapter 2.

2.
The history of corruption analysis

Much has been written about corruption in recent times. Indeed, as was noted on page 1, thousands of articles are written on corruption and related terms every year. This was not always the case. Indeed, corruption analysis was often seen as peripheral to academic life. Back in 1957, Eric McKitrick, writing in the *Political Science Quarterly*, bemoaned the fact that the "investigation of corruption" did not seem to be something of "very intense interest to social scientists" (McKitrick 1957: 502). Michael Johnston, one of the political scientists who has done the most to put corruption analysis back on the map, agrees; he noted in 2006 that "American political science as an institutionalized discipline has remained steadfastly uninterested in corruption for generations" (Johnston 2006: 809). Ten years later, he further lamented the fact that corruption had "more or less dropped off the academic and international policy agendas for nearly a generation" (Johnston 2016: 13).This former indifference of political scientists towards the study of corruption was best described by John Peters and Susan Welch at the end of the 1970s, in their now much-cited piece for the *American Political Science Review* (*APSR*), "If political corruption is in the mainstream of American politics, why is it not in the mainstream of American politics research?" (Peters & Welch 1978: 974).

Peters and Welch posed an interesting question. Even post-Watergate, an event that caused corruption to lurch into the mainstream of American public consciousness, corruption analysis remained notable by its absence. The leading social science journals in America rarely discussed it, and when they did, corruption was only infrequently regarded as a phenomenon that needed to be explained; it was corruption's impact on other things that generally grabbed people's attention. Peters and Welch blamed this apparent neglect on the challenge of defining the concept, but the prevailing analytical and methodological assumptions of their discipline no doubt also played a role. When your aim is to use data systematically to test hypotheses and you want to use increasingly sophisticated statistical techniques to do so, then corruption is by no means a straightforward concept to get a handle on. Given that, it should come as no great surprise that empirical political science did not – at that point, at least, and with a small number of notable exceptions – have much to offer in terms of corruption analysis.[1] The analyses that existed up until then tended to focus on one of three things: there were broad historical diagnoses of what was understood as corrupt practice; there were what Colin Leys has described as "inquisitional studies" of a broader range of predominantly English-speaking countries; and, finally, there were sociological studies, in which corruption appeared as just one of a number of phenomena to be unpacked (Leys 1965: 215).

This rather ad hoc analysis of corruption should not, however, disguise the fact that, as Peters and Welch noted, "corruption has been an ever-present part of American political life" (Peters & Welch 1978: 974). Indeed, it has been an ever-present part of life everywhere. The great nineteenth-century thinker Alexis de Tocqueville's analysis of democracy in America is a good place to start when looking for evidence of this in the US. And if we cross over to Europe, one certainly does not have to look too hard to find analyses of the corruption that plagued revolutionary France, or, indeed, the corruption that accompanied economic reform in eighteenth- and nineteenth-century Britain.[2] So, corruption clearly has been analysed, just not in the way that empirical political science has traditionally seen as appropriate.

When this is remembered, it becomes clear that the sudden (and relatively recent) burst of interest in corruption should not disguise the fact that the subject itself has a long history. As Bruce Buchan and Lisa Hill have impressively illustrated, corruption was an important issue in antiquity, just as it was through the medieval period and into early modernity and beyond (Buchan & Hill 2014). Given the prominence of corruption in analyses of these different periods, the notion that corruption did not receive much attention until the end of the twentieth century, therefore, has something of the absurd about it.

---

1. See, in particular, Heidenheimer (1970).
2. See de Tocqueville (1961), Maza (1993) and Harling (1996).

This chapter tries to do at least some justice to the issue of how corruption has been analysed over time. Corruption was often understood as being about moral aberrations and decay, and these moral issues are confronted head-on throughout the chapter. In the past two decades, corruption has risen to the forefront of academic attention, yet its focus is arguably narrower now than it was in the past. In the contemporary era, corruption is often understood as centering round individual indiscretions. Analyses of why and when these indiscretions happen have eclipsed much of the traditional thinking on what corruption was and what role it played in society. For many, as Chapter 3 illustrates in more detail, that in itself is a problem. Indeed, corruption analysts would do well to remember the concept's colourful and nuanced past when drawing conclusions about its role in the modern world.

STARTING AT THE BEGINNING

If one is inclined to look hard enough, it becomes clear that corruption and corruption analysis go all the way back to the very beginning. Indeed, if Christianity is taken as an example, then that means to the very beginning of the Bible. As Maryvonne Genaux notes, corruption is central to many of the Bible's teachings. In the Book of Genesis, for instance, it is made clear that humans can be, and are, corruptible, as Eve promptly illustrates by picking the forbidden fruit in the Garden of Eden. God, meanwhile, is not, and the very notion of corruption is what defines and signifies human "separateness from divinity" (Genaux 2004: 20). This understanding of corruption is not just something that appears in Genesis. As Genaux again notes, in the Book of Solomon, the kings are told that they are God's representatives on Earth, and that they therefore have to represent God's incorruptible state. The kings are reminded that it is their job to maintain and uphold God's teachings; if they do not do this, then they are by definition behaving corruptly (*ibid.*). Corruption, in other words, can be seen as a fundamental part of what makes humans "human".

It would, however, be a mistake to assume that corruption analysis has been a prominent part of our thinking since then. As Mark Knights has pointed out, in the case of the UK, "it is striking how few of our earlier struggles with corruption are known about, let alone reflected on as potentially useful data" (Knights 2016: 1). Corruption has (in the UK and beyond) often fulfilled a rather ambiguous and ill-defined role in political analysis. This is particularly true in terms of the contributions that analysts of corruption have made to both political theory and political philosophy. It is also not clear (even now) whether corruption analysis should be given greater prominence in these areas: "[t]hat is", as Mark Philp and Elizabeth Dávid-Barrett note, "a more complicated question to answer" than it might first appear (Philp & Dávid-Barrett 2015: 388). It is not that there is any dispute about the *existence* of corruption; there has never been any doubt about that. It is more that corruption is often seen as something that happens outside the realms of the permissible. It is something that exists beyond the boundaries of acceptability, and it therefore does not "compromise or put into question the values we advance" (*ibid.*). Arguments in defence of corruption are generally thin on the ground, which means they do not "challenge our sense that [it] is at best a marginal topic for political theory". To quote Philp and Dávid-Barrett once more, for political theorists, corruption is too often "a problem of implementation, not an issue of substance" (*ibid.*).

Be that as it may, corruption was certainly a prominent topic of discussion for many of the great early philosophers. None of them had a theory of corruption per se, but they did recognize that corruption was an important issue to be studied. Their understanding of corruption could nonetheless be very broad indeed; it was often viewed as "a decomposition of the body politic" that came about through "immoral decay". A panoply of behaviours were thus put into this general category, largely due to the belief that they were "dysfunctional and hence morally corrupt" (Friedrich 2002: 16). As a result, it tended to be the reasons behind these behaviours that caught the eye, rather than the corruption that such perversion led to (or stemmed from).

Aristotle's analysis of corruption in *Politics* is one of the most obvious early examples of this. His understanding of corruption centres around the dysfunctionality of states that have moved away from their "pure" state of being. He talks of how each constitution (of which there were three: monarchy, aristocracy and democracy) would be corrupted if it moved away from being guided by the rule of law. The "deviation" from monarchy, for example, would be tyranny: a single ruler ceasing to make decisions that were in the best interests of his subjects and beginning to do so for his own advantage. For Aristotle and a number of his contemporaries, this was the very essence of corruption, leading inevitably to decay, degradation and ultimately state failure.[3] Ramsay MacMullen uses a similar logic to argue

---

3. See the analysis of this in Heidenheimer (1989). For more on Aristotle, see *The Politics of Aristotle* (ed. 1946), p. 373.

that the ever-deepening problem of corruption is the primary reason the Roman Empire fell (MacMullen 1988). MacMullen's thesis is straightforward and well documented: corruption led successive governments to concentrate more on the need to generate private gains for themselves and their supporters, and less on the demands of running a large and complex empire. The moral core that characterized much of the thinking of Rome's founders had withered away over time; subsequent Roman leaders not only lost control of the government, but the government lost sight of what it existed to do. Even when it became apparent that corruption was at the core of the administration's work, attempts at reform came too late. Like a cancer, corruption had penetrated too many parts of the public ethos. The fall of Rome was also pivotal in Montesquieu's thinking on corruption (and state failure). One of his major works (*Considérations sur les causes de la grandeur des Romains et de leur décadence*) explained in detail how the virtuous thinking of Rome's founders helped it become an empire, but how the corruption of Rome's moral fibre ultimately brought the empire down. For Montesquieu and MacMullen, as well as many others, corruption was at the very core of Rome's descent into dissolution.

As time went on, corruption often ended up being analysed through the lens of what has been termed classical republicanism. Although developed largely in the Renaissance period, this strain of republicanism owed an intellectual debt to the likes of Aristotle. Notions such as civic virtue and civil society were seen as vital tools in developing a fair, just and ultimately corruption-free polity. The very existence of corruption was, for these thinkers, the antithesis of what they thought an ideal state should look like.

The Renaissance thinkers took this a step further, arguing that mixed government and power sharing was vital in creating good government and fighting corruption. For the likes of Machiavelli, Montesquieu and Rousseau, corruption was a disease that could beset any and every polity, and it remained very much at the forefront of their thinking as a result (Friedrich 2002: 17–18). Machiavelli, for example, argued that most people were weak and susceptible to the temptations of fame and fortune. Corruption subsequently had the potential to lure citizens away from an upstanding and virtuous state of being. Machiavelli declared that only great leaders could keep political order, and this they would do by inspiring citizens to overlook the temptations of corruption and uphold what he regarded as virtuous, patriotic values (Friedrich 1967: 138). As noted above, Montesquieu spent a considerable amount of time outlining how

21

corruption had developed in Rome.[4] Indeed, for him, Rome was the ideal type of regime: in essence, it was both noble and virtuous, but, over time, it had been perverted. The victories Rome enjoyed could not prevent moral corruption (and demise) from eventually setting in.

Like many of his contemporaries, Rousseau, meanwhile, talked more about moral corruption than he did about corruption in the political process, even though he clearly saw the two as interlinked. Rousseau argued that corruption was an inevitable fact of life, appearing as and when political power struggles developed. Rousseau started from the position that equality is a natural state, and well-organized polities look to achieve it through the rule of law. Only this will maintain virtue in the face of "the corrupting influence of power-hungry individuals" (Friedrich 2002: 19).

These thinkers worried predominantly about those active in politics having their heads turned by the lure of patronage and power (Sparling 2015: 618). They therefore grappled with the consequences of what they regarded as corruption as well as how best to structure a state so that politicians were not able to follow their inner demons and go down the corrupt route in the first place. These positions were particularly prominent in Florence, a city that regularly sought to stress its own virtues over Rome (where republicanism's proponents were less vocal). These thinkers bought into a long tradition of republican thinking that "hinged on the sense of an ideal order under the constant threat of corruption" (Philp & Dávid-Barrett 2015: 388).

It was not just in Europe that corruption occupied the thinking of prospective state-builders. As Heidenheimer and Johnston have noted, the early Americans also looked on with interest at how corruption was ruining (in their minds) the British system of government. The likes of Robert Walpole were not averse to crafting majorities in parliament by spending money on dissenting voices and "the trading of patronage favors" (Heidenheimer & Johnston 2002: 4). It was behaviour like this that contributed to would-be Americans breaking away and forming what became the United States.

Analysing the early Americans is particularly interesting, as it shows how opinions can vary regarding what should be understood as corrupt. They certainly did not see Walpole's actions as simply being part of the way politics functioned; instead, they argued that a line had clearly been crossed. Quite where that line lies remains just as much a bone of

---

4. See, for example, Montesquieu (1999).

contention today as it was then. There is more on this in Chapter 3, but it is worth noting here that, for American observers, George III and his ministers had become ever more adept at subverting parliament for their own means. Parliamentarians could be coaxed and cajoled, by foul means as often as fair, to support policies that arguably served the executive much better than they served the country as a whole (Heidenheimer & Johnston 2002: 4). For many outside observers, this was corruption personified.

There is a case to be made that many of these early analyses of corruption played small but significant roles in the development not just of practical politics but also of social science more generally. Woodruff Smith, for example, argues that understanding what he calls "mapping", a process by which rational thinkers work out what humans can logically hope to explain, has played a noteworthy role in defining the boundaries of what can be understood as corrupt. Smith argues that the mapping of "conceptual and discursive spaces" requires some important and obvious patterns of behaviour to be "conceptually quarantined". These behaviours are not, in other words, to be explained as such. Much of what has ended up in these spaces, over and beyond the reach of the logical explanation, comes under the rubric of corruption (Smith 2009: 261–2).

Smith uses the example of John Locke, the seventeenth-century English philosopher, to explain the role that corruption played in this process. Smith argues that in the *Second Treatise of Government*, Locke tried to understand the logic and motivations of the "wrongdoer" (Locke 2005). Because Locke understood natural law to be based on reason, wrongdoing posed a problem for him; how could he explain the behaviour of those who went against natural law and committed criminal acts? Locke's way of dealing with this conundrum was to introduce the idea of "degeneracy", a notion that fitted easily with the language that many before him had used to describe corruption. As Smith notes, Locke does not explain why this degeneration (or corruption) happens, but he does outline that even rational individuals who follow the rule of law need "rational restraint". Otherwise, they, too, will leave themselves open to the degeneracy that could afflict all of us (Smith 2009: 261–3). This is, even if Locke did not necessarily describe it that way, the beginning of an attempt to outline what could and could not be rationally understood.

Corruption, as has been briefly illustrated above, makes a regular appearance in the thinking of a range of scholars across a variety of epochs. But it was rarely the core of what drove these thinkers on. There was, as Philp and Dávid-Barrett note, a "pragmatic, instrumental interest in corruption", but this often came about through thinking about its impact on something else (Philp & Dávid-Barrett 2015: 388). This "something else" was often how states fail, how effective institutions are perverted and how honourable people come to behave in dishonourable ways. No one was trying to explain corruption per se; they were simply taking it as a given, something that was both inevitable and to be condemned. At the centre of all of these analyses, however, was indeed an assumption that corruption is "wrong" and represents a move away from what we might understand as "good" (or "right") behaviour. But adjudicating on what is right and wrong requires subjective judgements to be made, and that leads us to our next problem.

CORRUPTION AS A MORAL DILEMMA

Corruption, no matter how it is defined, has a moral dimension to it. That remains so regardless of the fact that economists in particular would prefer to couch their analysis, and, indeed, their prescriptions, in the language of rationality, interests, costs and benefits. Much of the recent literature on corruption – produced largely by those with the economist's mindset – has purposefully avoided the moral minefield and instead aspired to embrace "'objective' or 'scientific' approaches to the study of corruption" (Bukovansky 2002).

Given how slippery the issue of morality traditionally is, might the economist's approach not make sense? Would it not be easier and more consistent to simply give the whole morality debate a wide berth? There are understandable reasons for doing that; for example, it helps researchers avoid normative questions wherever possible, making it much easier to meet academic standards of rigour and robustness. However, effectively imagining that moral dilemmas are not there does not make them go away, and that is so even if "the contours of the moral person" remain very difficult "to research empirically" (Hallisey 2015: 307).

Bringing issues of morality back into our analysis helps us comprehend much more about what we understand corruption to be (see Chapter 3) as well as how (and, indeed, whether) we go about tackling it (see Chapters 7–9). The moral dimension to the corruption challenge, therefore, cannot be an optional extra, even if some argue that in defining it as a moral problem we are rendering it both "immeasurable and imponderable" (Wraith & Simpkins 1963: 17). Many anthropologists, sociologists and political analysts do not have much of an issue with corruption being (apparently) "immeasurable" (see Chapter 4 for more on this); but we can choose to ponder whatever issues we please. In other words, just because moral questions are awkward to answer does not mean we should not try to do so.

DEFINITIONS OF RIGHT AND WRONG

Claims that we should bring the issue of morality back into our corruption-thinking are one thing. Actually doing so is much more difficult. First, morality is clearly not a constant. It changes over time and, indeed, across space. John Noonan has colourfully illustrated this in a discussion of gifts and bribes in the Ancient Near East (starting around the fourth millennium BCE). Here, reciprocity (or the giving of gifts) was part of the moral foundation of life. "The bribe", Noonan notes, "did not exist and was not known". As and when strangers met, they gave each other gifts to avoid hostile reactions; to go empty handed was not an option, and chances were you would be encouraging an aggressive response if you did. The gift bought you a peaceful hearing. You bribed the stranger into reacting peacefully towards you. As Noonan further notes, it was simply "unnatural to depart from reciprocity", and no one thought of the process as anything other than normal and above board (Noonan 1986). Now, however, turning up and giving powerful strangers expensive gifts may be viewed altogether differently.

In the modern era, moral dilemmas often get wrapped in the language of ethics. Indeed, the two concepts cover very similar territory, and at times it can be quite hard to tell them apart. However, the two words are not synonyms, and there is a basic, if nuanced, difference between them. Morals are personal. Your moral positions will help shape your own understanding of what is right and what is wrong. When, if at all, is it right for humans to condemn other humans to death via capital punishment? When, if at all, is it right for humans to permit other humans to allow themselves to be killed (euthanasia)? When, if at all, is it right to terminate the life of a human foetus? These are all questions with a very obvious moral dimension.

That political issues such as these are specifically regarded as moral questions has led some Commonwealth countries to allow what have come to be known as "free votes" in parliament. Parliamentarians, in other words, are free to follow their respective consciences without any input from the party of which they are a part (and which normally strongly directs their voting behaviour). That other acts (going to war, deciding on how much support the state gives the poor, and so on) also involve clear moral choices can sometimes get overlooked; but the moral dilemmas are there nonetheless.

Ethics, meanwhile, is slightly different. Ethics does not centre on individuals: it concerns systems. A system of ethics is one where individuals are guided when it comes to applying their particular moral standards. Ethics, in other words, are standards that have been developed to shape the behaviour of individuals within a given group or setting. These standards could be within parliaments, they could be within companies, they could be within professional groups (such as doctors or lawyers), or they could be within families. All of these systems guide members as to what is appropriate behaviour in any given setting.

To give an example of how morals and ethics differ, it is best to think about a straightforward case. A criminal defence lawyer may well find herself defending someone who she thinks is guilty. Indeed, her client could be guilty of a crime that more or less everyone abhors (murder or rape, for example). The morals that shape the lawyer's own private life will lead her to reject the defendant's behaviour as immoral. However, she knows that in Western systems of justice everyone – absolutely everyone – has the right to have their case heard and their position defended. The ethics of the legal system mean that the morals of the individual defending the case cannot take priority.

Be that as it may, one is still left with the challenge of not just working out one's own moral positions, but also developing broader systems of ethics to shape behaviour in particular settings. Sometimes these ethical systems are vague and largely undefined. The public ethos of the UK civil service, for example, has traditionally been one in which civil servants are socialized into making ethically appropriate decisions based on the public interest as well as their own judgement of what that interest is. Recent trends towards (and, in places, subsequently away from) so-called new public management have challenged this (Hood 2011). More detailed guidelines have become the norm, directing and shaping the responses of public servants to the moral challenges they may face. While for a time this was very fashionable, there have been plenty of critics who believe it leads to a culture of box-ticking, whereby public servants concentrate rather more on what is not wrong and rather less on what is right (Heywood & Rose 2015; Heywood 2012).

In terms of corruption more broadly, the debate is less fiddly. Many argue that corruption is morally and ethically always a "bad thing". TI certainly adopts a zero-tolerance attitude towards corruption, and many in academia start from precisely the same position. "Corruption", argues Geetanee Napa, "in absolute terms is unethical".[5] Even in cases where someone with the power of discretion is faced with two "bad" options, they, if they are behaving in a morally upstanding manner, will choose the "least bad" option available. The logic of that position would seem to be unquestionable.

That logic only fits together, however, if there *is* a "least bad option"; there is then an assumption that an objectively correct decision can be made. But what if people disagree on what the right moral or ethical behaviour is? What if we cannot agree on what the "least bad option" is, and what if there is no consensus on what the most appropriate response to a given situation might be? It is not that we might disagree on the outputs; it is more that we can disagree fundamentally on the processes that get us into the positions where these outputs are produced. As quickly becomes apparent, there are a number of moral and ethical dimensions that bring any one-dimensional understanding of appropriate behaviour into question.

The point is not to agree that we should all condemn grand corruption involving many millions of pounds, or, indeed, the traffic police officer who extorts a bribe in exchange for overlooking a traffic offence. It is more that, when anti-corruption laws are created and policies and strategies are suggested, those involved are calling instinctively (albeit often indirectly) on their own understandings of right and wrong. In that sense, they make subjective rather than objective calls. Working out what is ethically acceptable is subsequently important in helping us understand whether there might be cases in which one person's "appropriate" behaviour is another person's "inappropriate" conduct.

THE HEAD TEACHER AND THE PROBLEM OF STUDENT ADMISSIONS

The above point is probably best made using a hypothetical example. Imagine a scenario in which pupils have to pass a series of tests in order to be admitted to what is the only good school in a big city where the schools are known to be generally poor. Students from right across the city

---

5. For more on TI's attitude to corruption, see Transparency International (2016c) and Napal (2006).

compete via these tests to try to gain entry to the school. Competition for places every year is intense. Entry is granted to students who pass all the tests. Should, for practical purposes, too many students pass the tests, then students with the highest overall average will be admitted.

The head teacher of the school is the first to see all of the results. She notices that one prospective pupil from a very poor area of the city has passed all of the exams except one: they have narrowly failed physical education (PE). This student is top of the class in all of their other subjects. Based on this information, the head teacher should reject that child's application to come to the school, as, although the child has performed admirably in all but one of their subjects, they did not make the grade in PE. Furthermore, the head teacher knows that, in a country where corruption is a real problem, it is important to keep illustrating that entry to her school is based on merit and not personal favours. The results of the tests are not announced publicly, but the head teacher is aware that if for any reason she lets the pupil in and the results somehow become public, then she will have some explaining to do.

However, the head teacher is also well aware that most of the students who pass the exams come from good, middle-class families. They have often paid serious money for hours and hours of personal tutoring, and they have been preparing for these exams for many months, indeed, in some cases, years. The culture within their families will be one in which passing exams is encouraged and expected. The head teacher knows that the case in front of her involves a student from the very poorest part of the city. The student did not go to a particularly good primary school but has still performed remarkably well in the tests. They are unlikely to have benefited from the (expensive) personal tutoring that others have had. The head teacher is aware that students such as this only get this far very infrequently, largely because the structural constraints on them are so severe.

Additionally, in the head teacher's opinion, narrowly failing PE is not the same as narrowly failing, say, maths or one of the natural sciences. There is no evidence at all of any cheating. Given all of this, and after much head scratching, the head teacher offers the child a place.

The head teacher has clearly broken the rules, and she has done so deliberately. However, she feels that she is entitled to in this context. Indeed, not just entitled but morally obliged to. The good that will be gained by admitting the child is greater than the harm that overlooking one failed test might do. For some people (although not everyone), the head teacher's behaviour will be morally acceptable. For others, through clenched teeth perhaps, it will not be. She knows this is an abuse of her position, but she feels that the student will be detrimentally affected by a rejection, and that this could quite plausibly have a profound effect on their future. Indeed, the head teacher thinks it would be an abuse of her position *not* to offer the child a place; the system is stacked against children from poor neighbourhoods and very much in favour of perpetuating a cycle of middle-class achievement. She feels that she has a case here of someone – surprisingly and unexpectedly – beating that system. Indeed, the head teacher feels that other children (and their parents) from similar backgrounds might be inspired by seeing this child admitted to her school.

DOES IT MATTER WHAT WAS INTENDED?

The dilemma that our fictional head teacher has just faced is one that philosophers have pondered before. Indeed, a number of philosophers have specifically thematized the relationship between corruption and ethics in settings very similar to this. The German philosopher Immanuel Kant was one of the foremost thinkers in this regard. He argued that the outcome of the act in question is only of secondary importance when compared with the intent of the actor involved in the process. Kant claimed that if a person in power acts in a way that they believe is morally right, then they are indeed acting morally.

The flip side of this, of course, is that an act cannot be regarded as moral if the actor is simply doing it out of duty. The actor may be following all of the rules, all of the conventions and all of the norms of behaviour, but, in the end, if they are doing something simply because they have to, then it cannot be regarded as a moral act. For example, a batsman in cricket claiming that he "walks" (i.e. acknowledging that he is out before the umpire officially makes his decision) is no good if he only does so because he is sure the umpire would have given him out anyway. To claim that you are a "walker" – a type of person that is still held in high regard by many cricket aficionados – when, secretly, you know that you do not walk all the time would be the very opposite of morally upstanding behaviour.

Given this, it is clear that for thinkers like Kant corruption is all about the process and not about the outcome. A theoretically corrupt act can be fine and upstanding as long as it is done for higher, morally acceptable reasons. This also means that there will be circumstances in which personal gain could theoretically ensue but would not make the act corrupt. The point, however, is that the decision was not committed for personal gain; that is a completely independent side effect of the morally upstanding act.

CORRUPTION AS PART OF THE SOLUTION?

Kant's point about process and outcome poses interesting questions for policy-makers. Is corruption justified if it can be shown to lead to more-rather than less-agreeable policy outcomes? To be clear, the vast majority of evidence indicates that corruption has a negative impact on many public policies (see Chapter 6). It leads not just to lower levels of economic growth, but also to a range of other negative developments; higher levels of infant mortality, shorter life spans and the like. In the 1950s and 1960s, there was, however, an attempt to rethink corruption's role in economic development (see pages 95–7 for more on this). Indeed, this movement also represented an attempt to face down some of the moral dilemmas that have made corruption analysis so difficult to undertake. As noted above, until this point corruption was overwhelmingly seen as a "bad thing" with corrosive effects. Philosophers tried to unpack the moral and ethical dimensions of this "badness", but in essence everyone still agreed that corruption was by and large something to be avoided.

The revisionists' starting point was an interesting one. They argued that despite the fact that corruption made periodic appearances in Western political thought, it was still rather patronizingly understood as a developing-world problem. According to the prevailing consensus, corruption happened in premodern states, which, as and when these states "caught up", would inevitably tackle corruption as part of the process of modernization. The West, so the logic went, once had a corruption problem too, but it tackled this as democracy set in and as countries got richer. Corruption was subsequently squeezed out of the system.

There were, so the revisionists argued, two problems with this narrative. The first was that the West was certainly not free of corruption, either at that time, or at any time before or since. While for much of the twentieth century it was easy enough to write off incidences of corruption as the work of rogue individuals, the sheer scope and scale of the corruption cases that hit the Western world in the immediate post-Cold War era rendered this position increasingly untenable. The West had corruption problems too; these problems simply differed from those in other parts of the world. The nature of the corruption challenges evident within the West differed starkly from one polity to another, whether this was the clientelistic politics of Austria, the perennial party-funding scandals in Spain or, indeed, the troubles surrounding London's financial sector. Many may still argue that the world of anti-corruption sounds too much like Westerners talking down to non-Westerners, but there is little doubt that a penny has dropped somewhere. Corruption is a challenge for everyone, and it is a challenge that comes in many guises.[6]

The second problem with the prevailing consensus of that time was that a number of the reforms that should, in theory, have led to both greater economic development and the embedding of democracy were seen to be failing. The "modern" states that were apparently going to bring with them fewer corruption problems did not seem to be materializing. Decolonization had been a much more difficult process than many thought it was going to be, as democratic development stalled and many citizens were forced to live in (often abject) poverty. This brought corruption on to the radar. Many mainstream economists argued that tackling corruption was the key to generating economic wealth; corruption was the brake that was holding reform back. Not everyone agreed, but corruption certainly rose up policy agendas as a result. Others went the opposite way, arguing that corruption might have a role to play as a force for good (see pages 95–7). Corruption could help breathe life into stultified economies by enabling efficient economic actors to get around self-serving bureaucracies. The bribes they paid did not just help them make a profit: they gave others jobs and subsequently income that they otherwise would not have had. If this argument were to hold up, then corruption's moral dilemma was going to get even more complicated. What was morally reprehensible about a process that actually helped individuals prosper a little and rendered communities just a bit better off? Chapter 6 deals with how this thinking pans out in the real world in more detail.

CONCLUSION

This chapter has illustrated that corruption analysis has a long history. It has also illustrated that, for much of that history, notions of corruption have centred around ideas of moral decay. Corruption was nonetheless

---

6. Particularly sharp criticisms have come from the likes of Steven Sampson and Mlada Bukovansky; see, for example, Sampson (2008) and Bukovansky (2006).

often analysed with a view to explaining something else: why states failed, or how to create legitimate government, for example. Attempts were only sporadically made to unpack corruption as a concept, and that reluctance prevails in some disciplines right up to the present day. Despite the fact that for many philosophers morals were at the core of much corruption analysis, it has long been clear that getting to grips with corruption's moral dimension is not easy. If, however, the analyst wants to understand the concept's richness, then bringing morals, values and ethics into the discussion is unavoidable. That this has not been the case during corruption's recent resurgence as a topic of interest has much to do with the problems inherent in defining it. Indeed, changes in the way corruption has been defined have had clear effects on our understanding not just of what corruption is but also of what should be done to try to fight it. The definitional challenge has been touched on already, but the next chapter takes these issues apart in much more detail.

3.
The definitional challenge

The last chapter looked at the history of corruption as an idea, but it skirted around the vexed question of what precisely corruption is. We know that the meaning of the term has changed over time, and that traditionally this meaning had a lot to do with morals and ethics. We also know that when morals are brought into the debate – as they arguably have to be – we are faced with the tricky conundrum of right and wrong as well as the inherent challenge of subjectivity. This particular set of challenges has often made conducting empirical research difficult, which is the main reason that until the 1990s corruption remained a subject of largely secondary interest in academia.

Paradoxically, the problem of pinning down a definition of corruption led to a plethora of potential definitions developing. What you do not specifically explain will often be interpreted in ways that suit those doing the interpreting. Nevertheless, in the world of Western policy-making, at least, this has not prevented an emerging agreement on corruption's definition from developing (see below). Be that as it may, corruption remains "a capacious, changing and contested term" (Knights 2016: 3). This chapter unpacks the most important of these definitional dimensions, identifying not just the strengths and weaknesses of the definitions used but also how useful they are for understanding real-world corruption challenges.

One part of that definitional challenge is undoubtedly linguistic. On the one hand, this comes from the way that the term corruption is used in public discourse. The term is now often utilized as a stick with which to beat political opponents, and it frequently appears to be more of a term of abuse than a statement with any basis in reality. Indeed, there are times when it appears to be fine to label virtually anything you do not like as corrupt. Whether it is Donald Trump claiming that Hillary Clinton may be the "most corrupt person ever" to run for president, or tabloid newspapers bemoaning the "corruption of the political class", we are in danger of turning the term into an empty box, into which you can simply place things of which you do not approve (Gambino 2016; McKinstry 2010). It is not that there are no processes (or, indeed, politicians) out there that deserve to be branded corrupt; it is more the apparently indiscriminate nature of the term's usage, and the willingness to tar those one does not like with this particular brush that is problematic. To put it bluntly, understanding corruption simply as a term of abuse is of no use to anyone.

The second part of the linguistic challenge comes from the fact that the term exists in many languages, yet the nuances that shape and mould its precise meaning differ considerably. As Arnold Heidenheimer wrote back in 1970, "any attempt to analyze the concept of corruption must contend with the fact that in English and other languages the word corruption has a history of vastly different meanings and connotations" (Heidenheimer 1970: 3). In Mandarin, for example, one can talk of fǔbài ("corruption"), but also of Wǔbì ("fraud"), Huì Lù ("bribery") and guān xi ("relationships"). All four terms can be translated into English, but the deeper meanings that come from their use in a Chinese context are inevitably very tricky to accurately convey.

Guān xi, for example, can be nothing more than a network of friends and acquaintances, or it can be something rather more complex that helps you circumvent problems and challenges as and when required. Guān xi certainly needs to be cultivated, and the best and most obvious way of doing this is through the exchange of gifts. But what gifts should be given when and to whom? The etiquette is complex. Gifts can range from small amounts of money, given (in what often appear to be ubiquitous red envelopes) to friends and family, to much more expensive tokens of appreciation, given at specific times of the year to officials and business acquaintances. Expensive "moon cakes", for example, are often gifted to those in authority during the second biggest festival of the year, the Autumn Festival. In addition, taking someone out for what is often quite an expensive meal is another way of ensuring that they know you appreciate them.

However, the advent of a significant anti-corruption drive by Chinese President Xi Jinping changed the country's gift-giving dynamics considerably. Gifts needed to be significant enough to show appreciation but not so ostentatious that they might catch the attention of members of the Communist Party's anti-corruption bodies. One would not want to "lose face" by dining in a restaurant that looked too cheap, but the days of banquets were (at least for a time) apparently over. The fortunes of Pernod Ricard through the Spring Festival (Chinese New Year) of 2013 illustrate the type of dynamics that were in play. Pernod Ricard is one of the biggest distillers of Scotch whisky in the world. In mid-2013, it announced that its sales in China had dropped by "double-digits in percentage terms" during the New Year period. Giving whisky was often previously viewed as a good way of shaping and moulding a relationship to one's advantage; people were, however, becoming more careful with regard to doing that. They had to think of other ways of cultivating guān xi. The nature, timing and value of gifts all have meanings that help build trust and credibility (Nie & Lamsa 2015; Smart 1993). Getting this gift-giving right can be hard for the Chinese, and it borders on impossible for foreigners (Lucas 2013).

Furthermore, in a country where the state has often been a distant entity, where the rule of law has had a decidedly chequered history and where rules and norms are subsequently interpreted flexibly, having a well-developed guān xi network is vitally important. These are connections that you can rely on in times of need. The participants subsequently often put more value on these relationships than they do on the often ill-defined rules and norms imposed on them by the state. In this context, drawing a line between where corruption begins and where simply keeping a well-developed network of contacts ends requires a well-developed understanding of both Chinese culture and Chinese norms. Again, these are things that foreigners will always find difficult to make sense of.

THE DEFINITIONAL MINEFIELD

"It's complicated" is not a satisfactory answer when trying to define a term. So, where does one begin when attempting to make sense of corruption? In essence, there are four types of contemporary definition. First, there are those that are based on legal understandings of corruption. Second, there are definitions that centre around an abuse of entrusted power. Third, there are those that involve business-to-business transactions. Finally, there is a relatively new and developing set of definitional claims made by those who analyse what has been termed "legal corruption".

Approaches that take the law as their starting point begin, unsurprisingly, with a given state's legal framework. This has the advantage of giving the corruption analyst clear markers as to what is corrupt, bringing much-needed clarity to what can become a confusing debate. If an act is committed that breaks a law designed to tackle corruption, then the act in question is understood as an act of corruption. On the flip side, if an act – no matter how morally questionable – is legal, then it cannot by definition be understood as corrupt. The clarity that a legal understanding of corruption offers is seen as outweighing the nuances and depth (but also confusion) of definitions that look to bring in either morals or ethics.

Furthermore, there is a growing body of international law that provides a framework for universalizing our understanding of corruption. UNCAC (see Chapter 7) is the most high-profile source of anti-corruption law, and, over time, more and more states have passed national legislation that brings their own legal frameworks in line with it. In other words, we are slowly gaining some clarity and consistency in our understanding of what corruption is. There are those who argue that universalist understandings of corruption are fundamentally misguided, but that certainly has not stopped the universalist logic from being embraced by the most prominent international institutions in this area.

There are, however, a number of problems with using the law as your starting point. First, the internationalization of anti-corruption thinking has not prevented states from having very different sets of national legal provisions. What might be seen as corrupt in one country may be seen as perfectly acceptable in another. Even in countries that have similar historical, cultural and economic backgrounds, variations in legal norms, traditions and provisions may be considerable. There is, therefore, a danger that using the law as your benchmark can lead to a false clarity. Indeed, important nuances in our understanding of corruption can be overlooked on largely procedural grounds.

Second, many acts that could legitimately be understood as corruption are captured under pieces of legislation that were not really made for that purpose. In and of itself, that is not a problem; if a person breaks a law then all that matters is that they are brought to justice. However, in terms of understanding whether an act is corrupt or not, this can lead to no little confusion. Not every crime is an act of corruption, just as not every act of corruption is a crime. For example, the UK's anti-corruption legal infrastructure throughout the twentieth century comprised three acts: the Public Bodies Corrupt Practices Act 1889, the Prevention of Corruption Act 1906 and the Prevention of Corruption Act 1916. The Anti-terrorism, Crime and Security Act 2001 added more depth to this, including as it did a number of clauses on overseas corruption. There were, however, a number of other acts in place that ostensibly looked to do other things but also had a corruption element to them. The Honours (Prevention of Abuses) Act 1925 is arguably the most prominent case in point. This hotchpotch did little to clarify precisely what corruption was or where the difference between criminal and corrupt behaviour lay. This may not appear to matter much, but if you are explicitly trying to tackle corruption, it is useful to know exactly what corruption is legally understood to be.

Third, public servants are not daft; they know that breaking the law normally leads to trouble, so they do not (generally) do it. Rather, they may well find ways of bending the law or, indeed, skilfully circumventing it, getting what they want while legitimately claiming they have done nothing wrong. The 2016 case of then Icelandic Prime Minister Sigmundur Gunnlaugsson offers a good example of this. Gunnlaugsson owned an offshore company, the details of which he had not declared to parliament. Details of the offshore assets of both Gunnlaugsson and his wife only became public after the release of over 11 million documents by the Panamanian law firm Mossack Fonseca. Gunnlaugsson stood accused of concealing millions of pounds worth of family assets and skilfully (and legally) protecting them while Iceland's banks collapsed. He had done nothing wrong in a legal sense, but the impression that he was more interested in his own (and his family's) financial future than those of the many Icelanders whose assets were being threatened saw him quickly forced to resign.

In countries such as the US, meanwhile, the legal definition of corruption is now so narrow that, unless an official is actually caught red-handed paying off someone, it is very hard to imagine situations in which officials can still be prosecuted for corruption. The case of Bob McDonnell, the former governor of Virginia, is particularly insightful here. In 2016, McDonnell had a conviction for corruption overturned by the Supreme Court. The Supreme Court was passing judgement on the nature of the relationship between McDonnell (and his wife) and Jonnie Williams, an entrepreneur who was trying to develop a business selling dietary supplements. Williams went to considerable lengths to develop that relationship, so much so that he gave gifts totalling $175,000 to the McDonnell family. McDonnell, meanwhile, set up meetings for Williams, called other officials on his behalf and hosted events for him. Indeed, on one occasion in 2012, McDonnell allowed Williams to shape the guest list at a reception for state health care leaders (Zapotosky *et al.* 2014).

McDonnell insisted that he never did anything specifically *because* he had been lavished with gifts. There was, his lawyers argued, never a quid pro quo. Indeed, McDonnell was simply supporting a local business-man, and he would have done much the same for any other local busi-nessman who needed a helping hand. The Supreme Court agreed. Chief Justice John Roberts argued that although what McDonnell did – taking gifts of Rolexes, wedding gowns and such like – may well have been dis-tasteful, there was no evidence that he specifically changed his behaviour on account of those gifts.

What the court effectively decided was that unless you had a clear piece of evidence documenting that X agreed to use their office to help Y on account of a gift that Y had given X, then you could not call it corruption. If you did, then a lawmaker would never be able to do anything for anyone who ever donated money to any of their campaigns, lest it look like they had been bribed. On the one hand, this may sound logical, but what is also being said is that, given that we can never know exactly what a poli-tician (or, indeed, anyone else) is thinking at any given time, it has now become virtually impossible – assuming the politician is smart enough to not inadvertently document a bribe in writing – to convict on the grounds of corruption (Cillizza 2016). This case prompted the *Washington Post* to claim that in the US it was now "almost impossible" to imagine scenarios in which politicians could be successfully prosecuted for indulging in cor-ruption (*ibid.*; see also Toobin 2016).

ABUSES OF ENTRUSTED POWER

Many analysts look to move beyond legal definitions by bringing context back in to the discussion. They try to understand corruption in slightly broader terms. These definitions centre around the abuse of entrusted power for private gain. Elected politicians and appointed public servants are expected to act in line with what is effectively a job spec. If they deliber-ately – corruption is never accidental – act in a way that is in line with their own interests, or, indeed, the interests of friends, family or other preferred parties, rather than the way that that job spec proscribes, then they are perceived to be acting in a corrupt fashion. These definitions nonetheless involve a subjective judgement on the part of the analyst as to when "abuse" is actually taking place. That judgement call is often much more difficult in practice than it might seem in theory. For that reason alone, it is very unlikely that there will ever be any agreement on an objective set of criteria against which potential acts of corruption can be understood.

Be that as it may, arguably the most well-known definition of corruption can be found in this category. Back in 1967, Joseph Nye claimed that

> corruption is behaviour which deviates from the formal duties of a public role because of private-regarding (personal, close family, private clique) pecuniary or status gains; or violates rules against the exercise of certain types of private regarding influence.
>
> (Nye 1967: 417)

Nye's definition has been followed by many others, often with only small modifications. TI, the world's leading anti-corruption NGO, talks of "the abuse of entrusted power for private gain", while the OECD believes corruption to be "the active or passive misuse of the powers of public officials (appointed or elected) for private financial or other benefits" (OECD 2013; Transparency International 2016e). The IMF follows Nye almost to the letter, claiming that corruption is "the abuse of public office for private gains".[1] The World Bank uses very similar language ("the abuse of public office for private gain").[2] Thus, the understanding of corruption as a deliberate act in which an official uses the discretion at their disposal to deliberately skew a process or an outcome in their favour is now very widely followed. However, it is also often cited, taken as a given and then simply forgotten about. Any further digging around and "corruption" suddenly gets fiddly and complicated as well as very difficult to get a handle on analytically. This prompts many analysts to steer well clear of becoming further engaged with definitional issues.

The (at times uneasy) consensus around Nye's definition has, however, far from ended the debate about precisely how corruption should be understood. This debate is nonetheless livelier in some academic fields than it is in others. In economics, for example, discussions on the nuances of what we should understand "corrupt practice" to be are particularly underdeveloped. This is the case despite some economists warning that, although it may appear to many to be a semantic issue, it does affect what questions you seek to answer and how, indeed, you seek to answer them (Jain 2001: 73). In the words of Toke Aidt, "the definition of the concept determines what gets modelled and what empiricists look for in the

---

1. International Monetary Fund (2016a). For a good summary of what the IMF believes corruption's negative effects are, see Schiller (2000).
2. World Bank (1997), "Helping countries combat corruption". URL: http://bit.ly/2b4hOnV.

data" (Aidt 2003: 623). Sloppy definitional work can and has led to both skewed measurements and ultimately to inappropriate policy suggestions (Hodgson & Jiang 2007: 1043).

Political scientists and anthropologists are rather more alive to these concerns, and definitional debates in these discplines continue unabated. Most recently, Bo Rothstein, for example, has argued that it might be helpful to turn the debate about corruption around. By this he means that very little thinking has been done on what the polar opposite of corruption might be. He subsequently claims that if we think about that, then we might be in a better position to understand more about corruption's key attributes. For Rothstein, the opposite of corruption is impartiality. He goes on to argue that those who try to unpack corruption's constituent parts need to think about where they stand on four dimensions: (a) universalism versus relativism, (b) uni- versus multi-dimensionality, (c) the normative versus the empirical and (d) whether their preferred definition relates to policy outcomes or the way that politics produces those outcomes. For Rothstein, the answers are clear. He sees corruption as a universal concept that is one-dimensional. He also embraces the need to look at the way the world should be (i.e. normative) rather than the way the world actually is (i.e. empirical), and he rejects the notion of judging a definition by the outcomes it produces, preferring instead to stress procedures and processes. This leads Rothstein to regard "impartiality as the basic norm for the implementation of laws and policies" and acting in any other way than impartially as being, to a greater or lesser extent, corrupt (Rothstein 2014: 737).

Rothstein certainly does not sit on the fence. He is far from shy in placing himself squarely in a camp that critics would argue is firmly rooted in the Western world, and which, subsequently, embraces Western norms of what is appropriate. These Western norms are then expanded to being universal assumptions about the way politics is and should be. Rothstein would not necessarily disagree (Rothstein & Teorell 2008). Unsurprisingly, anthropologists, another group whose disputes about definitions are frequent, are fiercely critical of many of the assumptions that underpin this sort of thinking. Elizabeth Harrison, for example, criticizes what she claims is a very Western understanding of both public office as a concept and the notion of rational-legal bureaucracy more generally (Harrison 2007). These Weberian ideas, so anthropologists argue more broadly, do not always travel all that well. Indeed, in some places elected politicians are actually expected to "abuse" their public roles to enrich their family and friends. As Michela Wrong once said of Kenya, win an election and "it's our turn to eat".[3] It does not say this in the Kenyan constitution, of course, and there are certainly no rules and regulations in which this is stipulated. Yet even the most cursory glance at how Kenyan (and many other states') politics works will reveal that the notion of public office being exclusively about public service often corresponds imperfectly with reality.

This clash between those who embrace what are in essence universalist understandings of corrupt practice and those who argue that there are many realities that prevent universal truths from emerging is an enduring one. Indeed, it leads to one of the most longstanding problems in the world of corruption analysis; ultimately, one's understanding of the corrupt will be indelibly linked with one's understanding of the political. As Mark Philp noted in 1997, the values, norms and ideas that shape our understandings of what politics actually is will be fundamental to understanding what is and is not an acceptable part of the process (Philp 1997, 2006). It is therefore hardly surprising that an interdisciplinary theory on the causes of (and solutions to) corruption remains elusive. This is not only because understanding corrupt behaviour is inherently complex, but also because "corruption research attracts people whose ideas on what the social world is are so fundamentally different" (Graaf et al. 2010: 166).

BUSINESS-ORIENTATED DEFINITIONS OF CORRUPTION

While political scientists and anthropologists wrestle with these difficulties, a third dimension to this debate has recently developed. The aim here is not necessarily to challenge legal or entrusted power definitions, but simply to broaden our understanding of how they work in practice. This broadening involves highlighting and analysing the role of the private sector in corrupt transactions. This certainly makes sense. While much of the social science literature on corruption is fixated on the public sector, work on compliance, business and, indeed, organizational behaviour more broadly has regularly touched on corruption issues. Daniel Kaufmann, former head of the World Bank's governance team, has been prominent in pushing this change in focus, highlighting what he terms "the privatization of public policy" (Kaufmann 2005: 82).

This increased interest in the role of the private sector has come about for two quite specific and distinct reasons. First, business has traditionally

---

3. For a review of Michela Wrong's thought-provoking book, see Bonner (2009).

been seen as responding to the incentives placed before it by more or less corrupt public officials. Economists in particular have been keen to understand the relationship in this way. Business responds to the incentives that power brokers offer it. The corruption therefore starts in, and analysis of it should be focused on, the state. Recently, it has been recognized that firms can also play a more proactive role in shaping potentially corrupt opportunity structures. There is, subsequently, a growing scepticism of the blind eye that can be turned to corrupters, and particularly of the assumption that the private sector is simply reacting to opportunity structures created by public officials, when, of course, it might well be that public servants are being well and truly worked over by skilful private actors (Brown & Cloke 2004: 283). The cases of Siemens, Daimler and Badische Anilin und Soda Fabrik (BASF), to name just three, illustrate that there are occasions when companies interact with the state in a fashion that can certainly be termed corrupt. The fact that Siemens used a wide-ranging system of bribes to help it achieve its business goals is now widely known, and this led to a $1.6 billion legal settlement in the US in 2008 along with total costs to the company of €2.5 billion (Watson 2013; Sidhu 2009). Daimler, meanwhile, paid $185 million to settle charges that it had used bribery as a fundamental part of its business model when trying to win government contracts in no less than 22 countries between 1998 and 2008. BASF was caught fixing the prices of vitamins and subsequently paid fines in both North America and Europe, totalling over half a billion US dollars (Dougherty 2007; Rubenfeld 2011). These are not just drops in the ocean; this is the type of behaviour that is planned, orchestrated and, in some cases, part and parcel of particular business models. These examples offer strong evidence as to why business behaviour is an important part of the corruption mosaic.[4]

Second, there has been some interesting work done recently on how transactions that ostensibly have nothing to do with the public sector can and should be understood as corrupt. The logic here is that although the state has nothing directly to do with the transactions in question, it is clearly affected by them. The case in 2012 of bankers manipulating the LIBOR interest rate in London illustrates the point well. This manipulation involved a series of fraudulent actions that were undertaken by banks to influence the rate of interest that they paid when borrowing money from one another. This might sound like an issue for the banks (and probably their lawyers) alone to resolve, but the LIBOR is, among

---

4. For more on these cases, see Hough (2017).

other things, used as an indicator when setting interest rates in the UK as a whole. Given that around seven million people in the UK are paying back mortgages on their homes and the rate of interest they pay on those mortgages is affected by that national interest rate, banks were effectively (and deliberately) defrauding UK mortgage payers to enrich themselves (Osborne 2015). The bankers involved were therefore affecting public policy for their own ends.

LEGAL CORRUPTION

The increased tendency to bring the behaviour of firms into the corruption discussion has contributed to the development of a final set of definitional issues. This involves what has come to be known as "legal corruption". Although hardly a new phenomenon, it crashed into the public spotlight in the spring of 2016 with the publication of the so-called Panama Papers. As noted above, the leak of over 11 million documents from the Panamanian law firm Mossack Fonseca revealed widespread attempts by well-off individuals to place funds in secretive, low-tax jurisdictions. That these practices took place was widely known, but the nature and extent of this illicit behaviour nonetheless came as a surprise to many. It led to a range of high-profile individuals having to defend their behaviour when, in the vast majority of cases at least, those involved had taken part in what were perfectly legal transactions.

That legality did not, however, shield those who had made use of Mossack Fonseca's services from accusations of inappropriate behaviour. There may be a clearly discernible line between, say, tax avoidance and tax evasion, but this was not a nuance that many observers were willing to take at face value. There was also a (perhaps unfair) feeling that the secrecy that underpinned all of these transactions was only necessary because something untoward was being hidden. The revelations in the Panama Papers looked and felt like (yet another) example of a distant ruling elite rigging the rules to suit their own needs.

The feeling that politicians are rigging a system to suit themselves is, of course, nothing new. Commentators have long pointed to processes of what is often termed state capture as evidence of that. State capture is when ostensibly legal processes and transactions take place that are widely regarded as corrupting the norms and values that should underpin an upstanding political process. Politicians are seen to systematically skew rules to suit their own interests. These very same politicians can then claim that their behaviour is perfectly legal and that they have no corruption case to answer. Often they will be correct, mainly as they themselves will have drafted the rules in the first place.

Examples of this sort of rule-shaping range from managing a state's affairs to enable them, or their allies, to pocket profits running into the billions of dollars, to small, low-scale indiscretions of an almost petty nature. In the case of the former, state capture often sees powerful non-government actors influencing and, indeed, manipulating the creation of new rules and regulations explicitly to their own advantage. They do this by bribing public officials and offering lucrative kickbacks when laws, rules and processes are shaped in ways that suit their interests. This generates huge rents for those in power, often while strengthening their control over political and economic processes. It also does much to exacerbate many of their countries' social, political and economic ills. Despite the fact that researching these questions empirically can be very challenging, there is now plenty of evidence that both resource-rich and transition countries in particular have fallen prey to these forces.[5]

The case of brothers Atul, Ajay and Rajesh Gupta in South Africa is indicative of how these processes tend to work. Despite having no formal role in government, the Guptas were accused in 2016 of exerting considerable influence not just on the appointment of government ministers but also on (in one high-profile case, at least) the sacking of them. They were also alleged to have had a considerable hand in the appointment of board members of major parastate companies. Indeed, their interests in coal, gold and uranium seemed to be particularly well catered for by the South African government of the time (see Monyake 2016). In the autumn of 2016, a damning 355-page report was published on the brothers' relationship with important members of the South African government. It talked openly of state capture (indeed, that is what the report was titled) and used unusually frank language in expressing concern about the Guptas' influence on South African public life (Public Protector of South Africa 2016).

Cases such as those involving the Guptas have prompted Joel Hellman and Dan Kaufmann to state that this issue has become "the most pernicious and intractable problem in the political economy of reform". Hellman and Kaufmann go on to decry the relative paucity of effort spent

---

5. See, for example, Innes (2014) and Hellman *et al.* (2003).

on disentangling it from other forms of corruption. The reason for that is not hard to discern. Data is devilishly difficult to come across, and actors on both the public and private sides of the divide have plenty of reasons to cover up their behaviour. Hellman and Kaufmann nevertheless attempted to do something about this paucity of data by developing a "state capture index" (Hellman & Kaufmann 2001; Hellman *et al.* 2000). Others have since risen to the challenge by developing competing approaches to getting more of an empirical handle on the phenomenon (see, e.g., Fazekas & Toth 2016). Methodological challenges abound (see Chapter 4 for more on those), but the aim is nonetheless clear: to gain more in-depth knowledge of the role that outside actors can play in distorting government affairs in their own interest.

Legal corruption does not have to come in such grand fashion. It can come in a decidedly down-to-earth, positively mundane manner, too. The 2009 UK parliamentarians' (MPs') expenses scandal has become a paradigmatic example of that. The *Daily Telegraph*, a UK newspaper, revealed that MPs were claiming expenses and allowances for a weird and wonderful array of activities, mostly in relation to their second homes. Some, for example, were found to be redesignating (or "flipping") their homes, enabling them to claim refurbishing and renovating costs on more than one property. That led to an array of what soon came to be regarded as questionable expenses claims being made. These included £2,115 for cleaning a moat (Douglas Hogg, Conservative) and £980 for bookshelves (Peter Bottomley, Conservative), right down to 49p for a doormat (John Barrett, Liberal Democrat), 30p for a jam doughnut (Rosie Cooper, Labour), 7p for a paper clip (David Cameron, Conservative) and even 4p for travel (Tristram Hunt, Labour). Five Sinn Féin MPs claimed over £500,000 in second-home allowances, despite never having even taken up their seats in parliament.

The vast majority of the claims made were not only legal but also within the specific rules stipulated by parliament. Fewer than a dozen parliamentarians broke the law, and those that did found themselves in court defending themselves (generally unsuccessfully) against (for the most part) accusations of false accounting. False accounting, however, has long been a criminal offence, irrespective of why you are indulging in it. On the other hand, the majority of the approximately 400 parliamentarians who chose, on account of the public outcry, to return money to the UK state did so without ever having been shown to have broken any rules.

The problem, of course, is that until the establishment of an independent oversight body immediately following the expenses furore, MPs regulated their own conduct. The expenses and allowances regime was brought in under Margaret Thatcher's tenure in the 1980s. It was allowed to expand in scope largely because giving MPs pay rises was seen as publicly problematic. Yet, many in and around Westminster were acutely aware that if MPs opted to throw in the towel and work five miles along the Thames in the City of London, they would not only enjoy a much quieter life but also very likely be able to stick an extra zero on the end of their salaries. That prompted the expenses and allowances regime to be developed in both a more generous way and to be exploited for purposes that it was not originally intended for.

These niceties were lost on many observers. They saw a simple case of power-holders shaping rules and regulations to suit themselves. And, in the strictest sense of the term, they were right. MPs did indeed have the power to decide their own expenses regimes, and that left the door open to some behaviour that MPs were uncomfortable defending in public. The problem, of course, is working out what an appropriate expenses regime should look like. The Independent Parliamentary Standards Authority (IPSA), the institution that now regulates such things, has not been without controversy, largely as the problems it faces are fundamental ones.[6] As noted above, understanding what is appropriate will always be linked to the morals and values that help individuals shape their own understandings of what is right and wrong, corrupt and non-corrupt. In that context, lawmakers are best placed allowing external bodies to regulate their affairs. If nothing else, it makes accusations that they are sneakily indulging in legal corruption much easier to fend off.[7]

CONCLUSION

It is highly unlikely that there will ever be one definition, or even one set of definitions, that keeps everyone happy. In the Western world, it nonetheless remains clear that when a politician or public servant deliberately chooses to look after her interests (or those of her friends, family or supporters) over and above those of the general public, then she is drifting into territory that

---

6. *Daily Telegraph* (2011), "Ipsa: the MPs' criticisms", 5 January 2011. Available at http://bit.ly/2kKNTpY, viewed on 5 December 2016.

7. For more on the MPs' parliamentary expenses episode, see van Heerde-Hudson (2014).

many would regard as corrupt. That may involve breaking the law, but in truth it usually does not. Everyone, more or less, knows that breaking the law can plausibly lead to very negative consequences, and it is subsequently avoided if at all possible. It is much safer to bend laws, rules or regulations than break them.

This has led to definitions that centre around the abuse of entrusted power gaining the most traction. But even then there are problems. In reality, a judgement has to be made as to when "abuse" takes place, and it is no longer always clear (if indeed it ever was) whether actors have to have clearly defined "public roles". If four bankers from Barclays can go to prison for a total of 17 years for rigging interbank interest rates and we can make a case for understanding that as corruption, then we can also make a case that the terminology of "public roles" is no longer as useful as it once was (Kirton 2016). People, in other words, are involved in corruption without necessarily having public roles, as the vast and growing literature on private sector indiscretions in this area illustrates. Our understanding of what is and what is not corruption has moved on from being almost impossibly broad and intertwined with notions of morals and ethics (see Chapter 2) to, by the 1990s, being excessively narrow and focused on private gain by public officials. Through the twenty-first century there has been a slow but necessary move back towards a much broader understanding of all the complexities that corruption entails.

However, the fact that the term "corruption" is being used increasingly loosely in public discourse does not help. The logic behind this understanding of corruption runs the risk of turning what are really disagreements about politics and policy into debates about corruption and, indeed, broader notions of legitimacy. As noted above, someone is not corrupt just because they say things you do not like, or do things with which you disagree. Indeed, making mistakes, or simply being incompetent, is not the same as being corrupt. We need to be clear in demarcating the concept from the rough and tumble of everyday political life. The real world of politics to one side, using corruption as a device with which to fling mud at your opponents does nothing to facilitate a serious discussion of what the term actually entails. We can, and must, do better than that.

4.

The measurement challenge

When policy-makers claim that they want to tackle corruption, they are making a statement about how much of it they think exists. For many, the answer to that question is likely to be simple: "too much". As a result, politicians are often happy to concentrate on tackling the problems that they see before them, without worrying unduly about broader issues of quantification. There is still, however, the nagging problem of how one empirically illustrates that an anti-corruption policy or approach is working. Before long, that inevitably brings you back to the thorny problem of measurement in some form.

Trying to discern how much corruption exists is nevertheless a task fraught with difficulty. For some (see below), the task is bordering on pointless. You cannot know for sure, so why bother spending lots of time and effort trying to find out? This has not stopped a growing number of organizations and individuals from trying to do justice to the measurement challenge. Some of their approaches are based on perceptions of corruption, some on individual experiences. Others use a range of proxies to measure what they argue might well be corruption. This means that, despite the deep-seated problems inherent in trying to quantify the phenomenon, we now have a range of tools at our disposal. This chapter outlines some of the most well known of these tools, illustrating both what they do well and where they fall down before moving on to analyse how their findings can inform the real world of anti-corruption policy.

As we saw in the previous chapter, there is still no agreement on what corruption precisely entails. Given that, what hope is there of reaching an agreement on how much of it exists? This leads critics to argue that, while most attempts to quantify corruption are no doubt well intentioned, corruption remains a classic contested concept that is, in effect, immeasurable. Corruption, in other words, is like the notions of fairness, freedom, democracy and justice: we know what they are when we see them, but knowing how much we have at any one time is, in any practical sense, impossible.

For others, this approach smacks of defeatism. Those of a more positivist persuasion will understand and acknowledge the difficulties and challenges that are inherent in trying to measure each and every social science concept, but, so they argue, that should not put us off trying to do it. For the most fundamentalist of the quantifiers, everything can be categorized as either a 1 or a 0. There are not, however, many of those fundamentalists about. In reality, the best and most useful attempts to quantify corruption recognize the shortcomings of their work and are careful in discussing their findings. They are also generally very quick to explain that their data should be used with caution.

Furthermore, it is not just certain academics who see the value in trying to measure corruption. Part of the drive towards quantification comes from the development and donor communities. They are particularly keen to know how much corruption is about, as they are often under real pressure to show that they are getting both results and value for money. This means being able to measure how much corruption you had in the first place, so that you can illustrate the impact of the policies/strategies you have implemented. Given this, issues of how to measure corruption deserve serious discussion.

THE QUANTIFICATION OF CORRUPTION

The idea of quantifying social science phenomena is a relatively new one. Indeed, it can be traced back to the onset of the "behavioural revolution" in the middle of the twentieth century. The turn towards analysing the social world through a more scientific lens had its roots not just in the advancement of the technology that enabled sophisticated data analysis to take place, but also in a growing disillusionment with the outputs of traditional political analysis. There was a particular disdain for the normative underpinnings of political research as it had been conducted up until then, and a belief that if political analysis wanted to remain relevant then it had to adopt the methods and approach – as far as possible – of the natural sciences (Dahl 1961). To analyse, in other words, what is, much more than what should be.

This change in approach revolutionized American political science in particular. Much of the rest of the world followed suit (Crick 1959), and the challenge of measuring contested concepts was subsequently embraced. Corruption certainly was not the first of these concepts to come in for systematic quantification, but by the 1990s it was attracting more and more attention. This was largely the case thanks to the pioneering work of a small group of people in what was then a relatively unknown NGO based in Berlin: TI. It was founded by Peter Eigen, a former employee of the World Bank, and has risen from humble beginnings to become a complex, international organization, with a yearly budget of around €27 million, representations (or "chapters") in more than 100 countries and a secretariat in Berlin (Transparency International 2015b).

TI's most well-known publication remains the annual CPI. The CPI (see Table 4.1) is a composite index. A variety of data sources are used to create what is in effect a poll of polls on perceptions of corruption in a given country. Data is gathered from surveys of business people and country experts, with the aim of measuring "the perceived levels of public sector corruption worldwide" (Transparency International 2016b). TI provides a detailed account of where its data comes from as well as how it uses it, and this is accessible via TI's own website.[1] The CPI was first published in 1995 when it included 41 countries, with New Zealand achieving the best score (i.e. nearest to 10) and Indonesia the worst (nearest to 0). Over the years, TI has changed the way it presents and produces its results, with the range of scores now stretching from 100 (no corruption) to 0 (complete corruption).

By 2016, the CPI had expanded to 176 countries (although in 2011 it included as many as 183), with Denmark (90) at the top of the pile alongside New Zealand, and Somalia (10) registering the lowest score (i.e. most corruption). When they couple this information with some further methodological tweaks, analysts can now (since 2013) compare the data across years, something that TI previously advised people not to do. The data is used, in varying ways and for varying purposes, by journalists, other anti-corruption organizations and politicians. The CPI has developed into a key brand name in the study of corruption worldwide.

Predictably, the best-performing countries share a significant number of characteristics. They are open, liberal democracies with a free press. They embrace the notion of transparency, helping citizens see where their

---

1. See, for example, the methodology and data section at Transparency International (2016f).

hard-earned tax money gets spent. They have independent judiciaries, and all support long-held assumptions about increased accountability leading to lower levels of corruption. The Nordic countries always do very well, as do countries in western Europe more generally. There are, however, always

Table 4.1 The Corruption Perceptions Index (selected scores).

Rank	Country / territory	2016 score	2015 score	2014 score
1.	Denmark	90	91	92
1.	New Zealand	90	88	91
3.	Finland	89	90	89
4.	Sweden	88	89	97
5.	Switzerland	86	86	86
6.	Norway	85	87	86
7.	Singapore	84	85	84
8.	Netherlands	83	87	83
9.	Canada	82	83	81
10.	Germany	81	81	79
10.	Luxembourg	81	81	82
10.	UK	81	81	78
18.	US	74	76	74
23.	France	69	70	69
27.	Bhutan	65	65	65
35.	Botswana	60	63	63
79.	Brazil	40	38	43
79.	China	40	37	36
79.	India	40	38	38
131.	Russia	29	29	27
166.	Iraq	17	16	16
173.	Syria	13	18	20
174.	North Korea	12	8	8
175.	South Sudan	11	15	15
176.	Somalia	10	8	8

Source: Transparency International (2017), "Corruption Perceptions Index 2016", Berlin: Transparency International. Available at http://bit.ly/2jo7IKy, viewed on 12 February 2017.

interesting outliers when some nations are compared to their regional peers: Singapore (7th in 2016) regularly appears in the top 10, while Botswana (35th in 2016) leaves many of its African counterparts in its wake. The countries at the bottom, meanwhile, also have lots in common. Leaving North Korea (12) to one side, these countries are often war-torn and bordering on ungovernable. The fact that South Sudan (11), Syria (13), Yemen (14), Sudan (14) and Libya (14) are immediately above Somalia (10) is evidence of that.

The CPI's prominence has certainly not shielded it from criticism. Indeed, criticizing the methodology that underpins the CPI has become a veritable cottage industry.[2] These criticisms cover a number of issues. To start with, boiling down a country's corruption troubles into one score is, to put it mildly, methodologically problematic. The type, scope and extent of corruption evident in, say, the city administration of Chicago is likely to be altogether different to that found in rural Wyoming. Computing one score to accurately cover such variety is always going to be very difficult. Plus, if a state were ever to register a score of 100, what precisely would that mean? What would a country with no corruption at all look like? Conversely, what would a country that scored 0 (i.e. was totally corrupt) look like? Any discussion of utopias usually ends in disagreement, and it is very likely that this would be the case here, too.

Furthermore, and as noted above, measuring concepts such as democracy, justice, fairness and corruption is hard at the best of times, but those who do it well acknowledge that their attempts are always approximations. Indeed, statisticians have developed their own language to discuss the problems in getting these measurements right. Even though the CPI's methodology has undoubtedly become more rigorous over the years, none of this is overtly acknowledged. This has led some researchers to cast doubt on whether such data can be put to any real use at all (Thompson & Shah 2005).

One type of potential bias concerns the issue of definitions. It is not always clear what respondents to surveys on this topic actually understand the term "corruption" to mean. On the one hand, the terms "bribery" and "corruption" often appear to be used interchangeably. On the other hand (and as was discussed in Chapter 3), there are plenty of definitional challenges around that may confuse respondents. Furthermore, responses to the various surveys on this issue are very likely – whether directly or indirectly – to be shaped by the assumptions and attitudes of the Western

2. See, for example, de Maria (2008), Andersson & Heywood (2009) and Hough (2016).

business community. This is simply because the majority of people asked have roots in this particular milieu (Andersson & Heywood 2009: 752–3).

The CPI also measures perceptions of corruption rather than corruption itself. TI regularly and consistently acknowledges that this can be problematic. While knowing more about how citizens perceive a phenomenon certainly has its uses, it is also plausible that perception and reality might differ considerably. The CPI may even be (inadvertently) distorting reality, simply reinforcing stereotypes and clichés. In TI's defence, there is a case to be made that perceived reality is actually more likely to shape their actions than reality as it truly is. If someone is on a bus and they think that a tiger is also on board, they are very likely to attempt to quickly get off. This would be the case regardless of whether the tiger was real or simply a figment of their imagination.

A further limitation is that the CPI focuses on perceptions of public sector corruption, that is, the corruption that takes place in and around governments and public servants. It says nothing about corruption in private business. As noted in Chapter 3, the rigging of LIBOR in Britain, for example, or the VW emissions controversies in the US (and, indeed, elsewhere), involved private actors; but they have very real public impacts, whether on the interest rates that people pay on their mortgages or on public health (BBC News 2015b; Spence 2015).

These problems have prompted a significant number of analysts to be quite scathing about the CPI. Steve Sampson, speaking for many in the development studies community, is sceptical of what he regards as "corruption becoming a scientific concept", as measurement tools such as the CPI can, and have, easily become objects of manipulation (Sampson 2007). Even fellow quantifiers such as Stephen Knack and Anwar Shah (from the World Bank) have criticized some of the statistical techniques that TI has employed in the past (Knack 2007; Thompson & Shah 2005). Indeed, Shah and Theresa Thompson leave no one in any doubt as to how grave they think the CPI's methodological shortcomings are when they state that "closer scrutiny of the methodology ... raises serious doubts about the usefulness of aggregated measures of corruption" and "potential bias introduced by measurement errors lead[s] to the conclusion that these measures are unlikely to be reliable, especially when employed in econometric analyses" (Thompson & Shah 2005: 8–9). Knack's careful dissection of the CPI also makes uncomfortable reading for TI defenders; he argues, for example, that no eastern European or central Asian state's score in 2005 was based on the same set of sources used in 2004. This is evidence, he claims, of the unreliability of scores even within one country, let alone on a cross-national basis (Knack 2007: 265). He also raises further significant issues about the independence – in a statistical sense – of the data used, claiming that many of the "statistically significant" changes that TI claims to have uncovered would not be so in reality if "appropriate corrections for interdependence" had been made (*ibid.*: 267).

For its part, TI has certainly tried its level best both to be open about the methodological shortcomings of the CPI (as well as its other corruption indices) and to adjust them wherever possible. For example, the founder of the CPI, Johann Graf Lambsdorff, is careful to acknowledge some of the methodological issues inherent in all composite indicators; he is always careful to describe changes in country scores from year to year as changes in perceived corruption, rather than in actual corruption levels (see, e.g., Lambsdorff 2005a, 2005b). TI has also tacitly admitted that the CPI has its limitations by the very fact that it has developed a whole host of other indices – such as the BPI and the GCB – to look at both the perceptions and experiences of specific groups of stakeholders (ranging from business-people to households) (Transparency International 2011, 2013b). One of TI's founders, Jeremy Pope, has been rather more explicit, claiming that "the CPI's major usefulness is in the past" and the TI has to be "a lot more sophisticated these days."[3]

Yet, all of these criticisms not withstanding, the CPI has done one indisputable thing: it has put the issues of corruption and anti-corruption well and truly on the policy map (Johnston 2005b: 875). As Andersson and Heywood observe:

> We should not underplay its significance in the fight against corruption: its value goes beyond the stimulation of research activity, since the publication of the CPI each autumn has generated widespread media interest across the world and contributed to galvanising international anti-corruption initiatives, such as those sponsored by the World Bank and the OECD.
>
> (Andersson & Heywood 2009: 747)

Even staunch critics of the quantification of corruption have begrudgingly admitted that, "whatever its limitations", the development of the CPI has "undoubtedly done much to promote the anti-corruption agenda"

---

3. As quoted in Andersson & Heywood (2009).

(Brown & Cloke 2004: 275). It is also doubtful that any of the more-nuanced indices that TI itself and other organizations have developed would have seen the light of day if the CPI had not existed before them (Andersson & Heywood 2009: 747).

OVER AND BEYOND THE CPI

The CPI is, however, not the only game in town. In terms of composite indices, the most highly regarded challenger comes in the form of the Worldwide Governance Indicators (WGI). One of the aims of the WGI is to measure the extent to which states "control corruption". The WGI represent one of the most ambitious attempts not only to measure corruption specifically, but also to measure the quality of governance more broadly. Given that governance as a concept is every bit as contested as corruption, this is no simple task. Yet, measuring governance has become one of the growth industries across the social science world, and there are now dozens (and even, some claim, hundreds) of attempts to do precisely that (Norris 2010; Arndt & Oman 2006). Governance, or "the traditions and institutions by which authority in a country is exercised", is clearly a term that goes over and above corruption (Worldwide Governance Indicators 2016a). However, tackling corruption is regarded by many as an important part of getting governance right.

The WGI have long been overseen by Daniel Kaufmann, Aart Kraay and researchers at the World Bank.[4] First published in 1996, they are composite indices that seek to measure perceived levels of governance quality across six specific dimensions. The sixth and final of these dimensions focuses on "control of corruption" (CoC), and seeks to provide comparative data on how successful the over 200 states and territories in the data set are at achieving this. According to the WGI, their measure of how effectively states control corruption "captures perceptions of the extent to which public power is exercised for private gain". It includes "both petty and grand forms of corruption" and incorporates notions of state capture "by elites and private interests" (Worldwide Governance Indicators 2016b). The WGI are clearly trying to understand corruption pretty widely. Over 30 data sources are used with the aim of taking "the views and experiences of citizens, entrepreneurs, and experts in the public, private and NGO sectors" into account (*ibid.*). The data comes from four different sets of

---

4. For more on the WGI, see, for example, Kaufmann *et al.* (1999) and Kaufmann *et al.* (2009).

sources: surveys of households and firms (such as the Business Enterprise Environment Survey, the Gallup World Poll or Latinobarómetro); data produced by commercial business providers (such as political risk analysts or the Economist Intelligence Unit); NGOs (such as Freedom House or Global Integrity); and public sector organizations (such as regional development banks).[5]

These often quite wide and varied data sources are reorganized and aggregated by what statisticians would call an unobserved components model. This effectively means that WGI researchers try to find ways of assessing whether variables they cannot immediately quantify are affecting the variables they can. For the uninitiated, this process can be quite challenging, but in essence WGI researchers are trying to produce comparable data to generate scores that reflect how confident they are in that data; "margins of error", as they are known, basically give us a feel for how close the answers we get from our sample of data are to the answers we would get if we asked everyone we could possibly ask. The larger the margin of error, the less confidence we should have in the data being genuinely representative. Wonkish though this may all sound, this sort of approach does help us make international comparisons (across time and space) that are, in theory at least, more robust than those produced in the CPI.[6] Indeed, Dan Kaufmann and his colleagues are very keen to stress the "unavoidable uncertainty" that goes hand in hand with the process of measuring any abstract concept (Kaufmann *et al.* 2009: 2).

As with the CPI, the methodology that underpins the WGI has not remained constant. Over time, a number of revisions have been made, some of which affect data from previous years, and some of which have affected particular countries more than others. All six aggregate indicators are nonetheless reported in two ways. First, all countries are given a score for each indicator (of which CoC is one) that represents their "standard normal units". This score ranges from roughly –2.5 to 2.5, with 0 being the mean of all the scores for all the countries; so, if a country achieves a score that is greater than 0, then it is performing better than the (mean) average. The data is also presented in percentile rank terms from 0 to 100. The higher the score, the better the performance on that particular indicator.

As Table 4.2 illustrates, the countries that perform well in the CPI also perform well here. There is some variation in scores, however. Denmark registered the highest score in the 2015 CPI, whereas New Zealand did so in the

---

5. For a full list of sources, see Worldwide Governance Indicators (2016b).
6. For more detail on WGI methodology, see Kaufmann *et al.* (2010).

WGI's CoC data. The Netherlands underperforms (as it were) in the WGI's index compared with how it does in the CPI. These differences, however, cannot disguise the fact that the same sets of states do well across the board. Table 4.3 illustrates that the picture is not dissimilar for the states that perform badly. North Korea does better in the WGI's index, but in general the pattern is much the same as in the CPI. Unsurprisingly, war-torn states such as Sudan, South Sudan, Somalia and Afghanistan perform woefully.

READING THE DATA

What does this data mean? On the one hand, it could mean that, regardless of the methodological challenges, we are getting a pretty accurate snapshot of what is going on. Very few people would be prepared to make the case that the countries at both the right and wrong ends of these respective indices should not be there. Denmark really is a state where corruption is, for the most part, under control, whereas the likes of Sudan and South Sudan face a whole series of governance challenges, of which controlling corruption is certainly one. The data, in other words, could be strikingly similar, as it is picking up on widely visible and largely predictable trends.

Table 4.2 WGI's control of corruption, 2015: top 12 ranked countries in TI's CPI.

Country	Number of sources	Governance score	Percentile rank	Standard error	2015 CPI position
New Zealand	9	2.29	100.00	0.15	4
Finland	9	2.28	99.52	0.15	2
Norway	9	2.26	99.04	0.15	5
Sweden	8	2.25	98.56	0.15	3
Denmark	9	2.23	98.08	0.15	1
Switzerland	8	2.17	97.60	0.16	7
Singapore	10	2.13	97.12	0.13	8
Luxembourg	6	2.12	96.63	0.18	10
Netherlands	8	1.89	94.71	0.15	5
UK	9	1.87	94.23	0.15	10
Canada	10	1.85	93.75	0.15	9
Germany	8	1.82	93.27	0.15	10

It can be argued, however, that the similarity simply shows that the different organizations which look to measure corruption inevitably call on data sets that have much in common and/or suffer from the same sets of biases. The data are generally collected by organizations that adopt – broadly speaking – similar approaches. We therefore should not be surprised when we get similar answers, and it would be absurd to expect results to be very different. The WGI's CoC measure certainly includes more data from a wider range of sources than the CPI, but it remains a composite indicator, and so it can be criticized on much the same grounds as all other composite indicators.

Table 4.3 WGI's control of corruption, 2015: bottom 11 ranked countries in TI's CPI.

Country	Number of sources	Governance score	Percentile rank	Standard error	2015 CPI position
Haiti	10	−1.26	8.65	0.16	158
North Korea	5	−1.29	7.69	0.19	167
Venezuela	14	−1.33	5.77	0.13	158
Afghanistan	10	−1.34	4.81	0.17	166
Iraq	9	−1.37	4.33	0.17	161
Angola	9	−1.40	3.85	0.16	163
Guinea-Bissau	6	−1.43	3.37	0.21	158
Sudan	11	−1.50	2.40	0.16	165
Somalia	8	−1.62	1.44	0.18	167
Libya	8	−1.69	0.96	0.18	161
South Sudan	9	−1.71	0.48	0.21	163

Kaufmann *et al.* (2009) are quick to recognize the limitations of the WGI data, but they defend their use for three specific reasons. Indeed, the authors are rather more combative in their defence of their indicators than TI is of its various indices. First, Kaufmann *et al.* are quick to point out that, as noted above in terms of the CPI, perceptions matter. In their words, "agents base their actions on perceptions, impressions and views", and if people believe something to be true then it will, by definition, affect their behaviour. Second, indicators that claim to be objective (such as those based on the experience of something as opposed to those based on perceptions of it) can never take subjective influences out of the equation completely. All humans come with baggage, and that baggage affects how we interpret not just what we see but also what we experience. Finally, even when "objective" indicators may be readily available – Kaufmann *et al.* give the example of laws, rules and regulations – how they *are* implemented can often be substantially different from how they *should* be implemented (Kaufmann *et al.* 2009: 4). The WGI subsequently use aggregate indicators to organize a large and diverse amount of data, and they report not only the generalized trends but also the disaggregated scores. Indeed, these can – with a few minor exceptions – all be downloaded from the WGI's impressive website.

Furthermore, Kaufmann *et al.* (2007) are robust in dismissing accusations that their indicators are not reliable enough as "entirely lacking in empirical support". Even when there is some empirical evidence supporting these criticisms, the authors argue that "the effects are so small as to be practically irrelevant" (Kaufmann *et al.* 2007: 30). They give a prescient example in response to criticism from Stephen Knack concerning the fact that the average indicators are scaled to give them a mean of 0 (Knack 2007). In practice, this means that the WGI look to have 0 as an average, with countries registering scores either above or below that score. Over time, however, the number of countries included in the WGI has increased; hence, a country may theoretically have registered the same CoC score across time but could see its performance affected without having done anything at all to warrant such a change. Kaufmann *et al.* enthusiastically take up this point. They illustrate that, in 1996, they possessed data on controlling corruption from 152 countries. By 2005, they had data from 204 countries. Over time, the averages will inevitably have changed, simply as a result of more countries coming on board. However, Kaufmann *et al.* ran a variety of tests on their data to discern the actual impact of this. Their results demonstrated that, again, although such criticism is technically correct, the net effect on the data as a whole is nothing more than negligible (Kaufmann *et al.* 2007: 4).

This defence has not prevented some from arguing that the WGI may still prove to be unreliable. The indicators continue to rely on relatively small numbers of national "experts" for the bulk of their data. Arndt and Oman make the further claim that governance indicators in general, and the WGI in particular, have a tendency to stress the opinions of business leaders over those of other stakeholders (Arndt & Oman 2006). There is, however, a real danger that critics can border on the obsessive when talking about the minutiae of these indicators' methodology (see, e.g., Thomas 2010). That is not to say there are not issues worth discussing; however, there is a real danger of throwing the baby out with the bathwater. As Pippa Norris says, "these [the WGI] measures provide some of the best available gauges of good governance" and they can – with suitable caution – offer valuable pointers for policy-makers (Norris 2010: 424). That is as true for the CoC variable as it is for the other five.

FROM BROAD INDICES TO SPECIFIC DETAIL

Given the methodological challenges inherent in creating broad indices, recently the emphasis has shifted towards greater detail and away from increased breadth. As a result, we now have indices looking at, among other things, state capture, the (legal and illegal) influence of the lobbying industry, levels of financial secrecy and the quality of the business environment. A range of organizations have now entered the quantification game, and TI's own GCB and BPI also remain prominent parts of this ever-expanding picture.

The development of the GCB in 2003 was a clear response to criticism that the CPI was too focused on the elite. The GCB moves its emphasis away from experts and business leaders and on to ordinary people. It is a public opinion survey that in 2013 asked 114,000 citizens in 107 countries about their "direct experiences with bribery", before going on to detail citizens' "views on corruption in the main institutions in their countries" (Transparency International 2013b: 3). The latest round of the GCB, published in stages through 2015 and 2016, is equally as expansive. The intention of the GCB is to bring ordinary people into a field where their experiences and perceptions have traditionally been neglected.

The GCB's findings give plenty of food for thought. In 2013, more than one in four people around the world admitted to paying a bribe at some point over the past 12 months. The police and the judiciary were the most bribe-prone institutions. Over half the people surveyed regarded their government as acting in the interests of preferred groups over the citizenry at large (*ibid*.: 3). The picture was in many ways as gloomy in the apparently less-corrupt Western world as it was in other places. In the 2016 survey, for example, 53 per cent of citizens in 42 European and central Asian countries believed that their government was doing a poor job in fighting corruption. Perceptions were particularly gloomy in Spain (where 80 per cent of people thought their government was doing badly in this regard), Italy (70 per cent) and France (64 per cent) (Transparency International 2016g: 4, 15). The 2013 survey asked a slightly different set of questions, and the resulting data revealed that 65 per cent of New Zealanders felt that over the last two years the level of corruption had increased in their country, while only 5 per cent felt that it had decreased. The outlook was little better over the Tasman Sea in Australia; over the same time period, 59 per cent of Australians thought corruption had worsened, whereas, as in New Zealand, only 5 per cent thought it had got better. Things were not dissimilar in Europe; 57 per cent of Germans believed that there was more corruption in their country than two years previously, while only 8 per cent thought there was less. Furthermore, 65 per cent of Germans thought political parties were in general corrupt, 54 per cent thought the same of the media, and 49 per cent thought civil servants were either "corrupt" or "extremely corrupt" (Transparency International 2013d).[7] Sobering numbers.

The GCB has now firmly established itself as an important part of the measurement mosaic. To TI's credit, they reacted to criticisms of the CPI by introducing a detailed survey that helps bring people on the street back into the discussion. Data such as this does nonetheless highlight two further potential problems. First, Claudio Weber Abramo has illustrated that opinions on corruption as revealed by the GCB "are strongly correlated with opinions about other issues". It may well be that rather than picking up specific attitudes to corruption the GCB is tapping into a much larger worldview. Indeed, Weber Abramo claims that the correlation is so strong that we could actually save ourselves the time and effort of measuring public opinion in this area by simply reading across from data on attitudes towards concepts such as human rights and violence (Weber Abramo 2008).

Second, many of the things we think can help predict levels of perceived corruption (economic development, press freedom and so on) are not good predictors of how much corruption people claim they have personally witnessed (Treisman 2007). In other words, there is at times a considerable difference between the amount of corruption that people perceive to exist and the amount that they themselves experience. Only 1 per cent of Australians over the 12 months to 2013 paid a bribe, for example, yet 53 per cent thought corruption was a problem. In the 2016 survey, no Britons (!) reported paying a bribe, yet 57 per cent of people

---

7. For more on Germany, see Hough (2017).

thought that the UK government was doing badly at fighting corruption. This discrepancy could, of course, be a reflection of citizens' awareness of grand corruption that they themselves have not experienced directly. The differences between what people think and what people experience are nonetheless often very large indeed (Transparency International 2013b). Furthermore, the size of these differences can differ noticeably from place to place (Weber Abramo 2008). Such discrepancies are not simply the domain of the GCB; Eurobarometer surveys reveal similar patterns. As Paul Heywood has noted, 74 per cent of European citizens questioned in the 2012 Eurobarometer surveys believed corruption to be a "major problem", yet only 8 per cent reported any experience of bribery or attempted bribery. Personal experiences of corruption in Europe clearly remain low (Heywood 2015: 138).

The BPI, meanwhile, assesses the likelihood that companies from leading economies will use bribery to win business abroad (see Table 4.4; Transparency International 2011). It aims, in other words, to capture "the supply side of international bribery", focusing attention on the private rather than the public sector (*ibid.*). The 2011 BPI includes interviews with over 3,000 senior business executives who were, at the time, working in 28 different countries (*ibid.*). The intention of this index is to link the real-world experience of those who do business across national borders with a single, easily definable act (i.e. bribery). As with the CPI, TI has changed the methodology used in the BPI over time. In 2011, 22 of the 28 countries appeared in the previous (2008) index. Given that the methodology for these two indices is identical, their scores can be compared and contrasted.

However, that does not hold for comparisons of the 2008 and 2011 data with the BPI indices that came before them. The 2006 BPI, for example, was based on the responses of more than 11,000 business managers, using two questions that were included as part of the World Economic Forum's Executive Opinion Survey. The questions were rephrased in the 2008 and 2011 BPI surveys. Furthermore, the 1999 and 2002 BPIs were based on data from emerging market economies only, with a much smaller sample of respondents (Transparency International 2011). The data in these prior indexes, therefore, are not "wrong", it is just not appropriate to compare and contrast them with what has followed.

These second-generation indices illustrate that TI is attempting to evolve with the times. They provide individual-level indicators, and there is much less chance of measurement error. They also, importantly, allow for specific margins of error to be recorded (Kaufmann *et al.* 2007: 1).

In other words, they are much better tools for working out what is really going on in the real world.

Table 4.4 The 2011 Bribe Payers Index (selected scores).

Rank	Country/territory	Score	Number of observations	Confidence array
1.	Netherlands	8.8	273	8.6–9.0
1.	Switzerland	8.8	244	8.5–9.0
3.	Belgium	8.7	221	8.5–9.0
4.	Germany	8.6	576	8.8–8.8
4.	Japan	8.6	319	8.4–8.9
6.	Australia	8.5	168	8.2–8.8
6.	Canada	8.5	209	8.2–8.8
8.	Singapore	8.3	256	8.1–8.6
8.	UK	8.3	414	8.1–8.5
10.	US	8.1	651	7.9–8.3
11.	France	8.0	435	7.8–8.2
11.	Spain	8.0	326	7.7–8.2
14.	Brazil	7.7	163	7.3–8.1
19.	India	7.5	168	7.1–7.9
22.	Saudi Arabia	7.4	138	7.0–7.8
26.	Mexico	7.0	121	6.6–7.5
27.	China	6.5	608	6.3–6.7
28.	Russia	6.1	172	5.7–6.6

Source: Transparency International (2011), "Bribe Payers Index". Available at www.transparency.org/bpi2011, viewed on 27 October 2016.

Of course, TI's indices are not, by any means, the only game in town, and the burgeoning survey landscape is testament to how important measuring corruption, or aspects of it, has become. Some scholars choose simply to count the number of corruption cases that have been investigated and/or prosecuted. This approach short-circuits any problems of perception bias and in many ways provides interesting and thought-provoking data. It does, however, produce a different type of problem. Imagine a state with 15 regions that are all equally prone to corruption; the only thing that differs between them is the willingness of their regional authorities to enforce anti-corruption laws. If more prosecutions are being recorded in a particular region, this should be seen as evidence that the region's governance structures and processes are helping it bring corrupt actors to justice. Yet, if we compare this data across all 15 regions, it could easily lead us to believe that more prosecutions is evidence of more corruption in that particular region. Whether there is really more corruption there than in regions where enforcement is not taken as seriously remains another matter.

A number of organizations have tried to nuance our understanding of corruption's relationship to business. Roughly every four years since 1999 (and most recently in 2014), the Business Environment and Enterprise Survey (BEEPS) investigates the experiences of business people with corruption in eastern Europe and central Asia. More specifically, the BEEPS asks people to quantify how much they have paid in bribes. In 2014, the BEEPS included data from managers in 15,883 enterprises across 30 countries (European Bank for Reconstruction and Development 2014). The World Economic Forum has also included several corruption-related questions in its annual Global Competitiveness Report (GCR). Section 2 of the first (of 12) pillars of the Global Competitiveness Index concentrates specifically on issues of ethics and corruption. More specifically, it includes data on the diversion of funds from the public sector, levels of trust in politicians and the number of irregular payments and bribes in a given economy. In 2014–15, New Zealand topped the pile with a score of 6.3 out of 7 (with 7 indicating no corruption in these specific areas and 0 indicating the opposite). Interestingly, and – in the eyes of many – quite provocatively, some of the countries on New Zealand's coat-tails were not the usual suspects; Finland was in second place (6.2 out of 7), sharing that accolade with Singapore, Qatar and the United Arab Emirates. Venezuela (1.7 out of 7) was 144th and last (Global Competitiveness Report 2015).

At the level of ordinary citizens, it is not just TI that has sought to probe deeper into the individual experience of corrupt practice. The World Values Survey now asks a number of questions on corruption, as do a number of the regional barometer surveys. The International Crime Victimization Survey also asks whether government officials have demanded bribes for the services they have provided over the previous 12 months (see World Values Survey 2016; Svensson 2005). In addition, using experts continues to be a popular choice. The World Governance Assessment asks 35 apparent experts 30 questions (including three that pertain directly to corruption) and its data covers 16 countries. The International Country Risk Guide (ICRG) also conducts surveys of those it perceives to be experts in risk analysis, and questions on corruption play a part in their analysis (see Overseas Development Institute 2007; PRS Group 2016).

PROXY INDICATORS

The challenges of measuring corruption directly have led some to approach the issue from a different angle. Recently, there have been a number of attempts at measuring phenomena that may indirectly shed light on how much corruption is taking place. These indicators act as proxies for corruption that is either very hard to see or very hard to measure (or both). On some level, all corruption indicators are, of course, proxies. Although notions such as bribery can (in theory) be measured with a degree of accuracy, corruption covers so many activities over and beyond this that it is impossible to claim with any certainty that any given approach can do justice to that diversity. Activities such as patronage, conflict of interest and abuse of power are exceptionally difficult to effectively and usefully quantify. This is where skilful proxy indicators have a role to play.

Ritva Reinikka and Jakob Svensson, for example, outline a whole series of micro-level proxies that have been developed to address the data-quality problem. These range from surveys of where and how money from the public purse gets allocated (and indeed misallocated) to surveys of service providers and enterprises (Reinikka & Svensson 2006). Advocates of using proxies as a measurement tool are often bullish about their usefulness. "A few well-chosen proxy indicators", argue Jesper Johnson and Phil Mason, "can be more informative than a sea of data or dozens of aggregate, cross-country indices" (Johnson & Mason 2013: 2).

Public Expenditure Tracking Surveys (PETS) are an excellent example of this. PETSs help highlight cases in which public money has either not ended up where it should have or cannot actually be accounted for at all. That money could, of course, have been misallocated or lost on account of incompetence, but when systematic patterns of misallocation are revealed, we have a framework of behaviour to hand that may well have corrupt practice at its core. PETS have subsequently become "effective in identifying delays in financial and in-kind transfers, leakage rates, and general inefficiencies in public spending" (Koziol & Tolmie 2010: 1). Indeed, it is those "leakage rates" that catch the eye not just of corruption analysts but also of the public at large. It is not hard to see why; unaccounted-for money is rarely dumped in a lake or burnt on a bonfire. It ends up somewhere, and frequently that somewhere is an illegitimate home.

Exploring patterns of leakage across space is therefore an attractive way of illustrating where problems may indeed lie. For example, Jonathan Stromseth, Edmund Malesky and Dimitar Gueorguiev have done this across China's 33 provinces. They used data from the Chinese National Audit Office to put together a data set illustrating how much money was misused as a proportion of each state's provincial budget. They wanted to know, in other words, how much money each Chinese province was unable to account for, and they used that figure as a proxy for what they term "macro-corruption" (Stromseth *et al.* 2017: 85). Some leakage will happen everywhere, and it is important to note that not all leakage comes about because of corruption. Sometimes things really do just get lost. However, in 2011, nearly 20 per cent of the budget of Heilongjiang Province (in China's north-east) was misused (see Box 4.1). It is highly unlikely that this was all down to honest mistakes (*ibid.*: 101).

PETS can also be effective at a much lower level. Indeed, that is in many ways the place where PETS show the greatest potential to impact both policy and service delivery. Being aware of the amount of money allocated to a primary school by a local authority, for example, might not tell you anything about how much corruption is taking place. Looking at the expenditures of the primary school in question, however, could help unpack whether the money has been spent, and on *what* it was spent. Doing this across a representative sample of primary schools in a district will help create a bottom-up set of indicators, illustrating where money is going and why, and whether there appear to be any anomalies in the process of getting it there.[8]

In 1996, Uganda became the first country where PETS were formally carried out. The approach was embraced on account of substantial increases in expenditure on education not trickling down to education providers. Or, indeed, they may have been trickling down, but there was a widespread belief that they were then being deliberately misallocated and misspent. The PETS approach was used to "compare budget allocations to actual spending through various tiers of government". This included "frontline service delivery points", all with the aim of working out where the money was actually going (Koziol & Tolmie 2010: 3; Ablo & Reinikka

---

8. For a good example of this in Brazil, see Ferraz *et al.* (2012).

1998). The results were chastening. In 1996, only 13 per cent of the government expenditure per student actually reached the school that it was theoretically destined for. A whopping 87 per cent, in other words, either vanished or was captured by local officials for private gain. Making sense of this large and off-the-books bargaining game between schools and local officials was key to understanding who ultimately ended up with what. On seeing these results, the central Ugandan government immediately recognized the problem and took action. Details of how much money was transferred to the local authorities began to be published in newspapers and via other media outlets, while primary schools were required to make public what they spent the money allocated to them on. With more information available, it became harder for the corrupt bargains that characterized relationships in the mid-1990s to keep hold. The government signalled that it was going to oversee, and indeed measure, the way that funds were spent (Reinikka & Svensson 2003b).

A number of other states followed this approach, and not all of the results were quite as dismal as Uganda's in the mid-1990s. Zambia, for example, saw 90 per cent of schools getting their non-wage allocation of funding. However, where officials had more discretion to allocate the educational budget, only 20 per cent of schools received anything at all (Koziol & Tolmie 2010: 3–6). Approaches such as this give us a more context-specific measure of where corruption might be lurking, and they have plenty of policy-related potential as a result. Indeed, they help policy-makers focus their attentions on particular parts of the political or bureaucratic system where problems are especially acute.

A set of proxies has been specifically developed to identify corruption risks in another area that has traditionally been seen as corruption prone: public procurement. These take advantage of the fact that large data sets (or "big data") of contracts are now published by many national and local governments, and thus can be analysed for evidence of irregularities that might be indicative of corruption. The approach relies on identifying a series of "red flags" that are often associated with corrupt practices in this area. These include, for example, a very short time period between the announcement of a tender and the deadline for submitting bids, which sometimes reflects hidden practices to favour a certain tenderer. Frequent use of non-competitive or "negotiated" procedures, perhaps citing "emergency" conditions, can be another red flag. By looking for systematic occurrences of these red flags in certain contracting authorities or relating to particular bidders, Mihaly Fazekas and colleagues have constructed a Corruption Risk Index (Fazekas & Kocsis 2015).

A variation on this approach combines the Corruption Risk Index with an examination of how contracting patterns are affected by a natural experiment – a change of government – to identify suspicious changes in winning bidders (Dávid-Barrett & Fazekas 2016). More broadly, there is potential for open data, that is, the publication of large data sets about government activities, to be used as an anti-corruption tool (see Chapters 7 and 8). However, researchers note that this potential should not be overstated, given that the process of publishing data remains highly political, and the ability to use open data to uncover or punish corruption depends on the existence of a wider ecosystem of accountability institutions (Dávid-Barrett *et al.* 2017).

CONCLUSION

In summary, data on corruption is now in abundant supply. It has made a significant contribution to the policy analysis of international organizations interested in tackling corruption. Although multidimensional indicators are clearly problematic in some respects, Sampson's claim that "the reliability of tools or other methodological issues are never totally brought out" is clearly unfair (Sampson 2010). Those who are fundamentally sceptical of any attempt to define, let alone measure, corruption may not like the turn towards quantification, but it is unreasonable to claim that these organizations think they are dealing in an exact science. All of the organizations that produce indices (no matter whether they deal with perceptions, experiences or proxies of corruption) point out, to greater or lesser extents, the weaknesses in their respective approaches. They may have a fundamentally positivist view of the world, but this does not make them boffins who have no concept of the world's complexity. TI and other organizations in the data-producing field may, in other words, talk up their respective efforts to quantify aspects of corrupt practice (and who can blame them?), but they do also realize that they are dealing in imperfections.

There is nevertheless a danger in taking these data too literally. Corruption is complex, multifaceted and riddled with nuances, and this makes reducing it to one number very difficult indeed. The very best of these indices can be used to help spot trends and illustrate the scale and scope of particular types of corruption. They can also help us to develop explanations of what might be causing corruption. They cannot, however, provide definite answers. But, if used carefully, the data produced by many of these indices can have a constructive role to play in helping us think just a little more about how the battle against corruption can be taken forward.

Box 4.1. Leakage as corruption: the case of China

Alternative, proxy measures of corruption have become increasingly *en vogue* in recent years. The efforts of Jonathan Stromseth, Edmund Malesky and Dimitar Gueorguiev are an excellent example of how this works. They use 11 years' worth of Chinese data (from 2000 to 2010) on both transparency and corruption "to demonstrate statistically that increases in government information on government structure and processes are strongly associated with reductions … in the misuse of public funds by provincial officials". They note, for example, that, in 2011, 9.68 per cent of funds in the median Chinese province were being misused. That translated to RMB8.3 billion (around $1.2 billion). They are also able to show that, since 2002, provinces such as Guangdong and Zhejiang have managed to reduce the amount of money that is "leaked", whereas other provinces have seen little change at all (they highlight Liaoning in China's north-east as an example). Some provinces, such as Jiangxi and Chongqing, have actually seen the situation get worse. Stromseth *et al.* (2017) are clear that they are not measuring corruption. But they are equally clear in stating that the levels of leakage they reveal give a good indication of how much corruption may well be taking place beneath the surface.

5.
Causes of corruption

Policies that have been developed to counteract corruption inevitably make a number of assumptions about corruption's causes. Indeed, in many cases, these assumptions are quite clear; people are rational, self-interested creatures, who, if the projected benefits outweigh the costs, should be expected to indulge in corrupt activity. These assumptions have led rational-actor and rent-seeking models to dominate much of the thinking on corruption's causes. Yet they clearly are not the only ways of thinking about this. Different disciplines approach the challenge of working out what precisely causes corruption in strikingly different ways. This has led to the development of a body of work that questions the dominance of these rational-choice approaches. This chapter unpacks both the dominant thinking in the field and the revisionist positions of its critics.

One thing that everyone can agree on is that understanding how to tackle something is much easier if you understand why it exists in the first place. Doing that, of course, is unfortunately not quite as straightforward as it might appear. There are often many factors that contribute to any given outcome, some much more obvious (and easily identifiable) than others. Assumptions that initially seem plausible can often turn out to be far off the mark. This is not just a problem for those looking to understand what drives corruption; pinning down causal effects in the social world more broadly is far from simple. There may well be strong statistical relationships between phenomena, but that does not mean that A is necessarily causing B. Between 1999 and 2010, for example, there was a strikingly strong correlation between the number of people in the US who drowned after falling out of a fishing boat and the ups and downs of the marriage rate in Kentucky. Between 2000 and 2009, the relationship between per capita consumption of mozzarella cheese and the number of civil engineering doctorates awarded was also remarkably strong and consistent.[1] Yet no one has (yet) come anywhere near to explaining how the relationships between these phenomena might actually function in practice; there are, in other words, plenty of spurious correlations that exist by chance and not by design.

It is not hard to work out that there is nothing that explains spurious relationships such as those outlined above. We can recognize those correlations for what they are: nonsense. But it is much harder to be clear about whether other, less overtly ridiculous relationships have anything in them. We know, for example, that higher levels of GDP go hand-in-hand with lower levels of corruption (see Chapter 6). We do not, however, know whether rich countries become less corrupt, or less corrupt countries become rich; or, indeed, whether a third (or fourth, fifth, sixth or seventh) variable is really key to understanding the mechanics of that relationship. On their own, the numbers do not mean anything, and what is causing something as opposed to being influenced by it is not clear.

Causation only becomes visible when there are theoretical explanations that plausibly illustrate how relationships might work. Convincingly setting that out is not easy. In essence, there are two approaches to pinning down when something is indeed causing something else to happen. On the one hand, it can suffice if a certain intervention produces a particular outcome. Smoking causes lung cancer, for example. Lionel Messi causes Barcelona to win football games. On the other hand, the bar for some is placed higher. Smoking does not always cause cancer, and, indeed, some people get cancer even though they are non-smokers. Barcelona often wins when Messi does not play, just as they sometimes lose when he does.

If one takes a probabilistic approach towards this, then it is enough to show that X increases the likelihood of Y happening (one is more likely to develop cancer if one smokes). If, however, more deterministic approaches are preferred, then we are trying to say more about under what conditions X leads to Y (smoking is likely to cause cancer if A, B and C are also in evidence). Deterministic causation is more the realm of the natural sciences, but there are many in the social science world who think that that is really what we should be aiming for. Only when you adopt this approach can you really say anything about under what conditions things are likely

---

1. For more on these and other incidences of spurious correlations, see Vigen (2015).

to happen. Doing justice to all of this in the world of corruption analysis is fearsomely difficult, but that has not stopped people from trying. It is to these attempts that we now turn.

STRUCTURES AND AGENTS

As noted at the beginning of this chapter, attempts to explain why corruption exists often start from the premise that people are rational actors. Those who buy into these ideas assume that all people act with self-interest at the forefront of their thinking. That might sound like a particularly gloomy understanding of human nature, but it does not necessarily mean that people act to the detriment of others all the time. Indeed, economists such as Adam Smith built longstanding theories based on the premise that – providing very basic rules of the game are adhered to – acting in your own self-interest is actually as good for the well-being of others as it is for you (Smith 1776). This approach nonetheless assumes that all people have interests and goals, and when push comes to shove, they will try to protect and achieve these over and above the interests and goals of others. In other words, people, all things being equal, will take decisions that "maximize their own utility".[2] This agent-centred approach stresses that if people are given opportunities to be corrupt, then we should not be surprised when they take them. If these opportunities are limited – maybe as the chances of being caught are high – then people are much less likely to act in a corrupt fashion. This approach subsequently puts the focus on people as individual actors, weighing up decisions on how to act based on their own sets of preferences as well as the costs and benefits of a likely course of action.

An alternative approach starts from a rather different understanding of human nature. Some argue that what can loosely be termed "structural forces" have a much more profound effect on human behaviour than those who stress rationality and incentives traditionally would like to acknowledge. We are creatures of habit, and a whole host of phenomena shape our daily lives, often without us even being aware of them. In terms of corruption, that can have both positive and negative consequences. On the positive side, if people grow up and are socialized into political systems where corruption is not seen as socially acceptable, then they are more likely to

---

2. For the first detailed explanation of utility maximizing, see Downs (1957).

turn down opportunities to act corruptly as and when they arise. Authors such as Alina Mungiu-Pippidi argue that this is the case in countries such as Denmark, where short-term corrupt gains are more likely to be over-looked in favour of longer-term societal benefits, as acting corruptly is not viewed as an "appropriate response" (Mungiu-Pippidi 2014). On the nega-tive side, so-called cultures of corruption can also develop, where behaving in a corrupt fashion is not just tolerated but widely expected. In some parts of the world, for example, it is widely expected that friends, family and those of the same persuasion will gain directly from a particular person being in power. As Michela Wrong impressively illustrated in Kenya, for example, if you win an election then it is "your turn to eat" (Wrong 2009). It is (direct and obvious) payback time for supporters and those who may have helped you get where you are today. Looking after your own is not only expected, it is accepted.

One of the most well-known structural accounts of why corruption occurs stresses the importance of both social capital and social trust. Put succinctly, the lack of both has been pinpointed as an explanation for a wide array of societal ills, of which corruption is just one (Putnam 1993, 2000). Quite how one measures these concepts remains (as is the case with corruption itself) a bone of contention; however, Bo Rothstein is still on strong ground when he suggests that where citizens possess high levels of generalizable trust, they are much more likely to believe that if you are honest, and refrain from corrupt acts, others will do the same (Rothstein 2011b). The setting within which you live and work will impact on what you see as suitable and appropriate sets of behaviour. Rothstein's position has been supported by Johann Lambsdorff, who, in a study of 33 countries, noted that trust does indeed correlate with lower levels of corruption. Furthermore, this remained the case even when variables such as GDP per capita were controlled for (Lambsdorff 2006: 18). Pinpointing these relationships is, however, the straightforward part. Isolating the causes of specific outcomes in particular places is far from easy, and, as Eric Uslaner notes, corruption does not just perpetuate such things as inequality, it also leads to both lower levels of trust and more corruption in an endless cycle (Uslaner 2013). This loop cannot simply be wished away by enacting institutional reform; bigger processes are at work (Uslaner 2008).

Both agent-centred and structure-focused approaches, therefore, have something to contribute to the debate on what causes corruption. The problem is untangling precisely what that something is. These starting points lead corruption analysts in very different directions. Be that as it may, the majority of corruption analysis still adopts what can broadly be understood as a principal–agent approach, which fits very clearly into the first of these two schools of thought.

PRINCIPALS AND AGENTS

Principal–agent thinking emerged in the 1970s as economists began to think about how to make sense (and subsequently model) ideas of uncertainty, risk and problems of informational asymmetry.[3] The approach that they developed has now been expanded to try to understand a range of problems across a number of disciplines. The key problem that principal–agent thinkers tend to grapple with is how to make sense of the decisions that a person (or agent) makes on behalf of another (a principal). The crux of this problem is that a principal will take a decision and then empower an agent to carry it out. Principals are power-holders. Shareholders (the principals) empower management (agents) to run their company. People (the principals) elect politicians (agents) to take decisions on their behalf. Politicians (the principals) empower bureaucrats (agents) to carry out the policies that they decide upon. And so on.

The "problem" as such is that the principal has to grant the agent a degree of discretion to carry out the task at hand. In modern democracies, for example, people cannot meet to make each and every decision that may affect their lives. They give politicians a (limited) mandate to do that for them, and they then pass judgement on those politicians' work every few years. Politicians, meanwhile, pass legislation, but they do not actually deliver on this in practice. They leave that to public officials. Corrupt acts come about as a result of "an information and interest asymmetry" between those who formally possess power and those who actually turn power-holders' decisions into action (Persson *et al.* 2010). A bureaucrat working in a country's embassy abroad, for example, will be given a set of criteria around which they can make a decision as to who should and should not be granted a visa to enter the country. The applicant will have to fulfil a set of predefined criteria, but it is up to the embassy employee to determine whether her or she has indeed done that. The employee is given discretion to make that decision. However, where there is discretion, we

---

3. For some of the initial thinking in this area, see Ross (1973) and Mitnick (1975).

find an opportunity (so the logic of this approach goes) for corruption to take place.

There is, by definition, discretion all over the public sector. Discretion brings with it the responsibility to act in the public interest and for the public good in the face of other incentives. Agents, like everyone else, are nonetheless assumed to be rational actors, calculating where and under what circumstances they can maximize their utility. If the principal puts in place suitable oversight mechanisms and generally increases the costs (in terms of being caught) of behaving corruptly, then it is argued that the agent will stay on message. The challenge, therefore, is to design institutions (and processes of institutional oversight) that strongly encourage upstanding behaviour. Anti-corruption efforts should concentrate on getting institutional frameworks right. If they can do that, then corruption is, in theory at least, solvable.

It is hard to overplay the significance of this approach. As Mehmet Ugur and Nandini Dasgupta noted in 2011, every single one of the 115 articles they found analysing the impact of corruption on economic growth used principal–agent thinking.[4] For many, understanding corruption through this prism was, and still is, the only game in town, and in the 1990s in particular the aim appeared to be nothing short of creating an intellectually coherent theory of corruption. This theory-building exercise became part of a move to use the tools, approaches and assumptions of economics in political analysis more broadly, and, as was noted above, was premised on a decidedly negative understanding of human nature. One of the advantages of this approach is its apparent analytical parsimony. The component parts are widely understood, and it can – in theory at least – be applied to a whole range of settings. It also talks to a series of eminently plausible assumptions about what makes people tick. It is perhaps for these reasons that such scholars have been very influential in shaping anti-corruption thinking in international organizations such as the World Bank and IMF (see Chapter 7).

DISCRETION, CORRUPTION AND THE STATE

Yet, on closer inspection, it becomes clear that many – although not all – of the analysts who use this approach have very particular (negative) attitudes

---

4. Ugur & Dasgupta (2011), as quoted in Marquette & Peiffer (2015, p. 2).

towards the state. The assumptions of the rational-actor model lead many to assume that the state will be used (and abused) for private gain unless very specific controls are put in place. Given this, the state should look to do as little as possible, leaving the market to allocate resources. The market, as a value and interest-free allocator of those resources, will simply allocate based on the grounds of economic efficiency. Providing it is appropriately regulated, and providing the state offers certain basic services, the human urge to utility maximize will be limited to doing things in a more efficient way than others are able to do.

The background to this is that politicians are believed to be rational actors. They are therefore expected to take decisions that will ultimately help them to fulfil their own particular objectives. Expect economic performance, for example, to be manipulated so that the economy is doing well in the run-up to an election. Expect politicians to privilege policies that help them get re-elected over, perhaps, tougher decisions that might be better for the population more broadly. Proponents of this approach to understanding why corruption flourishes may subsequently possess a deep scepticism about the ability of politicians to keep their own interests out of the decision-making process.

This has led some analysts to be highly critical of government interventions per se. Indeed, some believe that government intervention is the root cause of corrupt practices, and that "a large government increases corruption and rent-seeking" (Alesina & Angeletos 2005: 1242; see also Zhong 2010: 1). Even the less fundamentalist strain of this approach is still unambiguous in claiming that "excessive state intervention" would, sooner or later, directly or indirectly lead to "a range of ill-defined pathologies, ranging from low-level inefficiencies, through bureaucratic 'shirking', to out-and-out corruption" (Hopkin 2002: 580). For its most enthusiastic proponents, there is not only a highly sceptical attitude towards the state but also a deeply held belief that firms and private enterprises more generally only indulge in corrupt transactions as and when they need to in order to meet the demands of corrupt bureaucrats, or they are forced to do so on account of overwhelming state regulation. There is no, or very little, apparent thought that these firms may – at least theoretically – also be seeking to manipulate the environment for their own ends, so that policies can be developed and implemented that suit their own sets of interests.

Corruption analysis subsequently offered these scholars an opportunity not just to illustrate that the state was wasteful but also that the rent-seeking tendencies of politicians could, and indeed would, lead to an escalation in the number of corrupt practices.[5] Few went as far as Nobel Laureate Gary Becker, who claimed that "if we abolish the state, we abolish corruption" (quoted in Zhong 2010: 2), but the idea that the state could provide efficient and effective (and, by definition, corruption-free) services was dismissed as idealistic "romanticism" (Tanzi 2000: 19). "Corruption", in other words, "will be reduced mainly in those countries where governments are willing to substantially reduce some of their functions" (*ibid.*: 133).

Susan Rose-Ackerman's 1999 and 2016 (with Bonnie Palifka) works provide the most emblematic examples of this. Rose-Ackerman makes a number of eminently sensible suggestions for limiting incentives to act in a corrupt manner, such as keeping tax systems both simple and transparent, and avoiding over-regulation that may prompt firms to "cut corners" (i.e. bribe their way around them). But many of the suggestions are implausible in countries that do not have strong, well-organized, legitimate and effective states policing them. Creating, for example, "strong apolitical regulatory bodies" whose work is shaped by "transparent and open processes" is a task that states with high levels of corruption are unlikely to be able to fulfil. Rose-Ackerman herself claims that, for effective regulation to function, a "stable legal environment and credible enforcement institutions" are vital. Again, these may be to hand in low-corruption countries, but in the parts of the world where anti-corruption agendas are most needed they are most unlikely to exist (Rose-Ackerman 1999: 43–4; Rose-Ackerman & Palifka 2016). As Jonathan Hopkin notes, many of the assumptions on which this analysis is based actually regard – on account of their specific understanding of human nature – these aims as impossible anyway (Hopkin 2002: 584).

Even Robert Klitgaard's famous maxim that corruption is "discretion plus monopoly minus accountability" looks shaky when viewed in this context (Klitgaard 1988: 75). As Matthew Stephenson has noted, this "formula" is "not merely trite, but affirmatively misleading and therefore dangerous" (Stephenson 2014c). When analysed in more detail, it brings with it a whole series of assumptions that look questionable. Discretion, for example, may well provide officials with opportunities to feather their own nests, but "government officials who have too little (formal) discretion

---

5. See, for example, Rose-Ackerman (1978), Rowley *et al.* (1989), Rose-Ackerman (1999) and Tanzi (2000).

may be more inclined to bend or ignore rules that seem foolish, ineffi-cient, and contrary to prevailing social norms" (*ibid*.). Bringing in more rules and oversight procedures (and theoretically reducing discretion) can in certain circumstances simply lead to different types of corruption developing. Plus, there appears to be no acknowledgement that allowing discretion actually permits well-trained and thoughtful public officials to use their judgement and not simply make decisions of a tick-box nature. As Rose-Ackerman and Palifka note, "discretion is necessary" in complex bureaucracies. The aim should be to ensure that the decision-makers "have enough technical knowledge to exercise such discretion wisely", and not limit it as a point of principle (Rose-Ackerman & Palifka 2016: 527).

In the case of monopoly, there will indeed be occasions where the state's, or a public official's, monopoly control of something will lead to incidences of corruption. The evidence that replacing all monopolies with competi-tive processes somehow leads to lower levels of corruption is much less clear. A look at the privatization processes that many central and eastern European states undertook in the 1990s illustrates this nicely (see Box 5.1). Finally, Stephenson notes that if accountability means more targets and more controls, then, again, the stifling effect may paradoxically lead to a range of new forms of corruption. It may not, but that is the issue: context is important. Stephenson's narrower point is that understanding why cor-ruption happens as a formula, "which implies that it is an immutable law, is inaccurate and misleading" (Stephenson 2014c). His larger (more indirect) point is that there is an underlying scepticism towards the state that can often lead to policies that may well do little to help limit corrupt practices.

Alongside these theoretical problems, there is also a clear empirical problem that analysts who work in this tradition often overlook. Market mechanisms are believed to efficiently and effectively allocate resources in a neutral (i.e. non-corrupt) manner. The state, meanwhile, should limit itself to the most basic of tasks. Hopkin argues that these tasks can be summarized as "basic preventive health care, elementary education and national defence" (Hopkin 2002: 577). Yet the data on the relationship between levels of public spending and incidences of corruption remain ambiguous. The fact that some (although not all) countries that spend disproportionately large amounts of money on public services have low levels of corruption, while some (although, again, not all) states that spend comparatively little have high levels of corruption, is for the most part ignored. In 2016, for example, government expenditure in Finland repre-sented 57.5 per cent of GDP. In Denmark, that figure was 57.1 per cent, while in Sweden it was 53.2 per cent (Index of Economic Freedom 2016). These are three of the highest government expenditure–GDP ratios in the world, and yet all three of these countries also have, no matter how you measure it, some of the lowest rates of corruption anywhere. Politicians are clearly spending (lots of) money, and they would appear to be spending it reasonably well. This should not be seen as higher levels of government spending necessarily leading to lower levels of corruption: far from it. Perhaps asking *how* a government is spending taxpayers' money, rather than *how much* of this money it is spending, is a better starting point.

Box 5.1. Privatizing corruption?

Following the collapse of state-socialism in central and eastern Europe, decisions had to be made about how to revitalize flagging economies. With that in mind, all states across the region set out, to greater or lesser extents, to privatize state assets. The market, so they reasoned, would do a much better job of allocating resources and kick-starting economic development than the state would. Neoclassical economic thinking very much backed them up.

The scope and scale of the process was unprecedented. Whereas during the 1980s approximately 6,000 firms around the world were privatized, through the first half of the 1990s over 75,000 medium and large firms were sold to private bidders in central and eastern Europe alone (Kaufmann & Siegelbaum 2006: 1).

Privatization certainly helped these economies to begin the process of generating wealth; but it also brought with it widespread corruption. Well-placed actors bought state utilities on the cheap and, in the worst cases, effectively captured the state, using their powerful connections to further their own interests.

Corruption is not an inevitable part of the privatization process. However, where the state is either unable or unwilling to regulate the process, and where the government cannot ensure that transactions are carried out in a fair and transparent fashion, we can expect the worst. Privatization is much more likely to bring negative side effects where the state is weak and the institutions of government are fragile. In those cases, public monopolies simply become private monopolies, and there is a real danger of corruption being hardwired into the way countries operate.

Despite the catchiness and inherent plausibility of the idea of human fallibility leading us to be sceptical of giving too much power to public servants, the relationship between principal–agent problems and corruption is consequently not straightforward. Subtle shades of grey are evident in the real world, and they should not be overlooked or explained away simply as deviant cases. In certain situations (see below), the principal–agent approach can indeed be analytically very useful; however, we need to be careful not to see it as the only analytical approach available.

NORMS, VALUES AND APPROPRIATE RESPONSES

Much of the criticism of this approach comes from those who reject the foundations upon which it is built. For instance, a group of what Olli Hellmann calls neo-institutionalists have developed the most powerful and theoretically rigorous critique of the rational-actor approach (Hellmann 2017). The focus of much of the neo-institutionalists' analysis is the non-Western world, and the (often radically) different context within which politics takes place there. Principal–agent approaches, in other words, can make significant contributions when placed in a setting where the rule of law is strong, the regulatory climate is one of openness and transparency, and institutional frameworks stress the importance of accountability. In states where that is not the case, neo-institutionalists argue that principal–agent approaches "mischaracterize" the nature of the corruption problem (Persson *et al.* 2013).

The key assumptions that the neo-institutionalists make, however, undoubtedly have wider implications. In a theoretical sense, they reject the notion that actors' interests are exogenously fixed. They do not believe that interests remain constant and settled independent of the settings in which people exist. On the contrary, the interests and behaviour of individuals are shaped and influenced by their interactions with other individuals as well as the institutions within which decisions are made. This applies as much to advanced industrial democracies as it does to economically underdeveloped dictatorships (Hellmann 2017). Context, in other words, matters. It matters in shaping not just what corruption is understood to be, but also how patterns of corruption develop, and whether sets of proposed reforms are more or less likely to work. Context will therefore be crucial in understanding what an appropriate response to a particular problem might be and, subsequently, whether that response involves behaving in a corrupt fashion.

The problem that neo-institutionalists have is this: while rational choicers have a clear understanding of why corruption happens (self-interest), neo-institutionalists do not. The latter group rejects what it regards as the decidedly heroic idea that there can be a single, uniform cause for a phenomenon as widespread as corruption. For neo-institutionalists, working out what precisely causes corrupt behaviour requires a deep understanding of context as well as an appreciation of potentially multiple, interlinking phenomena.

Culture is sometimes used as a starting point in making sense of this, but the problem of defining what precisely that means leads us into yet another potential minefield. Indeed, it is often not at all clear what culture is, and it can often look suspiciously like a "residual explanation, brought into play for differences that are not explained by other factors" (Banuri & Eckel 2012: 52). Specific concepts such as (levels of) trust or religiosity are sometimes used; on other occasions, more nebulous ideas such as morals and norms are discussed (see, e.g., Marquette 2012). The rise in salience of experimental research on corruption has nonetheless led to a significant number of studies that try to pinpoint how, when and why norms, values and what can be more widely defined as culture affect behaviour. While this type of research was more or less non-existent before 2000, the scope and aims of its experiments are now broad and diverse. Unfortunately, however, these studies "have led to some puzzling, contradictory results", with research design problems preventing anything like a consensus from developing (Banuri & Eckel 2012: 51).

Difficult though it might be to illustrate the impact of culture empirically, more and more thoughtful research is at least giving us a feel for some of the patterns that are out there. One good example of this comes from a natural experiment conducted in New York involving United Nations' diplomats and unpaid parking tickets (see Box 5.2). Citizens of New York have long since had a love–hate relationship with the UN. One of their particular bugbears is that during the UN meetings, traffic around the city can often grind to a halt. The parking habits of UN diplomats do not help, either; many have been found to have parked illegally, safe in the knowledge that their diplomatic immunity means they can ignore the standard fines and tickets. This sort of behaviour fits nicely with many of the standard definitions of corruption: a deliberate abuse of entrusted power for clear personal gain.

Over a period of five years, Ray Fisman and Edward Miguel (two economists) analysed the data on diplomats' unpaid parking tickets with a view to pinpointing where the particularly bad parkers came from. The authors found that there was a strong correlation between illegal parking and existing measures of home-country corruption. They used the CPI as their measure but were quick to add that their findings would have been consistent if other corruption measures were used. This discovery suggests that cultural or social norms related to corruption are quite persistent. Indeed, "norms related to corruption are apparently deeply ingrained, and factors other than legal enforcement are important determinants of corruption behaviour". Fisman and Miguel (2006) subsequently concluded that diplomats from countries with low levels of corruption still behaved well, even when it would have been perfectly possible to have broken the rules and got away with it.

COLLECTIVE ACTION DILEMMAS

Work such as that by Fisman and Miguel illustrates that corruption takes place, and indeed often flourishes, because actors have learnt that it is an appropriate response to a given problem. Others have used these sorts of findings to argue that, while the principal–agent approach is a useful way of understanding corruption in some settings, adopting this approach in many parts of the world can lead to a fundamental misunderstanding of the corruption problem. Anna Persson, Bo Rothstein and Jan Teorell's analysis of the failure of anti-corruption reforms in Kenya and Uganda led them, for example, to theorize about corruption in settings that lack principled principals (see Persson *et al.* 2010, 2013). They argue that when principals oppose corruption and actively seek to counteract it then corruption can become a high-cost, and often a high-risk, undertaking. This is not, however, a situation that is to be found in many countries. Persson *et al.* subsequently make the case that "while contemporary anti-corruption reforms are based on a conceptualization of corruption as a principal–agent problem, in the African context corruption rather seems to resemble a collective-action problem, making the short-term costs of fighting corruption outweigh the benefits". We should not, therefore, be surprised when in those settings anti-corruption reforms that are based largely around principal–agent thinking fail. As Persson *et al.* further note, in states where corruption is systemic and systematic, people may disapprove of corruption and be fully aware of all the negative consequences it brings, but very few will see any value at all in putting their heads above the parapet to fight it (*ibid.* 2010: 1). This is particularly the case in developing countries, "where the Weberian state is weak and communal societies are strong" (Walton & Jones 2016: 2).

> **Box 5.2. Parking tickets and cultures of corruption**
>
> Do people possess a series of innate qualities that make them behave as they do, or are we creatures of environment, acting on and learning from our personal experiences? This debate (nature versus nurture) is a longstanding one; in the context of corruption, it poses an interesting question: can people be socialized into behaving in a non-corrupt manner? Raymond Fisman and Edward Miguel, two economists, devised a clever natural experiment to test these ideas out. Over a period of five years, they analysed which diplomats were given parking tickets across New York City. Given that the roughly 1,700 consular personnel in NYC enjoyed diplomatic immunity, they could, until 2002 at least, park where they liked and not have to fear the consequences. That led to a lot of bad parking: between 1997 and 2002, 150,000 of the parking tickets issued to diplomats (a cumulative total of $18 million to be paid in fines) were left unpaid. Nearly half (43 per cent) of those were for parking in "no-standing zones", 7 per cent were for parking in front of fire hydrants and 6 per cent were for expired meter readings.
>
> Fisman and Miguel analysed whether there were any particular patterns in this bad-parking epidemic. They found strong evidence indicating that there were. Furthermore, these patterns held even when national GDP, employee salary levels and a range of other potential explanatory variables were held constant. Fisman and Miguel unearthed a direct correlation between the number of people who parked particularly badly and the level of corruption (as defined by TI's CPI) in their home countries. The five worst offenders were Kuwait (246 violations per diplomat), Egypt (139 violations), Chad (124 violations), Sudan (119 violations) and Bulgaria (117 violations). Just 22 countries saw their diplomats register no parking violations at all. Fisman and Miguel subsequently concluded that "even when stationed thousands of miles away, diplomats behave in a manner highly reminiscent of officials in the home country". This remained the case even when it would have been perfectly possible to break the rules and get away with it. The culture of their home country appears to have been imported to New York, and they acted accordingly (Fisman & Miguel 2006).

Mancur Olson was the first to popularize talk of collective-action dilemmas, and Persson *et al.* clearly build on his thinking (Olson 1965). Olson argued that there are many cases where it is in everyone's interests to work together to solve large problems, yet these collective actions frequently do not happen. This is because the time, effort and cost involved to any one individual may be high; however, the aims of such actions will only be achieved if all members of the group are prepared to make the same contribution. Furthermore, problems are preordained when individuals can choose not to act but cannot be prevented from reaping the benefits of others' behaviour. In other words, free-riding is a real challenge when individuals know that their non-participation in a given initiative will not stop them from benefiting from its outcome. Taking action to mitigate the effects of climate change is a good contemporary example of this. An individual might know that reducing his reliance on a fuel-hungry car would be better for the environment, but driving a smaller, more fuel-efficient car might be less comfortable than driving a big 4x4. Plus, most pressingly, the effect of one person downsizing their car would be minimal. For any genuine impact on climate change to be discernible, lots of other people would have to do the same thing, and a rational actor is likely to come to the conclusion that this is unlikely to happen. If that is the case, why worsen your own driving experience when others are not doing the same, and there is effectively no larger benefit forthcoming? Furthermore, even if you were to drive a smaller, more environmentally friendly car, that alone would make only a miniscule impact on the earth's climate-change problem. The rational position would be to free-ride on the back of others' efforts elsewhere.

In this context, corrupt acts can be seen as akin to free-riding. Personal interests are put before the interests of the broader community. The latter's interests are taken to be clean government and the generally accepted benefits that come from it (Rothstein 2011a). Why, so the logic goes, avoid corruption when you will be worse off as a result (i.e. you will not get whatever it is you want the corrupt payoff to get you) and government structures are highly unlikely to be any cleaner as a result? As Marquette and Peiffer note, corruption also reduces the state's "ability to provide public services effectively and efficiently". The person who engages in corrupt behaviour – the free-rider – "reduc[es] or deplet[es] the capacity of the state to take care of all citizens to its actual financial potential" (Marquette & Peiffer 2015: 4).

In many ways, this approach sounds persuasive. It highlights the clear flaws in the principal–agent approach, and it explains that endemic corruption needs to be looked at and explained in an altogether different way (Persson et al. 2013: 450). It also taps into longstanding thinking on the problems of getting people to act collectively in situations where the immediate benefits are not always apparent and free-riders are known to be in play. Furthermore, Mungiu-Pippidi illustrates that facing down this dilemma and engendering approaches that consciously bring collectives together to tackle corruption can be a constructive way of tackling deep-seated problems. She uses examples from South Korea and Romania to make her case (Mungiu-Pippidi 2013, 2015).

Yet, Marquette and Peiffer persuasively point out that placing the emphasis on collective action may also lead these analysts to do exactly what they accuse principal–agent thinkers of doing: mischaracterizing the problem. They note that the language of principled principals is not helpful. Nice though the wordplay is, it represents a broad and widespread misconception. Principals should not be assumed to be principled at all (although in practice they certainly have the option of being principled if they so choose), but rather seen as having sets of interests. They empower agents to (help them) do justice to those interests. Indeed, Marquette and Peiffer claim that "there is no such thing, in theory, as a 'principled principal'" (Marquette & Peiffer 2015: 6). A look at the history of the principal–agent framework illustrates this; the principal–agent framework was originally developed to understand sets of behaviour within firms as opposed to between governments and those acting on their behalf. The relatively recent move to expand the use of principal–agent thinking from economics to other disciplines often overlooks this, leading to expectations of principals that are decidedly overambitious.

Furthermore, Marquette and Peiffer argue that the collective-action approach, as understood by corruption scholars, is not necessarily incompatible with principal–agent thinking. However, that is what the still-embryonic literature on collective action and corruption tends to suggest. As they note, "both theoretical lenses describe the same individual calculations made when deciding whether or not to engage in corruption" (*ibid.*). Rationality is seen to be at the core of human action, and interests are seen as driving behaviour. Both approaches ultimately end up talking about how to monitor and sanction miscreants. There is subsequently a lot more overlap between these approaches than many seem to acknowledge. Marquette and Peiffer are careful not to claim that these approaches are one and the same, and they are quick to acknowledge that they both shine light on particular dimensions of the corruption problem. Indeed, the usefulness of each approach will be determined by context. Others agree: Grant Walton and Ainsley Jones, for example, argue that, in the case of Papua New Guinea, "the relevance of principal–agent and collective-action theories are shaped by political, administrative, cultural and social factors which are place-specific" (Walton & Jones

2016: 2). Marquette and Peiffer do, nevertheless, have a point when they claim that the two approaches' starting positions actually have more in common than many care to realize.

CORRUPTION AS A PROBLEM-SOLVING DEVICE?

Marquette and Peiffer (2015) make a further point about potential causes of corruption. They start by noting, quite rightly, that corruption is almost universally seen as a problem. A small group of analysts to one side (see pages 95–97 for more on their ideas), analysts treat corruption as something to be both condemned and tackled. That makes sense, but, so they argue, in some parts of the world it overlooks one important point. Corruption is, on occasion, not the problem per se; it is a response to a problem, and may act as a – perhaps unwelcome, perhaps uneasy – solution. This point is important in understanding not just why corruption happens, but also why generating solutions to corruption problems requires a clear understanding of the context in which the activity is taking place. In other words, it helps us to fathom why in challenging situations corruption is a tool that a variety of people reach for in order to achieve broader aims. To reiterate, this does not make corruption "right", but it does help us to understand why corruption is a more or less widely utilized coping mechanism.

Marquette and Peiffer highlight a number of scenarios in which corruption functions as a solution to a given problem. First, in states where institutions are weak and often dysfunctional, the development of networks with strong ties of loyalty can be vital in helping maintain stability. In advanced democracies, stability and legitimacy are achieved in a number of different ways, but in states where the tax base is low and political redistribution is never likely to be sufficient to meet welfare needs, "political leaders … arguably face a more 'expensive' task of maintaining political stabilization than others" (Marquette & Peiffer 2015: 8; see also Khan 2004, 2006b). In other words, these states buy people off. The patron-client networks that ensue become necessities in helping maintain that (degree of) stability (de Sardan 1999: 41). The payoffs do not just enhance rulers' positions of power, they "ensure the public good of a sense of political stability for society more generally" (Marquette & Peiffer 2015: 8; see also Khan 2006b).

Second, and related to the first point, the inability of the state in many places to provide basic services leads citizens to revert to corruption to get what they need when they need it. If you are ill, then paying the relevant middleman to get you access to quick, appropriate medical care makes sense. As Grant Walton notes of Papua New Guinea, corruption can offer a form of social protection for when the time comes and you need to call on one of the patchy and often inefficient services that the state offers (see Box 5.3 for more on this; Walton 2013). The fact that paying what are in effect bribes to access these services will do nothing to help improve general service delivery is likely to be of little concern to you if a family member needs urgent health care and the only way to get it is to grease the appropriate palm. Corruption in contexts like this is how you get things done. As stressed above, it does not make corruption "good" or "right"; however, in some circumstances corruption is just one part of a much larger process.

CONCLUSION

Much has been written on the causes of corruption, and the debate is still an evolving one. For some, the most obvious starting point is expecting people to act rationally in order to do justice to their own particular sets of interests. If that involves acting corruptly, then, sooner or later, we should expect people to take advantage of the opportunities that come their way. Appropriate responses to this tend to focus on institutional tinkering: improve oversight mechanisms, make it clear that enforcement of the rules and regulations will take place, and generally get the cost and benefit equation right. If that happens, then the incentives to act corruptly will be much diminished, and we should see levels of corruption drop accordingly.

This approach makes sense in settings where the rule of law is strong, public officials work in a climate of transparency and accountability, and there is widespread trust in government (generally) doing the right thing. It makes less sense in settings where the state is weak and corrupt practices have become the norm. Citizens may be perfectly aware of corruption's deleterious effects, but collective-action problems will frequently prevent them from doing anything about it. Sullen resignation is often the response. Furthermore, there are contexts in which corruption is not so much the problem as a(n imperfect) solution to other sets of problems. In these situations, getting your child into a good school, for example, will simply take priority over more abstract ideas of fighting corruption. Corruption is a response to the poor services offered by the state.

Quite how these broad approaches to understanding corruption's causes play out in specific contexts will depend on a multitude of factors. There simply is not a one-size-fits-all explanation. The multiple potential causes of corruption, therefore, lead to a variety of potentially valid conclusions. Before looking at how this translates into anti-corruption mechanisms and policies, it makes sense to look at how these conclusions pan out in arguably the most important individual policy area: the economy. It is the impact of and responses to corruption in that area to which we now turn.

Box 5.3. Is all corruption dysfunctional? The case of Papua New Guinea

Very few people make the argument that corruption is a good thing, and those who do often find that their argument rests on shaky theoretical and empirical ground. There is, however, a significant amount of work in the development studies tradition which illustrates that corruption can have differing levels of dysfunctionality. Grant Walton's focus group work in Papua New Guinea (PNG) is a good example of this. Walton asked residents to evaluate the effects of different scales and types of corruption. He found that citizens in rural PNG did appear to have (at times quite widely) diverging views on the effects of particular corrupt acts. Indeed, most corrupt acts were perceived as leading to dysfunctional outcomes, but there were some types of corruption that drew much more ambivalent responses. What Walton termed "marginalized respondents" saw small-scale, day-to-day corruption as functional and nothing more than a way of getting by in a country where the state could not be trusted to provide good quality public services to everyone. Walton's findings are not just interesting in theoretical terms; they illustrate that anti-corruption reformers need to think carefully about who will be affected by reforms, and how they are likely to respond. That is true everywhere, but it is particularly the case in states with a poor capacity to deliver public services. A zero-tolerance policy in PNG, for example, is likely to lead to even more disillusionment among many who are already deeply sceptical of politics and political processes (Walton 2013).

6.
Business, the economy and corruption

This chapter analyses the relationship between the economy and corruption. In many ways, this relationship is a straightforward one; the effects of corruption on economic development are overwhelmingly believed to be negative. While it is impossible to quantify the costs of corruption, and, indeed, many of the figures that are quoted in this regard are nothing short of simple guesses, it nonetheless remains clear that corruption can be a debilitating drain on economic development. It is beyond question that corruption costs rich and poor countries alike significant amounts of both money and resources. This chapter begins by illustrating why that is. It explains that even the most cursory of glances at the data reveals that corruption skews the allocation of resources, often has a detrimental effect on economic growth, undermines both the rule of law and property rights and impacts negatively on standards of living.

Nevertheless, the following carefully points out that much (although not all) of the econometric analysis that is done in this area is conducted on shaky ground. None of the traditional measures of corruption are rigorous enough to facilitate the data crunching demanded of them; however, much economic analysis ignores this and carries on regardless. Simply noting that they are the best measurements of corruption we have is not a good enough reason to go on and use them as if they were actually reflecting real-world activity. This poses a real challenge for economists and those seeking to create economic models that can be tested with real-world data.

This chapter illustrates two further things. First, the economic impact of corruption is differential. Indeed, context is important in explaining why corruption can be so utterly corrosive in some places and have a much more sanguine effect in others. This does not mean that corruption is a positive influence, but it does mean that there are some awkward real-world situations involving what is clearly corruption that need explaining. How, for example, did the Asian Tiger economies of the 1980s and 1990s manage to mix dynamic growth with sustained and deeply ingrained corruption? How has China made such astonishing economic progress since Deng Xiaoping began opening up the country in the late 1970s, and yet corruption levels have remained stubbornly high? Could it be that corruption may, in some contexts, help to generate a stability that, in turn, helps – in the short and medium term, at least – to generate positive economic benefits? The answers to these questions are complex, but even where authors have argued that corruption can have "positive" economic effects, these still come at the cost of hardwiring in problems that future generations will ultimately have to deal with.

There is also a second, rather different, challenge that needs putting under the analytical microscope. In certain parts of the world, legal corruption has come to make a significant contribution to economic prosperity. Furthermore, these parts are often located in the richest, most well-developed corners of the globe (see also page 35ff) (Kaufmann & Gillies 2016). Legal corruption involves sets of activities that are all within the law and generally seen as both reputable and often part of everyday business. They can range from the system of offshore finance that was laid bare thanks to the Panama Papers, to the problem of state capture and actors legally shaping systems in their own interests. These processes can help foster economic growth, but they can also help "generate huge rents for the elite, increase their power, and exacerbate a country's political and economic inequality" (*ibid.*).

ECONOMIC DEVELOPMENT AND CORRUPTION: THE CLASSICAL APPROACH

For many, the debate about corruption's impact on economic development is actually a non-debate; they believe that corruption has deleterious effects on everything that can possibly be understood as positive in developmental terms. Having less corruption would lead to better policy outcomes. Well-known and oft-cited econometric analyses regularly posit a clear link between corruption and a range of variables, such as economic growth, economic freedom, per capita income and broader notions such as human development (as measured by standards such as the Human Development

Index) (see, e.g., Knack & Keefer 1995; Mauro 1997). Furthermore, corruption is seen as negatively affecting a broader range of issues that are posited as being linked to what can loosely be termed "quality of life" variables. Corruption and press freedom are negatively correlated, for example, as are corruption and life expectancy at birth, while more corruption leads to higher rates of infant mortality.[1] Corruption also clearly leads to worse outcomes in terms of health care provisions and educational outcomes (Ferraz *et al.* 2012). The list goes on.

The fact that the quality of data underpinning these statements is, on the corruption side at least (and as was discussed in Chapter 4), often anything but rock solid is widely overlooked. The relationships stack up statistically and seem eminently plausible; therefore, the same sets of apparent facts and figures tend to get wheeled out time and time again. That corruption almost certainly *does* lead to the types of problems mentioned above is not really the issue; it is that the data behind some of these claims are not reliable enough for them to be made in the way that they are.

So, what is to be made of all of this? In terms of the evidence, and putting those contributions that use dubious data to one side, it is still clear that corruption has a series of deleterious effects. Even then, some of the most paradigmatic pieces of research on corruption and economic development (stemming generally from the 1990s) are based on assumptions that have not held up well over time. However, they did still spawn an array of more sophisticated analyses that have been of real use in further testing out these perceived relationships. Matthew Stephenson, for example, spends quite a bit of time in a fascinating blog post explaining why one of the most well-known academic pieces purporting to show that corruption leads to lower levels of economic growth (by IMF economist Paolo Mauro) is, in reality, methodologically flawed (Mauro 1995). But, as Stephenson notes, "Mauro was one of the first scholars to try to figure this all out", and the more sophisticated work that has followed him "might not exist if he hadn't made a first, valiant attempt to try to evaluate the economic impact of corruption using quantitative data" (Stephenson 2014a). Learning by doing involves making mistakes.

Articles such as Mauro's are likely to have inspired the likes of Mushfiq Swaleheen to use dynamic panel data in trying to control "for the

---

1. For details of a whole series of correlations on corruption and the quality of government (including a significant number on corruption and economic development), see Holmberg & Rothstein (2014).

endogeneity of corruption and investment" on growth levels. Swaleheen recognizes the methodological imperfections that have plagued previous studies in this area and looks to face down what he calls the "four estimation challenges" that make pinpointing cause and effect so difficult. While recognizing that his approach is also open to criticism (largely on the grounds that he, too, uses a proxy measure for corruption), he is still on much stronger ground in claiming that the relationship between corruption and economic growth is significant. The impact of corruption is also differential; corruption in Finland (the least corrupt country in his data set) has a negative effect on growth, but, in states such as Egypt, after a certain point it ceases to have any quantifiable impact. Swaleheen (2011: 23–4, 38) even makes the claim that in states such as the Congo (the most corrupt country in his data set) there are scenarios where corruption appears to be (statistically, at least) growth-enhancing.

Raymond Fisman and Jakob Svensson, meanwhile, take an altogether different approach to what is essentially the same problem. They use a data set of estimated bribe payments by a random set of firms in Uganda in the late 1990s. These data help them to look at how the level of bribes affects growth in the number of firms across the country. They make a point of trying to deal with the endogeneity challenge by using what they term industry-location averages, coming to the conclusion that a "one-percentage point increase in the bribery rate is associated with a reduction in firm growth of three percentage points" (Fisman & Svensson 2007: 63). The evidence that studies like this provide is a much stronger indicator not just of corruption's (negative) influence on growth but also of which way the causal arrow is pointing. As these authors show, it is the corruption that is doing the impacting.

Attempts to avoid country-level corruption data have led to a slow but steady change in focus towards firms. This is despite the fact that, as late as 2009, Elizabeth Asiedu and James Freeman noted there were little more than a handful of articles that looked at the impact of corruption on the behaviour of companies.[2] The reason for this is obvious: a paucity of data. That has been changing of late, and, once again, it helps to flesh out our general understanding of corruption's relationship to economic behaviour. Asiedu and Freeman use country-level and, importantly, firm-level data from the World Business Environment Survey (with over

---

2. Asiedu & Freeman note only three studies in their own review of the literature: Gaviria (2002), Smarzynska & Wei (2002) and Batra *et al.* (2003).

10,000 respondents) to tease out more information on how corruption affects firm-level investment. They argue that the corruption–investment relationship varies across the world; corruption has a negative effect on firm investment in what they term transition countries, but no significant effect is discernible in either Latin America or Sub-Saharan Africa. The authors add that, in transition countries, "corruption is the most important determinant of investment growth", more so than the size of the firm in question; who owns it; what business it is in; or other factors, such as GDP growth or inflation (Asiedu & Freeman 2009: 201). That, however, does not appear to be the case everywhere.

GREASING THE WHEELS?

Analysis of corruption and economic development is therefore clear in terms of its general direction of travel; corruption is regarded as a negative influence, even if causal relationships are tricky to pin down and sometimes not quite as clear as many think (or, indeed, wish) (Khan 2004). However, the impact is differential, and there are a number of awkward outliers. This is not a simple story, and it has led contrarians to develop a number of theses that have challenged the prevailing consensus. The first of these came from a small but significant group of developmental economists in the 1960s, who argued that there might well be times when corruption can be a useful tool in helping to generate growth.

The background to this comes from what was in effect something of a rebellion against traditional economic thinking. Much economic analysis, both back in the 1960s and into the present day, sticks rigidly to neoclassical assumptions of how economies work. Public officials have the opportunity to use the discretion that they are granted to look after their own interests and thereby disrupt what would otherwise be efficient market transactions. The assumption is that public officials can both make life easier for outsiders (by clearing away potential hurdles) and more difficult (by introducing extra costs), all with the aim of maximizing their own utility (Rose-Ackerman 1978, 1999; Shleifer & Vishny 1993). Mainstream corruption analysis uses these assumptions, focusing on the opportunities for public officials to rent-seek and searching for ways to counteract these (allegedly natural) tendencies towards utility maximization.

Nathaniel Leff is probably the most well-known rebel who challenged this. Leff looked at market failure in the developing world and began to generate ideas around corruption not (just) being part of the problem, but also being part of the solution. In the real world of developing-world economics, he believed, innovative thinking was needed to try to kick-start malfunctioning economies. There was also a moral dimension to this. What, so the logic went, was morally acceptable about keeping people poor when there might be a way to do something about it? Leff was part of a group of revisionists who subsequently began to challenge the prevailing orthodoxy. He argued that many developing states were riddled with monopolistic structures, which were largely impenetrable to outside companies wanting to do business there. This was great for those who could control the means of production, but it was dismal for many citizens. They were destined to remain desperately poor while kleptocrats helped themselves to the state's bounty.

Leff subsequently argued not that corruption would solve all of a state's problems, but rather that it "may introduce an element of competition into what is otherwise a comfortably monopolistic" market (Leff 1964). Companies with an eye to sell products in competitive global markets would no longer necessarily be kept out of local markets purely on the grounds of not being part of the local clique. The bribes they paid to gain access to resources were in effect business transactions that brought with them "a tendency toward efficiency" in what was otherwise a chronically inefficient system (*ibid.*). As Leff famously put it, "if business groups are otherwise at a disadvantage in articulating their interests to the government, and if these groups are more likely to promote growth than is the government, then their enhanced participation in policy formulation can help development" (*ibid.*).

Leff was not alone in making this point. Two years later, in 1966, David Bayley argued along similar lines, noting that "corruption serves in part at least a beneficial function in developing societies" (Bayley 1966: 719). Bayley made the case that excluded groups could buy their way into a situation where they could take advantage of economic opportunities. The bribery they had to indulge in to get there simply helped mitigate the myriad sets of self-interested parties that had little interest in generating wealth for anyone but themselves and their cronies. Rigid bureaucracies could be bypassed, government planners side-stepped. Bayley's line of thinking was that, in making money themselves, these bribers would be able to bring life to economies where very little of it existed (*ibid.*).

The debates of the 1960s on corruption's impact ruffled feathers in a number of ways. First, and as noted in Chapter 2, they traditionally had something of a patronizing feel about them. Corruption was seen as "symptomatic of a 'backward' level of political development" or of an inability to "modernize" effectively (Perry 1997: 38). Given that the Western world was long since believed to have grown out of such behaviour, corruption was seen as something that "immature societies" suffered from; indeed, in the words of Samuel Huntington, "when the leaders of juntas and revolutionary movements condemn the 'corruption' in their societies, they are, in effect, condemning the[ir states'] backwardness" (Huntington 1968: 59; see also Brown & Cloke 2004: 280). For political anthropologists in particular, these positions simply were not tenable, and a considerable body of literature built up with the aim of refuting what they saw as culturally skewed analyses. Their aim was certainly not to defend the antics of anti-democratic leaders or the at times deplorable behaviour of some of the developing world's politicians; however, they argued, a little context is vital in understanding the processes and structures in which corruption is flourishing. The core tenets of this fight back were succinctly articulated by Elizabeth Harrison, who observed that "comprehension of how opportunities are shaped, both to engage in and to escape from corruption, is important" before acerbically adding that, unfortunately, "it seldom occurs" (Harrison 2007: 675).

Still, the ideas of Leff and co were certainly catchy, and much empirical work has been done to test them out. That leads us to the second problem: there is little evidence that these notions hold up in practice. Corruption may solve a short-term problem, but it hardwires in longer-term ones. It can do so by encouraging the creation of overtly complex sets of rules and regulations purely so that bribes can be extracted to get round them. It can do so by encouraging bureaucrats to use their positions as businesses, generating money via facilitation payments. It can do so by encouraging opacity and complexity in a way that goes against the grain of what we know can have at least some effect on corruption: increased transparency and accountability.

Encouraging bribery in these circumstances would pose an interesting challenge to the idea that corruption is "bad" if there was persuasive evidence that positive outcomes came about as a result. There is not. The judgements that the defenders of corruption made around half a century ago nonetheless prompted plenty of debate about what exactly the impact of corruption might be. We may dismiss their arguments as lacking in evidence, but accepting that corruption can lead to differential outcomes is important. Like many thinkers who thought differently, their ideas have ultimately turned out to be wrong; but they have prompted debates that have been, in the longer term, much more fruitful than many would perhaps give them credit for.

DIFFERENTIAL IMPACTS

The contrarians of today do not argue that corruption is "good". They try to unpack why states – by any definition – that have sustained corruption problems can still produce impressive economic development. Clearly, high growth and significant corruption can go hand-in-hand, even if that might only be in very specific settings. Japan, South Korea, Taiwan and China are all good examples of precisely this (see Box 6.1; see also Wedeman 2012). These sorts of uneasy illustrations have prompted the likes of Mushtaq Khan to note that "heterodox economics looking at late developers has identified an even wider range of rents and interventions that can potentially accelerate economic development if properly managed" (Khan 2006b). Corruption, according to this school of thought, produces additional incentives that might lead to the "acquisition of new technologies" or indeed help in generating a form of political stability that can have differential effects on economic outputs.[3] Khan is clear that, in the long-term, the "relationship between lower corruption and better development is not in question". But, in the short(er) term, the relationship between economic development and corruption is more complex than the traditional approach would have one believe.

What does this mean in practice? In the case of the Asian Tiger economies, developmental corruption saw power brokers work in cohorts with key figures in the business community. In the case of Japan, these power brokers could be found within the (once) hegemonic Liberal Democratic Party; in South Korea (in the 1960s and 1970s), in the military; and in Taiwan, within the Kuomintang. The alliances that these groups struck saw those in power pursue strongly growth-orientated economic policies, while the movers and shakers in the emerging business community provided funding to the organization in question to enable it to cement its dominant position in the country. The bargains were sometimes explicit and sometimes implicit; one thing they always were was focused on fulfilling the interests of both groups. These (at times unseemly) coalitions

---

3. For more on this, see Aoki *et al.* (1997), Amsden (1989) and Rodrik (1995).

subsequently enabled development and corruption to prosper together for significant periods of time.

Mushtaq Khan has done much to help us understand the contexts in which these bargains come to fruition as well as the effects that they have (see Khan & Jomo 2000; Khan 1996, 2006a). He posits four types of corruption that will, depending on context, lead to a variety of economic outcomes, some positive, some negative (see Table 6.1). Traditional approaches to understanding the corruption–economic development relationship are most at home in the bottom-left quadrant. Corruption is linked to the power of the state to legally intervene, whether this is via introducing regulations, allocating resources or carrying out specific functions. However, those interventions inevitably (and deliberately) distort market processes. The answer to this type of corruption is to get the state out of the process of allocating resources altogether: liberalize, privatize and increase the costs of corruption for public sector officials. Easily recognizable though this approach will be to mainstream economics, it is not usually the main problem in developing countries. Other types of corruption dwarf it in importance.

The second type of corruption (defined by Khan as "statist corruption") plays a more ambiguous role. As the author notes, it is "distinguished by being associated with state interventions that are legal and potentially beneficial for society" (Khan 2006b). The key issue is the extent to which subversion distorts the growth impulses that these state interventions may provide. The types of legal activity that could fall into this category encompass deeds such as the way credit is allocated, or the way infrastructure projects are prioritized. These interventions may well be of real importance in generating growth, but they are often wide open to political manipulation. Growth and corruption could go hand-in-hand.

The Elite Cartel corruption that characterized South Korean public life for decades is a useful example of this (Johnston 2005a: 89–93). For those in power through the 1960s, 1970s and 1980s, corruption was more a means of control than influence. They rewarded business leaders who made direct or indirect financial contributions to their pet projects, allowing a culture of crony capitalism to develop. This benefited both the politicians and the conglomerates (known as "chaebols" in South Korea), just as long as those same conglomerates used their privileged positions in growth-enhancing ways. This ultimately became a double-edged sword. On the positive side, the chaebols recognized their pivotal role in driving exports ever higher and therefore pushing the South Korean economy forward. On the negative side, the economy became extremely centralized and bureaucratic, deterring anything resembling a fair distribution of benefits. Development in South Korea was thus planned and strictly controlled by an authoritarian state, with resource allocation based overwhelmingly on the interests of politicians and the economic elite.

With the onset of democracy in the late 1980s, this slowly began to change. However, right up until very recently, there was still an institutional reflex that instinctively viewed corruption as being nothing more than an annoying side-effect if economic growth kept on coming. The case of Chung Mong-koo, chairman of Hyundai Motor Group, is insightful here. In 2007, he was convicted of embezzling $110 million, but was nonetheless exempted from going to prison. The presiding judge in the case, Lee Jae-Hong, noted that he (the judge) "was unwilling to engage in a gamble that would put the nation's economy at risk". He subsequently told Chung to return to his job, work hard and fulfil his social responsibilities (Lee 2007). The corruption was not to be condoned, but the importance of Hyundai to the South Korean economy was so significant that jailing its chairman for something as apparently trivial as embezzlement was seen as inappropriate.

Statist corruption takes place on a continuum that encompasses a wide range of positions. On the one hand, you have the economically advantageous behaviour of South Korean elites, while, on the other, you have the crass cases that are not always easily distinguishable from classical market-restricting corruption. Spotting the difference is not always easy. One thing is nonetheless clear: liberalizing reform will not necessarily lead to the better-quality infrastructure that developing states desperately need. As Khan notes, "strategies of state withdrawal risk throwing the baby out with the bathwater", and we need to be wary of propagating them just because it seems to fit with sets of preordained ideas of good practice (Khan 2006b).

The third and fourth types of relationship involve off-the-books interventions that are at worst blatantly illegal and at best ambiguously legal. There is also, crucially, little or no opportunity to actually make them legal. "Inadequate institutionalization" can drive power-holders to use off-the-books corrupt payments to buy stability. The country's tax base is likely to be far from able to redistribute enough resources to do this legitimately, so political elites have to find alternative ways of keeping potentially restless communities onside. In a theoretical sense, this can also involve getting resources in place to enable productive sectors to be at their most efficient and effective. This sort of arrangement may not appear to be a growth-enhancing one, but even in the face of widespread corruption it certainly can be. The outcomes are nonetheless highly context specific and not easily generalizable.

The bottom-right cell in Table 6.1 encompasses a range of activities that do not have productive side-effects. Those in positions of power and influence plunder and loot the state for their own purposes. Power-brokers at the top of the political pyramid lose control over those lower down the system, and a vicious cycle of self-enrichment develops. Economic development is not part of anyone's agenda, and little attempt is made to try and actively promote it. This type of corruption is clearly the most serious and leads not just to economic inefficiencies, but also to widespread poverty and, at times, state-collapse. The classical policy responses are of no use in this situation. What is needed is a form of political reorganization that can at least see states in this position move from widespread predatory behaviour towards the (still very imperfect) scenario of inadequate institutionalization. Khan points to Malaysia in 1969 as a case in point: in this instance, a national front government came to power and pulled the country back from the warlordism and anarchy that threatened it (*ibid.*).

The work of these revisionists is at once both useful and complicating. They highlight how there are multiple economic trajectories available and that corruption can play (more or less) negative and (more or less) positive roles in some of them. Their focus when doing this is generally the developing world, although it remains clear that the so-called developed world also has a rather more complex relationship with corruption than many would like to acknowledge.

LEGAL CORRUPTION

The economic impact of what Dan Kaufmann calls legal corruption is every bit as difficult to meaningfully quantify (see, e.g., Kaufmann & Gillies 2016; Kaufmann & Vicente 2005). Legal corruption concerns situations where economic and political elites can unduly shape rules, regulations and ultimately policies from within the system to suit their own interests. This generates huge rents, will be legal and comes about on account of an ability to dictate what is and what is not acceptable practice. The mechanics of this have been discussed elsewhere in this book (see Chapter 3), but in the context of this chapter it is worth noting that legal corruption may well have clear (positive and negative) economic impacts.

Table 6.1 Government behaviour, corruption and impacts.

	Legal interventions	Illegal interventions
Potentially beneficial interventions	Statist corruption	Inadequate institutionalization
Damaging interventions	Market-restricting corruption	Predatory behaviour, theft

Source: Adapted from Khan (2006b).

On the negative side, many would argue that legal corruption is most obviously at play in the area of tax collection. On the one hand, large companies are frequently able to game their tax payments in ways that are perfectly legal but still throw up a whole series of moral and ethical questions. As Kaufmann and Gillies noted in 2016, American companies have become adept at using foreign tax havens to limit their tax liabilities at home. They cite a 2016 Oxfam report that bemoaned the fact that, in 2008, 50 American multinationals reported that 43 per cent of their foreign earnings came from five tax havens, yet only 4 per cent of the companies' workforces were based there (Kaufmann & Gillies 2016). To use another example, is it right that Apple was able to avoid paying $13 billion in tax to the Irish government, even if the latter was both behind and perfectly happy with this arrangement? The European Commission did not think so, whereas the US government most definitely did (BBC News 2016). While neither of these cases constitute corruption in the classical sense, they do raise difficult questions about the relationship between powerful economic entities and the political actors who shape the rules by which they abide. Thinking about legal corruption also highlights why keeping morals and norms out of the process of judging these cases is impossible.

It is not just the area of tax in which issues of legal corruption are prominent. A whole range of what the UK Prime Minister David Cameron called "enablers of corruption" work across a number of the most profitable sectors in the UK economy (Elgot 2016). These enablers earn a good living by providing perfectly above-board services in areas such as accountancy, legal affairs, property management and other consultancy services to potential investors in the UK. For example, many non-UK citizens value the education that UK schools offer. They are not, however, generally thinking of comprehensive schools in sink estates, but rather of the UK's network of well-healed private schools. These schools charge significant fees, and they are under no obligation to ask where the money comes from to pay them. That is the case no matter how well known or suspicious the payer of those fees might be.

In addition, if an individual wants to invest in property in London then the estate agent that she chooses to use is under no obligation to do any background checks on where the investor has got her money from.

Box 6.1. China and the conundrum of corruption and economic growth

The Chinese are regularly revealed to be the world's most optimistic people. In 2016, 41 per cent of Chinese citizens thought that the world was becoming a better place. This result put them a full 18 percentage points ahead of Indonesians in second place. The French, meanwhile, came in last, with only 3 per cent feeling optimistic about the world becoming a better place; 81 per cent believed it was getting worse (Dahlgreen 2016).

The main driver of this optimism in China is the consistently impressive economic development that the country has enjoyed ever since it opened up to the world in the late 1970s. China gets richer, and its people remain optimistic. This development has nonetheless gone hand-in-hand with systemic corruption, which poses a challenge to the long-accepted notion that corruption stunts economic development. Following a nuancing of some long-standing assumptions about what drives development, China has now gone down as a classic case of developmental corruption engendering a stability that has helped the economy to grow. The Communist Party of China (CPC) under Deng Xiaoping set out to reform China's planned economy by opening it up to more market pressures. This process offered plenty of incentives for productive economic activity, just as it created myriad opportunities for self-enrichment, of both the corrupt and non-corrupt kind.

Introducing the market to help allocate resources stimulated growth and corruption alike. The problem, of course, is that corruption is now hardwired into the Chinese way of doing things. For as long as development advantage works for China, this is unlikely to matter too much. As soon as China runs into economically choppy waters, however, this endemic corruption will develop into a major problem. President Xi Jinping is well aware of this; the tens of thousands of corruption prosecutions which have taken place under his watch are a testament to that.

Corruption can work well when a country is in a state of development. As the other Asian Tigers have shown, that does not last forever. China's leaders would do well to take note of this, as when the slowdown inevitably hits, the Chinese are unlikely to remain the world's most positive people for too much longer.

Investing ill-gotten gains is much easier when a no-questions-asked culture exists, and it is for that reason that governments such as those in Nigeria and China (to name but two) get frustrated at their inability to get their hands on assets that they believe have been stolen from their jurisdictions and invested in places such as London (and other hotspots such as Geneva; see, e.g., BBC News 2015a; Xinsheng 2016). The UK government is looking to do more to help alleviate this situation, but as things stand it is still too easy for the proceeds of corruption to be reinvested in the UK. Neither estate agents nor private schools are doing anything wrong in a legal sense, but this may be because those with their interests at heart are reluctant to reshape the systems in place that allow them to behave as they do. It could, in other words, be good for UK PLC to have high-worth individuals continue to invest in Britain, even if we best steer clear of asking about the source of some of the assets in question.

Operationalizing the notion of legal corruption can be very difficult, but that should not detract from the observation that we need to try to recognize acts that fall into this category for what they are. At the level of the individual, the aim should not necessarily be to seek retribution from those involved, but rather to change the context in which they operate, so that the most appropriate response becomes not one of turning a blind eye but of walking away from the potential money-making opportunity. At the macroeconomic level, legal corruption can play important and, in some cases, pivotal roles in generating welfare. Expecting governments to simply sweep it away is therefore unrealistic. The interests of all parties involved need to be (however begrudgingly) noted. Only then can attempts at broad-based reform really begin.

CONCLUSION

The relationship between corruption and economic development is, in many ways, straightforward. The mass of research done in this area illustrates quite clearly that the general direction of travel is one where more corruption leads to a wide range of economically disadvantageous outcomes. Even when it is remembered that a significant portion of econometric analysis uses aggregate measures of corruption that are not adequate for the task, and that there are, and always will be, a number of other fiddly methodological problems to deal with, it is still clear that corruption is a serious hindrance to a range of policy outcomes.

However, the harder one looks, the more one realizes that the nature of the relationship between corruption and the economy is a complex one. Corruption can have a more or less significant impact on economic outcomes, depending on a range of factors. Indeed, there are occasions where corruption may even be a contributory factor in helping economies function more effectively. No one should understand this as a call for more corruption, but we should recognize that, in the cold light of day, there may well be scenarios where corruption is a better policy choice than anarchy or state failure. There are also scenarios where corruption is a solution that offers a policy outcome which would not otherwise have existed; the solution to the problem of needing to bribe a doctor to gain access to health care may be to improve oversight mechanisms across the health sector. Or it may plausibly be that the health sector itself needs investment, so that it can render bribes redundant.

Latterly, it has also been recognized that some settings thrive economically because they turn a blind eye to what can be termed enablers of corruption. This is not a simple story of greed and avarice; it is just what happens in an era of global capitalism. Money and assets travel seamlessly and speedily around the globe, and reforming the financial services sector in one jurisdiction is not likely to make much of a dent to the money laundering of those who are that way inclined. Concerted efforts to establish international rules and regulations as well as norms of behaviour are the only real way of dealing with such challenges. It is with this in mind that we move on to analysing quite how the international community has proceeded to try to do precisely that.

7.
Tackling corruption: the international dimension

Given the amount of time and effort spent analysing corruption in recent years, it should come as no surprise that there are a wide variety of potential remedies on the market. Indeed, the world is most certainly not suffering from a dearth of toolkits, action plans, agreements, conventions, treaties and agendas for change. The aim of this chapter and the two that follow is not to unpack every anti-corruption option available, but rather to look at the evidence for what seems to work and what does not. The latter point is particularly important. Despite the multiple calls to arms of recent years, the evidence that genuine progress has been made is disappointingly thin on the ground. There is subsequently a case for both rethinking what we think might work and assessing what indeed "success" might mean.

For starters, any anti-corruption attempt that claims to want to eradicate corruption or adopt a "zero-tolerance approach" should be treated with more than a dose of scepticism. The aims are too grand and, quite frankly, incompatible with the rough and tumble of everyday life. Corruption will often be deeply embedded in given social and political practices, and part of complex and ever-changing power relationships. This is all before, of course, any consensus has been reached as to what exactly the problem is, and what needs to be done to put it right. The specific aims of any attempt to tackle corruption, in other words, need to be carefully defined.

Successful anti-corruption is, by definition, a piecemeal affair. As Michael Johnston has noted, reforms often take a long time to work; they need a modicum of good fortune along the way and can be "a lot more messy and acrimonious" than is generally anticipated (Johnston 2013, 2016: 16). One-size-fits-all policies, even of the most obvious nature, can be counterproductive. A given anti-corruption mechanism may work well in one setting but have little impact in another, whereas it could cause far more problems than it solves in a third context. Carefully designed strategies focused on local contexts and specific problems are very much the order of the day, even if they, too, fail from time to time.

That may sound rather pessimistic. But there are, as these next three chapters illustrate, grounds for optimism. Not optimism of the "corruption can be swept away" variety, but hope based on the fact that ever more nuanced and potentially useful approaches to tackling this problem are being developed. Some of these are on the most local of local levels (see Chapter 9), while others stem from would-be reformers, who appear to understand that tackling corruption is not only the "right thing to do" but also in their interest. Before analysing some of these national and local approaches, it is worth starting with the most obvious and high-profile initiatives aimed at bringing corruption under control: those that have developed in the international arena.

INTERNATIONAL ORGANIZATIONS AND THE ANTI-CORRUPTION AGENDA

Of all the mismatches in the world of anti-corruption, using predominantly national efforts to tackle what is frequently an international problem is the most obvious. Assets that have been inappropriately acquired, for example, can be both quickly and easily laundered in far-off jurisdictions. Criminals of all shapes and sizes have long since become adept at using global networks to avoid national law enforcement authorities. One of the clearest and most challenging tasks for those looking to combat corruption is, subsequently, to face down an inherently international set of problems with what still remain (a wide and diverse set of) predominantly national tools.

The first international organization to rise to that challenge was the United Nations (UN). The UN's General Assembly adopted a resolution calling for international cooperation against corruption and bribery in international commercial transactions as early as 1975, although, given that other institutions failed to follow this lead, the resolution remained very much a paper tiger. It took fully 20 years for calls to be made for another resolution, this time for deeper and more sustained cooperation in halting the bribery of foreign officials. Eventually, the "United Nations Declaration against Corruption and Bribery in International Commercial Transactions" was passed, as the international community sought to pursue its development goals by opening up new, cleaner, more efficient channels of international commerce (United Nations 1996; see also Bukovansky 2006: 186–7). Following the 1996 breakthrough, the UN regularly passed resolutions imploring member states to do more to fight corruption (and, in particular, bribery).

The practical effects of the UN's resolutions have traditionally remained relatively small, mainly as the UN does not tend to have the tools to enforce (or even monitor) its own anti-corruption clarion calls. The UN has none-theless attempted to bring a more concerted and coordinated approach to its anti-corruption work via UNCAC. As of Autumn 2016, the convention had 140 full signatories, while 194 entities were "parties" to it (see Box 7.1).[1] UNCAC covers a considerable amount of ground, and there are provisions on law enforcement, preventative measures, international cooperation and technical assistance plus asset recovery. Parts of UNCAC are mandatory, while other provisions remain suggestive.

Since 2009, states' progress in meeting the obligations that UNCAC places on them has been assessed via the Implementation Review Mechanism (IRM). The IRM is aimed at helping countries use "a compre-hensive self-assessment checklist" to identify their progress and pinpoint areas where they are experiencing problems.[2] The progress of every state is reviewed (with the active involvement of the state that is under review) by two other states, the identities of which are drawn by lots. One of the states doing the reviewing will be drawn from the same region as the state that is being reviewed. In theory, the process is cooperative and collabora-tive, and the country under review actively contributes to the final report that is produced. The idea there is that it is much easier to make progress if a constructive dialogue is taking place.

The convention is certainly not lacking in ambition or high-minded ideas, but in the cold light of day the impact of the treaty remains ques-tionable. The "soft" nature of law in the international sphere means that implementation is always going to be more about persuasion than com-pulsion. One of the challenges that anti-corruption campaigners subse-quently face is how to embed these principles in national law and, most significantly, how to make sure national-level actors do justice to them in practice. As TI's Marie Chêne notes, "although legal measures, such

---

1. For a full and updated list, see http://bit.ly/1lvffOl, viewed on 20 November 2016.
2. Conference of the States Parties to the United Nations Convention against Corruption (2009), "Report of the Conference of the States Parties to the United Nations Convention against Corruption on its third session, held in Doha from 9 to 13 November 2009", p. 4.

as anti-corruption acts and agencies, have been established to execute UNCAC, there are local constraints to the full implementation of the Convention". Specifically, she pinpoints "under funding and lack of political will" as challenges (Chêne 2009: 1). She could, however, have gone further. In 2013, TI bluntly claimed that "the official process is not strong enough to keep countries on track". After having analysed 60 of the 69 completed reviews, TI stated that the process "contains inherent weaknesses that undermine its effectiveness" (Transparency International 2013d). Or, as Chêne put it four years previously, progress has undoubtedly been made in sharpening up legal frameworks and aligning domestic legislation with UNCAC's obligations, but "there are still major gaps to overcome for successful implementation". Furthermore, many governments remain reluctant to publish their own self-assessments, let alone the full reports that are ultimately produced. Clearly it is easier to talk a good game than it is to play one.

The UN is not the only international organization that has started to think in much more detail about the corruption challenge. The OECD is another relatively high-profile case in point. The background to the OECD developing an interest in corruption is, however, rather different. The driving force there has been the US. The reason for that is that the US government has had a longstanding interest in persuading the international community to develop rules, procedures and practices that mirror those the US itself has developed via its own FCPA. The FCPA (see Chapter 8) was passed in 1977 and, among other things, prohibits American companies from bribing foreign officials. As a result, American officials have been keen to level the proverbial playing field and prevent US companies from being in a disadvantageous position in relation to firms from elsewhere (who are implicitly still allowed to bribe). The US authorities have periodically lobbied countries to embrace a similar position on a bilateral basis, but they realized early on that these goals might be easier to achieve in a multilateral forum. Hence, the OECD became an object of focus. This led to a "Convention on Combating Bribery of Foreign Public Officials in International Business Transactions" being adopted in November 1997 (see Box 7.2) (Pieth 1997; see also OECD 1997). The convention is "the world's most ambitious global agreement to combat business corruption". It requires signatories to enact domestic legislation criminalizing the bribery of foreign public officials, and impose strong sanctions on those who break the law (Chapman *et al.* 2016).

However, while the influence of the US in promoting the convention has not been insignificant, it is not just an American policy that has been railroaded onto the international policy agenda. Indeed, if that were so, then it is unlikely that the Americans would have taken fully two decades to bring the convention to fruition. The fact that there was a growing consensus across a range of influential NGOs and academics (principally

---

Box 7.1. The United Nations Convention Against Corruption (UNCAC)

UNCAC remains the United Nations' flagship anti-corruption initiative. The first concrete move to establish what became UNCAC occurred in December 2000, when the UN's resolution 55/61 declared that there was a need to create a convention through which states could work together to find common anti-corruption ground. It took five years for UNCAC to be negotiated and then adopted, with resolution 58/4 coming into force in December 2005. As of November 2016, 140 states were signatories. While more or less all states that sign UNCAC then proceed to ratify it, it did take Germany until November 2014 to get that far, and, as of late-2016, Japan still has not ratified a convention that it signed in December 2003.

Antonio Argandoña has claimed that UNCAC is "the first truly global instrument to prevent and combat corruption", and that it is "built on a broad international consensus". That has not stopped critics from arguing that it is more warm words than concerted action (Argandoña 2006: 2). Signatories, for example, are under no obligation to criminalize certain acts that most people would clarify as corruption, the passive bribery of a foreign public official being one example. The language in UNCAC is also very careful: there are plenty of "shall endeavour to do", "may adopt" and "shall consider". Finally, there are a number of very clear caveats that allow states to dodge particular parts of the convention if they conflict with constitutional or legal principles at home. It is subsequently very easy to find fault with much of what UNCAC stands for.

Defenders of UNCAC, however, argue that it remains the best – and, indeed, only – international convention of its type, and that progress will always be slow and frustrating. They claim that having a forum via which countries can at least come together and talk about corruption issues is better than imagining that the problem simply does not exist. While it does take time for these conventions to have an impact, UNCAC's critics still have a point when they say that, when progress has been made, it tends to have precious little to do with UNCAC. The real question is what a replacement would look like and how we can be sure it would do a better job.

economists) that corruption was impeding economic growth, as well as development more generally, also played a significant role in moving the discussion forward (Bukovansky 2006: 191).

The first moves towards creating the convention came in 1989, when the OECD created an ad hoc working group to analyse legislation across member states on bribing foreign officials. Interest in creating a formal convention that would outlaw such practices grew throughout the 1990s, with the convention ultimately coming into force in February 1999. The current, revised version was passed in 2009 and has 41 signatories; these are all OECD countries, plus six non-member states (Argentina, Brazil, Bulgaria, Colombia, Russia and South Africa). The convention claims to establish "legally binding standards to criminalize bribery of foreign public officials in international business transactions", and there is an expectation that these standards will be translated into national legislation (OECD 2016a). Like UNCAC, the OECD's convention makes use of peer review to ensure that signatories make good on their obligations. The monitoring reports, therefore, contain recommendations that are "formed from rigorous examinations of each country" (*ibid.*).

However, as is the case with UNCAC, the OECD has no authority to actively enforce the convention. The OECD has developed an intricate four-phase monitoring process to oversee enforcement, but if states do not move to actively implement their promises then the OECD is powerless to compel them. The only power it has is the power to persuade. Unsurprisingly, this has led to a mixed implementation record. In 2016, TI noted that only four (Germany, Switzerland, the UK and the US) countries were actively enforcing the treaty, while six (Austria, Australia, Canada, Finland, Italy and Norway) were "moderately" enforcing it. In just under half of the signatory states (20), there was very little or no enforcement taking place at all. This group included Denmark, the state that came first in the 2016 CPI (Transparency International 2015a).

That mixed implementation record may, however, still be better than having no implementation record at all. As Jensen and Malesky have noted, bringing in a peer review phase made a clear difference to the bribery behaviour of signatory countries' firms that were active in Vietnam. They put this down to OECD signatory governments becoming more willing to police the behaviour of "their" firms abroad (Jensen & Malesky 2016). That is surely a positive development.

However, there may well be a cloud to accompany this particular silver lining. There is also evidence of a series of "unanticipated effects" on the behaviour of firms from states that do not participate in the convention. These firms, according to research by Terrence Chapman and his colleagues, are more likely to bribe than they were before the OECD brought in its system of peer review. Furthermore, firms from non-signatory states "will tend to increase their bribery effort", as less competition from firms across the 41 signatories "translates into a higher probability of accessing rents". To compound that even further, they add that this increased rate of bribery "is exacerbated as the quality of monitoring and the severity of enforcement under the convention increases". In other words, the more the OECD polices its own convention, the more bribery we see from the 150 plus non-signatory states (Chapman *et al.* 2016).

If the aim of the OECD's convention is to reduce overall levels of bribery, then this is clearly a worrying finding, and it poses plenty of awkward questions. Further research is needed before those findings can be generalized more broadly. Vietnam is, after all, just one country. But the conclusions provide plenty of food for thought. One way forward will be to sign up more countries to the treaty's aims. If those signatories are states with significant export sectors, then there is good reason to believe that the OECD's treaty can make a real impact on international bribery transactions. If that proves elusive, then the treaty's advocates may have a real problem. If nothing else, this is a perfect example of how the road to successfully fighting corruption is nothing if not winding.

THE WORLD BANK

Many would argue that the main institutions of the global financial order – the World Bank, the IMF and the World Trade Organization – are on the same winding road. They have registered some successes, but there are plenty of people who would argue that they have also played counterproductive roles. These organizations all have roles that go well beyond tackling corruption, but the World Bank in particular and the IMF to a lesser extent have, over the last 20 years, begun to think more about how they, too, can contribute to the anti-corruption effort.

The World Bank is principally tasked not with fighting corruption but with alleviating poverty. For many years, this aim ensured that World Bank officials expressly avoided analysing, or, indeed, talking about, corruption. They did this on account of the Bank's articles of agreement. These articles forbade the Bank from engaging in a nation state's domestic political affairs; commenting on corruption was viewed – rightly or wrongly – as engaging in national politics. That meant the Bank concentrated on providing loans to developing countries to help them tackle poverty.

Throughout the 1980s, criticism of the World Bank's work got ever louder, and that without anyone even mentioning the issue of corruption. Critics felt that the Bank had become a tool of the liberal West, lending money to struggling countries so they could service their (large and effectively unpayable) debts, and pushing them into structural adjustment programs that fitted its lean-government, small-state ideals. For many, the World Bank was a free market tool of Western powers that had nothing more than a passing interest in poverty reduction.

Over the course of the 1990s, however, the bank carefully redefined its role. The strongly ideological stances of the previous decade were watered down, and the Bank came to realize that corruption was a challenge that it could not in good grace continue to overlook. By doing this, it managed to increase the profile of anti-corruption work within the organization. This is best evidenced by then President James Wolfensohn's call to attack corruption's cancerous qualities, along with the publication of a number of policy papers outlining how the Bank planned to bring anti-corruption thinking into its work (Marquette 2004: 413).[3] In principle, the Bank pinpointed four things that it felt it could do: prevent fraud and corruption in its own projects; offer specific anti-corruption help to countries that requested the Bank's assistance; mainstream anti-corruption thinking throughout the Bank's work; and support the broader international anti-corruption initiatives that were developing at the time (Huther & Shah 2000: 1). By the 2000s, corruption had been positively transformed from a non-issue into being at the core of much of the Bank's work.

The Bank, however, has come in for more than its fair share of criticism. First, once the Bank decided to grasp the corruption nettle, its senior management was rarely slow in coming forward to give high-profile speeches about it. Wolfensohn, the Bank's president for a decade from 1995, famously started this trend in 1996, while his successor, Paul Wolfowitz, highlighted five anti-corruption objectives and a three-part plan for achieving them. Robert Zoellick, president from 2007 to 2012, looked to continue Wolfowitz's reform agenda. These grand designs are laudable, in and of themselves, but at times the Bank's senior management has seemed less than enthusiastic about putting them into practice (Wolfensohn 1996; Wolfowitz 2005).

---

3. One of the most prominent of these earlier policy papers was World Bank (1997).

Box 7.2. The OECD's Anti-Bribery Convention

The OECD monitors the effectiveness with which countries try to tackle bribery via its Anti-Bribery Convention. The 41 signatories are expected to implement legislation to incorporate the convention into domestic law, and then to make a clear effort to enforce it. The OECD evaluates progress towards these goals via what was until March 2016 a three-stage process of peer review:

- Stage 1 assesses to what extent the signatories' domestic legislation corresponds with that of the convention;
- Stage 2 assesses the mechanisms available to those looking to enforce the convention's demands;
- Stage 3 assesses the extent to which the mechanisms pinpointed in Stage 2 are actively utilized.

Latterly, a fourth stage looking at country-specific enforcement challenges has been introduced (Organisation for Economic Co-operation and Development 2016b). A report is then published on how effectively the country in question is implementing the convention.

The extent of enforcement across the 41 signatories can vary considerably and, indeed, year-on-year. This is reflected both in the assessments that countries are given as well as the number of anti-bribery cases that are investigated and prosecuted. In 2012, for example, Germany investigated 43 cases, while Denmark investigated 0; there were 113 investigations in the US, but just three in Japan (Fulbright 2012). Most external observers, and, indeed, many within the OECD itself, recognize that more work needs to be done to improve enforcement levels. There is also a strong case to be made that other large exporting countries (China, India, Indonesia and Saudi Arabia, to name but four) need to be brought into the convention. As noted on pages 112–113, without those players on side, there is growing evidence that the convention may be treading water in terms of taking the global fight against bribery forward.

Second, the Bank itself has, at times, seemed beset by internal corruption problems. The fine rhetoric notwithstanding, the Bank seems more intent on ensuring that loans are made than it does on ensuring that the money is spent wisely. Until very recently, putting oversight procedures in place to prevent corruption was often less than a top priority. In 2009, for example, the Bank's International Development Association (IDA), effectively the part of the Bank that makes interest-free long-term loans to poor countries, was accused of lacking "effective safeguards against corruption". Furthermore, the Bank's own evaluation of how the IDA oversaw its then $10 billion annual budget noted "[it] doesn't protect its funds adequately from theft and diversion" (Edwards 2009). Given that the Bank had by this point spent over a decade championing the anti-corruption cause, the attempts of management to stop the report being publicly released looked, at best, unedifying and, at worst, decidedly hypocritical. Some analysts have subsequently argued that up to 20 per cent of the funds that the Bank distributes are lost to corruption, while one of the Bank's most notable academic critics, Jeffrey Winters, has argued that almost $100 billion of World Bank funds have been lost to corruption over the years (McMahon 2006). The World Bank disputes these figures, but it nonetheless remains clear that corruption within its own programs is a challenge the Bank is finding difficult to face down. Indeed, internal problems at the Bank have led some critics to claim that rather than help tackle corruption the Bank has inadvertently been facilitating it. In the words of one report, the Bank has "abet[ted] corrupt regimes" by issuing loans that are devoid of "clear performance benchmarks", and doubts continue to linger about "the bank's ability to police itself" (*ibid.*).

Third, general oversight and management problems that might inadvertently facilitate corruption are one thing, but internal corruption scandals of the most basic order are quite another. The Bank has experienced a steady stream of these. Paul Wolfowitz becoming involved in negotiating both a new job and, more particularly, an eye-catching salary for his girlfriend, for example, falls squarely in this category. Wolfowitz arranged for his partner to move from the World Bank to the US State Department, which was his place of work before moving across to become the World Bank's president. The affair ultimately cost Wolfowitz his job (*Der Spiegel* 2007). Scandals are part and parcel of everyday life, but when you are banging an anti-corruption drum, such revelations do little for your credibility.

Finally, and most pointedly, there is a considerable body of evidence which illustrates that many of the World Bank's anti-corruption efforts simply have not been working. The Bank bought heavily into the principal–agent understandings of corruption outlined in Chapter 5, and this has led it not only to come up with particular policy prescriptions but also to buy into whole sets of assumptions about the role of the state. For much of the 1980s and 1990s, the Bank was seen to be using the fight against corruption as another tool with which to push through market-friendly and state-sceptic sets of structural reforms (Riley 1998: 138). It appeared to see counteracting corruption as being a technical issue, which could be solved with particular types of (essentially more liberal) economic policy, coupled with careful institutional reform (Brown & Cloke 2004: 289). Indeed, in an authoritative account of the World Bank's anti-corruption agenda in the early 2000s, Heather Marquette claimed that the considerable amount of research that World Bank experts have done, along with the Bank's practical efforts, "assume[s] away the negative links between economic and political liberalization and corruption", preferring instead to focus "on only one side of the debate" (Marquette 2003, 2004: 413). For much of the World Bank's existence, then, its economists have fallen into a misdiagnosis trap.

The Bank has, however, responded to these criticisms. Instead of defensively claiming that all is in fact fine and dandy, the Bank has chosen to develop a new set of tools to help it oversee spending on not just its own programs but also the anti-corruption efforts of states that ask for assistance. The Bank's critics often overlook its willingness to be at the forefront of actually doing things to fight corruption; this willingness may well lead to mistakes being made, but it is also a way of trialling innovative ideas. For example, the World Bank has created an independent Integrity Vice Presidency unit that "investigates and pursues sanctions related to allegations of fraud and corruption" within the Bank's own projects.[4] The Bank now lists the number of referrals it receives for allegedly corrupt activities (there were 22 in both the 2015 and 2014 fiscal years), and it provides a publicly available list of debarred firms and individuals.[5]

In order to prevent corruption on the ground, the World Bank has developed more precise and sophisticated monitoring and evaluation tools. In 2010, across South Asia, a number of "remote compliance oversight-focused strategies" were tried out. To be more precise, in Afghanistan, as part of a program called the Emergency Irrigation Rehabilitation Project, the World Bank sponsored the use of GPS-enabled cameras "to capture geo-referenced photos of irrigation project[s]". The data could then be sent to the project coordination unit at the Afghan Ministry of Energy and Water and viewed via Google Earth, showing the exact time and location of the observation. The aim was to ensure that funded projects were making the progress planned of them (World Bank 2013: 35).

---

4. For more on the Integrity Vice Presidency, see http://bit.ly/2kW4QAf, viewed on 7 December 2016.

5. For a list of the corruption-related referrals as well as more on the internal investigation process, see http://bit.ly/2kNfOFn, viewed on 7 December 2016. For the list of debarred entities, see http://bit.ly/1gwzXF5, viewed on 6 December 2016.

The World Bank's position in the anti-corruption fight has changed considerably over time. It has gone from being an institution that was viewed with scepticism and, in some quarters, no little scorn to being an increasingly thoughtful contributor to anti-corruption practice. The challenge of rooting out corruption where it is deeply embedded remains fearsomely difficult. Plus, the World Bank has to weigh up whether a more rigorous approach to overseeing where its funds go would simply lead to the world's poor being in a worse position than they already are. This circle is anything but easy to square.

However, the Bank is still, at times, adept at talking eloquently about fighting corruption without effectively illustrating how it has made progress in doing so. This applies both to the billions of dollars it spends on aid every year as well as the way it deals with corruption allegations within its own four walls. The Bank's inability and/or unwillingness to be open and transparent about some of its own procedures and practices, along with its willingness to launch review after review, the results of which often get buried deep on its unwieldy website, sends out its own clear messages. The Bank's anti-corruption agenda, it would seem, remains something of a work in progress.

THE INTERNATIONAL MONETARY FUND

Like the World Bank, the IMF does not exist primarily to fight corruption. Its aims are focused squarely on macroeconomic policy: ensuring global financial stability, facilitating trade and generally fire-fighting when economic crises develop. It also plays a role in offering economic advice to member states (through so-called Article VI consultations) (International Monetary Fund 2016b).

Yet it, too (like the World Bank), really "discovered" corruption as a public policy challenge in the 1990s. IMF scholars began publishing working papers and academic journal articles looking at corruption's impact on a range of economic issues as well as possible remedies for tackling it. Unsurprisingly, they came to the conclusion that corruption had a negative influence on a range of economic indicators such as growth and investment.[6] By September 1996, the IMF had developed a "Partnership for Sustainable Global Growth", in which tackling corruption was seen as an

---

6. See, for example, Shleifer & Vishny (1993), Tanzi (1994) and Mauro (1995, 1997).

"essential element of a framework within which economies can prosper".[7] This interest in corruption initially paralleled that of the World Bank, but it soon became clearer and more obvious to track. The IMF consistently calls for states to implement good governance strategies, and combatting corruption and successful integrity management are core tenets of that approach (International Monetary Fund 2016a).

It would be disingenuous to claim that the IMF's much-increased interest in corruption was ill-conceived; it is clear that it was not, and that the IMF and scholars closely linked to it are right to point out the array of damaging economic effects that corruption brings with it (see Schiller 2000). The IMF's mandate and resources also demand that it analyse corruption purely through the prism of whether, and how, it affects macroeconomic performance. However, the default position of many IMF scholars – the more the state does, the more likely it is to foster corrupt activity – does consistently come through. Christian Schiller, then Deputy Division Chief in the IMF's Fiscal Affairs Department, recommended specific sets of measures – liberalizing trade systems, decontrolling prices, broadening the scope of marketization – that were intended to both improve the quality of governance and fight corruption. Schiller claimed that such approaches have successfully "helped curtail that fertile ground for rent-seeking" (*ibid.*). Furthermore, in 1994, Vito Tanzi openly claimed that opportunities for corruption increase along with the size of a state's role in the economy; in 1998, he developed this further by adding that government regulations per se and the public provision of goods and services at below-market prices in particular prompt corruption (Tanzi 1994, 1998). When many of those active and influential within the IMF develop remedies from the philosophical and ideological starting points of the rational choice school, it is not surprising that the policy advice the organization gives is unlikely to actually lead – in a sustained and systematic way – to reductions in corruption levels.

REGIONAL ANTI-CORRUPTION INITIATIVES

As Table 1.1 (page 3) illustrates, there are a number of regional initiatives that are looking to set common anti-corruption standards. Indeed, most

---

7. International Monetary Fund (1996), "Partnership for Sustainable Global Growth", Interim Committee Declaration. See also International Monetary Fund (1997), "The role of the IMF in governance issues", Guidance Note. Available at http://bit.ly/2lSipyK, accessed on 22 November 2016.

regional governance bodies now talk about corruption in some way, shape or form. Quite how they talk about it and what types of action such discussions are leading to is, however, another matter. In Europe, for example, the CoE has developed both civil and criminal law conventions on corruption. In 1999, the CoE also set up the Group of States against Corruption (GRECO) in order to monitor compliance with both of these conventions as well as with its other anti-corruption initiatives. More specifically, GRECO uses the now familiar tools of mutual evaluation and peer pressure to "identify deficiencies in national anti-corruption policies". It also claims to provide a forum that enables member states to share best practice in preventing and detecting corruption.[8]

The EU also has a number of quite clear anti-corruption provisions. Judicial cooperation between EU member states to prevent corruption by EU-level or, indeed, nation-state-level officials has existed since 1997; and, before they were abolished in the Lisbon Treaty, the EU passed a number of framework decisions – decisions that required member states to achieve a particular outcome without being told specifically how to do it – that looked to combat corruption.[9] The EU has also set up its own anti-fraud body (the European Anti-Fraud Office, or OLAF) to try to prohibit fraud within the EU budget and across its institutions as well as to develop broader anti-fraud legislation. With over 1,400 investigations and €3 billion recovered between 2010 and 2015, OLAF has clearly been busy.[10] The EU is also keen to stress the importance of anti-corruption in the accession process, and both Romania and Bulgaria had their applications for EU membership delayed on account of making too little progress in this area.

The impact of all this activity remains harder to discern. Persuading states to pass legislation has often been much easier than coaxing them into actively enforcing it. The EU has little power to compel nation-states to take action in this area, and where anti-corruption progress *is* made, it is not always easy to see the EU's hand at play. Liljana Cvetanoska has nonetheless illustrated that the accession process is one area where some progress can be made. Even then, substantive moves to enact anti-corruption legislation are much more likely to happen early on in the accession process (when states

---

8. Council of Europe (2014), "Group of States against Corruption (GRECO)". Available at http://bit.ly/2iiMvNL, viewed on 23 November 2016.
9. European Council (1997), "Convention against corruption involving officials", 26 May. Available at http://bit.ly/2lnlidi, viewed on 23 November 2016.
10. See http://bit.ly/1VSWxB1, viewed on 23 November 2016.

theoretically have the most ground to make up), but only when it suits the needs of those in power. In Macedonia, for example, the pull of belonging to the EU was simply not as strong as the desire to defend systems that were working very nicely for those at the top of the pyramid (Cvetanoska 2017). In situations like this, the EU's power to persuade remains much weaker than it might like.

It is not, of course, just the EU and European states that have been thinking about corruption. In Africa, the "African Union Convention on Preventing and Combating Corruption" came into force in 2003 and has 35 signatories. This convention covers a wide range of issues in both the public and private sectors, and all provisions are mandatory. Issues such as recovering stolen assets and improving regional cooperation figure prominently. The Arab League also has a "Convention on Corruption" that came into force in 2010, where restituting assets and providing mutual judicial assistance are flagged as being particularly important. On the other side of the world, the countries in the Organization of American States ratified the "Inter-American Convention against Corruption" as long ago as 1996. The focus there is more on the public sector, and it represents an effort to find a regional consensus on a range of corruption issues. Even in East Asia, traditionally something of an outlier, China has been working with other Association of Southeast Asian Nations (ASEAN) states to develop regional anti-corruption legal frameworks (Yan 2016).

On paper, these initiatives sound impressive. When the complex and challenging nature of tackling corruption is remembered, however, it would be unreasonable to expect too much from them. Successful anti-corruption work takes time. Nevertheless, there are good reasons to wonder whether these regional bodies represent a coherent way forward. A number of regions do not have regional bodies at all, and Matthew Stephenson has outlined why, perhaps, they should not bother creating them. UNCAC, Stephenson notes, claims to be the global instrument for tackling corruption. If international efforts are subsequently going to work, then UNCAC would appear to be the most appropriate vehicle for helping them do so. Plus, the majority of the regional conventions existed before UNCAC came along; creating new ones now would seem a little odd.

As Stephenson points out, it may be argued that regional conventions can conduct more frequent reviews and build on the base provided by UNCAC, but there is also a real danger of "convention overload" and "peer review fatigue" (Stephenson 2014b). The impression would become ever more prominent that more time was being spent talking about corruption than actually tackling it. On top of that, the idea that local neighbours work better together can often be a long way removed from reality. Furthermore, the temptation may also be there to "respect local values" and, in effect, nicely undercut UNCAC. As Stephenson persuasively notes, the "focus both within the region and outside should be on pressing for compliance with global norms" that everyone understands and can sign up to (*ibid.*).

CHASING THE MONEY

Over and beyond these conventions, there is a plethora of more-focused initiatives aiming to do something about particular parts of the corruption problem. Given that corruption often has a strongly international dimension, this makes sense. These initiatives range from quite expansive attempts to tackle money laundering (Financial Action Task Force) and foster more transparency in the extractive industries (Extractive Industries Transparency Initiative) to the creation of much lower profile initiatives in quite specific sectors.

FATF is a good example of an organization that is dealing with a complex, international problem (money laundering and, latterly, terrorist financing), which is exceptionally difficult to uncover, let alone root out. FATF was founded in 1988 on the initiative of the then G7. Its initial aim was to come up with "legal, regulatory and operational measures" that could help tackle money laundering (Financial Action Task Force 2016b). It has since developed a series of recommendations (49 as of 2016), and signatories are expected to enact them into their domestic legal frameworks. FATF, again via peer review, assesses their success (and failure) in doing this. This organization currently has 37 full members and eight associate members, as well as many more countries that have generally endorsed FATF's standards and made a commitment to upholding them.

Tough though FATF's task is, there is certainly reason to believe that it has made a difference. Sabina Kook from the US Treasury, for example, noted in 2013 that FATF is almost "unique among the scores of global governance bodies" as it does actually appear to have been "largely successful in pushing countries forward to comply with its standards". The process of reviewing promises to commit to FATF's standards has been useful, while the "strong multilateral action" that has ensued when states have not played ball has garnered attention (Kook 2013). The strongest of these actions involves FATF effectively blacklisting any of the jurisdictions around the world that it deems uncooperative. In 2000, it published a list of 15 juris-dictions that it officially called "non-cooperative countries or territories". By October 2013, that list included 13 jurisdictions, but by June 2014 the number had fallen to six (Iran, North Korea, Algeria, Ecuador, Indonesia and Myanmar). By October 2016, only Iran and North Korea were left on the so-called blacklist (Financial Action Task Force 2016c). The impact of being blacklisted has arguably been more significant than the recommen-dations that FATF has developed, and a number of countries have reacted quickly (and often grumpily) to being described as non-cooperative.

How successful the EITI has been is rather more contested. Formed in June 2003, it has developed a global standard to promote and ensure open-ness and transparency in the way that the gas, oil and mining industries – industries that have traditionally been plagued by corruption – manage their affairs. The logic of the EITI is simple: information on every part of the resource extraction process should be publicly shared. That includes how much companies pay for licenses to do the extracting, how much of that resource they then produce, what they charge for it and who pays them for it. Governments, for their part, need to reveal their incomings from the extractives sector and explain how that money is then spent (see Box 7.3). Membership of EITI is not just limited to countries; companies and civil society initiatives are also welcome to join. In May 2005, EITI stakeholders worked together to establish six criteria outlining the mini-mum transparency requirements they felt should be required. By 2011, these rules had developed into 23 specific criteria, and in May 2013 these became the "EITI Standard".

A total of 51 countries have committed themselves to upholding that standard, and every one of them is required to publish an annual report disclosing all information on each part of the resource extraction process. In theory, the EITI sets a high barrier. Furthermore, it has been "an impor-tant and innovative actor", leading the way in "developing consultative pro-cesses" that have had a clear impact in terms of opening up discussions on transparency across the extractive industries and, indeed, beyond (Brown 2015). In terms of oil and gas, there has been a move towards openness that simply did not exist just a decade ago. This, in anyone's book, should be counted as success of a sort. This move has necessarily been piecemeal, and at times cumbersome, but it is a move in the right direction nonethe-less. In addition, before EITI there was no global discussion at all about the behaviour of those in the extractives sector; so, this really is a case of something being better than nothing.

Box 7.3. The Open Contracting Partnership (OCP)

One example of how governments are being encouraged to commit themselves to international agendas of openness comes through the Open Contracting Partnership (OCP). OCP began in 2012 in South Africa, when around 150 participants took part in a process that aimed to pin down what open contracting meant and how it could be implemented. This ultimately developed into the Open Contracting Standard, published in 2014.

OCP coaxes and cajoles governments into opening up their processes of contracting. The aim is to ensure that the "huge sums of money involved are spent honestly, fairly, and effectively". OCP works across sectors and claims that it wants to save governments time and money while enabling citizens to enjoy the benefits of getting better goods and services.

OCP subsequently aims to create a "global norm in public contracting", moving the default position from closed to open decision-making processes. It also aims to offer assistance in helping create open contracting best practice as well as gather evidence about open contracting's impact.* It has a way to go before achieving these aims, but it is one example of how international initiatives can quickly develop.

---

* See "About the Open Contracting Partnership". Available at http://bit.ly/2kNpdwU, viewed on 29 November 2016.

It is nonetheless intriguing that some of the countries that are most prone to corruption in the area of extractives have still been keen to sign up to EITI. At first sight, this would appear to be a paradox. Why commit yourself to more transparency when that very commitment is likely to prevent many government insiders from reaping the rewards of the deals they have struck? Elizabeth Dávid-Barrett and Ken Okamura offer an explanation for this. They argue that "EITI serves as a reputational intermediary" for an array of stakeholders. Governments intent on reforming (at least some) of their ways "can signal good intentions", while actors in the international arena "can reward achievement" by those who make substantive progress. Transparency becomes the norm to which ever more governments (at least appear to) want to subscribe, and a small but noticeable virtuous circle is therefore created (Dávid-Barrett & Okamura 2016: 227).

Be that as it may, the EITI has nonetheless been faced with a string of criticism. In the cold light of day, the EITI does not possess many teeth, and its options for sanctioning miscreants are only weak at best. ExxonMobil, for example, is a member of the EITI US multi-stakeholder group, but it still refuses to share information on the taxes that it pays in the US (Rucker 2015; see also Brown 2015). There are also questions regarding what precisely EITI should demand of signatories; should the barrier be high in the knowledge that some countries (and companies) will fail, or should it be low with a view to slowly coaxing and cajoling everyone forward? EITI participants have had plenty of internal arguments about precisely this.

There has also been criticism of the way that civil society organizations have allegedly captured the EITI board (where they occupy a third of the seats). These organizations have often been impatient with the apparent lack of progress made, and critics of their shrillness have argued that this has ended up politicizing the EITI. As Michael Chadbourne and Parke Washington noted in an industry journal in 2012, the EITI is becoming "as much a tool of interest-group politics as it is a mechanism of transparency" (Chadbourne & Washington 2012). At the very least, and as former chair of the EITI board Clare Short once noted, "conflict is entrenched in the very model" of organization that EITI has developed.[11] There has also been criticism that EITI does the very opposite of what these predominantly business-based critics claim. Rather than dance to the tune of civil society members, they say, EITI may not have been outgoing enough in getting involved in the affairs of states that do not uphold the rules. EITI's unwillingness to sanction Azerbaijan on account of an alleged "breach of the initiative's requirements for fostering an enabling environment for civil society" is a case in point.[12] In addition, there have been questions about EITI's credibility, particularly after it allowed Ethiopia to join in 2014 (Biron 2014). EITI is nevertheless working in a high-profile, highly problematic (in corruption terms) set of industries. It is also trying to bring together quite different actors with different interests. It is, therefore, no surprise that progress is subsequently too slow for many. Indeed, expecting radical change would simply be unrealistic.

One initiative that has nonetheless made a clear impact on its industry is the "Shipping and Maritime Initiative" at TRACE International. Its focus is tackling bribery (and corruption more broadly) at ports. It has a narrower focus than EITI, and this may be one of the reasons it appears

---

11. Short (2015), quoted in "NGOs and governments grapple over ownership of mining and energy firms", *The Economist*, 24 October. Available at http://econ.st/1W35AMl, viewed on 24 November 2016.

12. Extractive Industries Transparency Initiative (2016), "Human rights groups call to suspend Azerbaijan from participation in EITI", *Netherlands Helsinki Committee*, 21 October. Available at http://bit.ly/2lW6Mq6, viewed on 24 November 2016.

to have been more successful. The initiative was developed "in response to the direct request of vessel owners, shipping agents and freight forwarders", and it aims to develop focused solutions that will rise to the not insignificant compliance challenges faced by this sector.[13] The activities included in this initiative are quite wide ranging: knowledge-sharing and benchmarking take place through an anti-bribery customs working group, for example, along with due diligence reviews of third-party companies active in the sector (the results of which are provided to shipping and ports agents). Although TRACE International's efforts will not eradicate corruption in the maritime industry, this initiative represents the type of collective-action thinking that long-time advocates of such ideas – such as Mark Pieth – have championed: stakeholders working together on discrete challenges to come up with mutually agreeable solutions (Pieth 2012).

CONCLUSION

As this chapter has illustrated, a wide and varied array of international anti-corruption initiatives exist. Some are genuinely global in scope, while others focus on particular parts of the problem in specific industries. Some have broad aims, while others have much more precise objectives. None have achieved all of their goals, which leaves us asking the following question: how much progress should be regarded as "enough" for the initiative to be merited a success? Given that, as was noted at the start of this chapter, successful anti-corruption work is time-consuming, messy and, at times, downright frustrating, there is a case to be made that these attempts should – all things being equal – be given a little leeway. It took some of the world's cleaner states centuries to be sure that they had genuinely tackled the worst of their corruption problems. None of these initiatives have been around anything like that long, and they all exist in a complex international system populated by a wide range of actors with multiple interests. International anti-corruption efforts are very easy to criticize, but, in truth, there is no plan B. All of these anti-corruption organizations and ideas may need to mutate and develop, but no one is making the case that the world would be a better place without them. If Rome was not built in a day, then a corruption-free world certainly will not be built in a decade or so.

---

13. For more, see Trace International (2016), "Shipping and maritime initiative". Available at http://bit.ly/2lWr3M4, viewed on 25 November 2016.

8.
National approaches to anti-corruption

The international approaches to tackling corruption discussed in Chapter 7 still inevitably have as their focus the work and behaviour of governments, businesses and civil society organizations that work largely within national boundaries. Corruption is, in other words, a transnational phenomenon that requires internationally agreed responses to be translated into the frameworks and cultures of national political life. This ensures that the divide in this book between international and national approaches is, by definition, something of a false one. International approaches are translated into national contexts, while national (and, indeed, local; see Chapter 9) approaches often have their roots in – or, at the very least, a relationship with – initiatives that began either in the international arena or simply in other places. The notion that there is a clear divide between the national and international arena therefore needs to be dispelled right at the beginning.

There has also been a fair amount of diffusion in anti-corruption thinking. Throughout the 1980s and 1990s, the institutions of the Washington Consensus (World Bank and IMF), for example, had a considerable influence over how states thought about anti-corruption. Still, some of the most popular tools that national governments use start out as discrete responses to specific national (or subnational) problems. They can prompt copycat actions elsewhere; in terms of national anti-corruption commissions, for example, the creation of the Hong Kong Independent Commission against Corruption (ICAC) in 1974 prompted scores of similar (although rarely identical) institutions to be created in other jurisdictions.[1] The ICAC was a genuine trailblazer. The American FCPA, passed in 1977, has become a

---

1. For more on the Hong Kong model, see Scott (2011).

piece of legislation that firms all over the world, and not just those who conduct most of their business in the US, are aware of.[2] National anti-corruption initiatives can, and do, have international effects.

This chapter analyses how national governments tend to approach the anti-corruption challenge. Given that many anti-corruption reforms are not particularly successful, this chapter begins by grappling with a potentially tricky question: how does the outside observer know that a given authority is actually serious about wanting to tackle corruption in the first place? Just about every politician everywhere decries corruption's deleterious effects, and they all claim to want, in some way, to do something about this. If these claims are all genuine, why do so many of these politicians fail to make progress? It is often claimed that it is down to a failure of political will; a failure, in other words, to make the tough decisions that come with taking on vested interests and opposing deeply entrenched political forces. For many critics, anti-corruption talk is a smokescreen that politicians use to make themselves look good. How, then, do we know whether a politician is really serious about taking the fight against corruption forward? How do we know that the political will is really there?

Once this issue has been unpacked, the chapter moves on to analyse some of the ways that governments address the problem. In recent years, one-size-fits-all agendas for change have become a lot less fashionable, and a lot more thinking has been done about what might work where.

Countries with relatively strong governance institutions and relatively low levels of corruption will face one set of problems.[3] These governments are often dealing with so-called influence markets, where an anti-corruption agenda built around accountability drives, transparency initiatives and nuanced efforts to tackle particular (national) variants of "legal corruption" make sense (Johnston 2005).

Countries with governance institutions of a more mixed quality tend to face rather more overt sets of corruption challenges. There may be a mixture of both grand and petty corruption; in some ways, corruption may take on systemic traits, whereas in other situations it will still be a crime of opportunity. Possible remedies will therefore be more varied and arguably in even greater need of translation into a national context. It is also easier to pinpoint a number of quite popular anti-corruption mechanisms that

---

2. For more on the FCPA, see Koehler (2013).
3. For a much more detailed analysis of governance regimes and anti-corruption, see Hough (2013).

patently have not worked. These range from bringing in anti-corruption commissions to developing ever more intricate sets of laws and regulations. In this context, the commissions are rarely able to stay above the political fray, and they are frequently deprived of the resources and competences (not to mention a receptive broader institutional environment) necessary to make an impact. Rigorous legal and regulatory frameworks are indispensable in the anti-corruption fight, but the real issue remains not what is written on paper but how it is translated into practice. That is where this middle group of states runs into difficulties.

Finally, there are an awful lot of states in which corruption is both systemic and systematic. In these contexts, simply talking anti-corruption can be counterproductive. Those in power look to defend (for better or worse) their positions and often see anti-corruption rhetoric as a direct attack on what they are doing. Frequently, of course, it is. In these states, the best anti-corruption tools often have surprisingly little to do with corruption at all. In a state where the rule of law is patchy or non-existent, anti-corruption laws (or, indeed, laws more generally) mean very little. The challenge here is to improve the basic tools of governance in the knowledge that then and only then can the issue of corruption be brought onto the agenda.

DO THEY MEAN WHAT THEY SAY?

It is tempting to conclude that political leaders who "fail" to root out corrupt practices have done so because they did not have the drive and determination to see things through. Other issues got in the way, and tackling corruption somehow became less important than they might have claimed previously. Many a critic, citing the old adage "where there's a will, there's a way", has subsequently claimed that there was not enough political will about. Those critics could indeed be right: some politicians do talk a good game that they have no intention of playing. But we cannot know that for sure.

Those who think political will is a concept worth pursuing have created frameworks to try to operationalize it. Derick Brinkerhoff's ideas are the most prominent: although he certainly recognizes the notion's inherent slipperiness, he still claims that there is "a set of action-based components" that are both "observable and measurable", and can help us pinpoint when the will to enact anti-corruption policies really is there (Brinkerhoff 2000, 2010). Brinkerhoff disaggregates political will into seven discrete components that he claims are all quantifiable. These range from where an initiative stems from, to "the extent to which government actors consult with, engage, and mobilize stakeholders". They include the amount of resources an administration puts into the anti-corruption cause as well as whether "well-crafted and enforced" sanctions are in place (*ibid.*: 2).

In many ways, Brinkerhoff is trying simply to encourage governments to think just a little more about how they action their policies. Much of what he advocates can quite plausibly be put into a box titled "good practice". It certainly makes sense to resource any and all attempts to implement policies, just as consultation with end users and those impacted is also likely to be a sound strategy. Failure to do this, however, does not mean that political will is lacking. It is not hard to think of situations where "reveal[ing] … policy preferences publicly" would not be such a good idea. Highlighting that you want to tackle black money in an economy, for example, may well prompt those involved to quickly move their funds to offshore or otherwise inaccessible jurisdictions (*ibid.*: 3).

Turning attempts to unpack the real intentions of practitioners into a scientific concept remains a task that is at best fraught with difficulty, and at worst downright impossible. As Michael Johnston has noted, "political will is a tempting, but ultimately empty slogan". We cannot get into decision-makers' heads, so there is no way we can tell for certain what is driving them; knowing what is really going on inside the minds of policy-makers places us in the realm of unknown unknowns. Much as Brinkerhoff's framework is an interesting approach to understanding how good policy might be made, the notion of political will still remains to all intents and purposes analytically useless (Johnston 2016: 14).

WHAT TO DO WHERE

If trying to empirically illustrate the authenticity of a politician's attempt to tackle corruption is an intellectual cul-de-sac, then how do we find a way through the maze of potential anti-corruption options? There is no perfect answer to that question, and, throughout history, many of the most effective anti-corruption tools have been implemented with other goals in mind. As Johnston and Kpundeh note, corruption is often reduced not because reformers have a long-term reform vision, but rather due to "the growing ability of people and groups outside the state to defend themselves against official abuse and to check the unfair advantages of others" (Johnston & Kpundeh 2002: 1). This is achieved by creating fora in which individuals can legitimately contest decisions and defend their interests. That only happens slowly. There may well be lots of false starts along the way, but it is this process of empowerment that has the most discernible impact. Potential reformers in the contemporary era, however, cannot wait decades to see the fruits of their labour; they need results in a much shorter time span.

Given this, we often find ourselves limited to tools that talk to the interests of power-holders. Those power-holders may, of course, have plenty to lose, but the reality is that reforms work best when it is in the interest of the reformers themselves to make them work. This can be an uneasy finding when those potential reformers are known to have indulged in corruption in the past, but if change is going to happen then a broad coalition of supporters is usually necessary (*ibid.*). Even in situations where one charismatic individual is intent on driving change, they will need to think carefully about ensuring that they take reform laggards along, too. Anti-corruption is very much a team event.

Jeff Huther and Anwar Shah from the World Bank have tried to turn these broad ideas into practical politics by linking the quality of the governance regime with the type of anti-corruption activity that is most likely to succeed (Huther & Shah 2000: 9–10). As noted earlier, the notion of governance is every bit as slippery as that of corruption, but Huther and Shah's starting point is nonetheless a sensible one. They look at states' performances regarding the WGI and broadly bracket states into high, fair and low regime types. Then, they note that states with a high quality of governance generally have relatively low levels of corruption. Correspondingly, states with a poor quality of governance have high levels of corruption. The authors' aim is not to then say that state A needs to do X, while state B needs to do Y; rather, they posit a range of possible actions that probably deserve some consideration.

Huther and Shah (and others) do not claim to be able to micromanage the anti-corruption strategies of particular states. Instead, they try to flag what will, might, could and probably will not have a positive impact. In other words, their research helps those who want to tackle corruption to rise to "the challenge [of] … identify[ing] structural factors that create favourable conditions for reform" (Rose-Ackerman & Palifka 2016: 415). In states with good-quality governance regimes, corruption tends to take place away from the prying eyes of people on the street. It is not petty corruption that provides the challenge but the wheeler-dealing of a capitalist class that seeks to earn profits and exert influence without the wider world being aware of it. The responses to corruption in these influence markets subsequently tend to centre around the notions of transparency and accountability. In recent years, a number of attempts have been made to do justice to one or both of these concepts. Indeed, they frequently go together; it makes little sense to increase the transparency of government if the overall aim is not to enhance accountability mechanisms as a result.

GETTING THE LEGAL FRAMEWORK RIGHT

One of the most fundamental parts of any move to tackle corruption involves prosecuting those who break the law. Indeed, if anti-corruption is going to be a successful long-term venture, then potential miscreants need to know that there is a cost to being caught. All states need to develop a legal framework that makes clear what is and what is not legally permissible. In places where the rule of law is patchy (or indeed non-existent), there is little point in crafting detailed anti-corruption legislation. It is very likely to be ignored or even hijacked for political gain. The challenge in these states is much more fundamental, and involves creating functioning institutions that are based around an independent judiciary and a power-holding class that respects the law of the land.

The anti-corruption drive of Xi Jinping, president of the People's Republic of China since 2012, is an example of this. Before 2012, China prosecuted around 20,000 individuals annually for corruption-related activities. Since then, millions of officials have been investigated, around 750,000 have been disciplined and 35,000 have been expelled from the CPC. That includes around 200 at ministerial level. The Chinese state was keen to be seen taking on both the "tigers" (powerful figures in leadership positions) and the "flies" (much lower-ranked officials) within the Chinese system. Xi was also keen to stress that China was becoming a state governed by law. On 5 December 2012, for example, he noted that the CPC's sole aim was "to fully implement the Constitution" and to build "a socialist nation ruled by law" (quoted in Yinan 2012).

However, being "governed by law", as Xi meant it, has an altogether different meaning to being governed "by the rule of law"; legal issues in states that abide by the rule of law are overseen by non-partisan, independent judges, free from the influence or indeed control of the executive. In Xi's China, rule by law implies that the CPC is creating laws it can then use to ensure that Chinese officials (and Chinese citizens more broadly) act in a way that it believes is appropriate. The aim for the CPC is to create a legal framework that helps it fulfil the goals that it has set for China. An independent judiciary is not part of that understanding.[4] The effect CPC rule has had on China's recent development is certainly debatable; in terms of anti-corruption policy, however, it will – sooner or later – run into trouble. One can throw as many people behind bars as one likes, but when arbitrary behaviour is at the core of the decision-making process, then, ultimately, any and every anti-corruption drive will flounder.

In states where the rule of law is widely apparent, the focus moves on from these fundamentals towards getting the specifics of the corruption framework right. This is by no means easy. As the UK entered the twenty-first century, for example, its anti-corruption body of law was described by the then Lord Chancellor (i.e. the highest legal authority in the country at the time), Lord (Charlie) Falconer, as "complex, inconsistent and outdated". The former UK Home Secretary, Jack Straw, added that it was both "old and anachronistic".[5] In Germany, meanwhile, awareness of corruption took a long time to filter into legal and procedural changes, and until 1999 it was perfectly legal to bribe foreign officials to gain contracts. Furthermore, these bribes were even tax deductible (Abdelal *et al.* 2008: 2).

Both the UK and Germany (and others) subsequently found themselves playing a form of catch-up. Indeed, it was the US that first stuck its metaphorical neck out and drafted anti-corruption legislation that had real teeth. The 1977 FCPA became for many a standout piece of legislation, largely because it was the first attempt by any single country to prevent its citizens from bribing abroad (see Box 8.1). Developed in the immediate aftermath of Watergate, the act was only enforced infrequently until the late 1990s, when the second of two revisions (in 1998) broadened its scope and empowered and emboldened investigators. Up until that point, more or less "nothing happened", as the FCPA "effectively lay dormant" for the best part of a quarter of a century (Malesky 2013). As enforcement has become (much) more aggressive, that has changed significantly: awareness of the FCPA is now high; a number of other countries have followed

---

4. *The Wall Street Journal* (2014), "'Rule of law' or 'rule by law'? In China, a preposition makes all the difference", 20 October.

5. Lord Falconer, 24 March 2003. Quoted in Brown (2007), "Prevention of corruption: UK legislation and enforcement", *Journal of Financial Regulation and Compliance*, 15(2): 180. Jack Straw, March 2009. Quoted in Michael Osajda (2012), "The UK Bribery Act of 2010: Whiter the FCPA", p. 4.

> **Box 8.1. The US Foreign Corrupt Practices Act (FCPA)**
>
> The FCPA may well have been largely ignored for 25 years after its inception, but, in recent years, it has been the focus of much attention and no little controversy. It has now led to over 200 cases, covering activity that touches on around 80 countries. A look at the informative http://fcpamap.com/ reveals that around US$7.8 billion worth of fines have now been levied, with US$3.8 billion having been paid by businesses in the energy sector; they are thus far and away the largest sinners (in financial terms). People's Republic of China is the country that pops up most frequently as a place where bribes are paid, with 36 different cases appearing to have touched on its soil (see Mintz Group 2016). As of Autumn 2016, only three of the 10 biggest cases have involved American firms: KBR/Halliburton (third, fined US$579 million in 2009), Och-Ziff (fourth, fined US$412 million in 2016) and Alcoa (eighth, fined US$384 million in 2014). This illustrates that if companies plan to be active in the US or use US banks, they need to be up to speed with the provisions of the anti-corruption world's most prominent piece of legislation (Cassin 2016).

the US's lead in enacting similar anti-bribery laws; and the OCED has developed an anti-bribery convention that follows very much the same logic (see Chapter 7). Indeed, there is evidence that where the FCPA is used to investigate the behaviour of companies in a territory, that territory is more likely to go on and develop and enforce its own anti-bribery laws (Kaczmarek & Newman 2011).

The FCPA has risen to such prominence because it now allows American officials to prosecute both US and non-US citizens who work for companies (American and non-American) that have a presence in the US. That "presence" can entail something as obvious as being listed on the US stock exchange, but it can also be something as specific as using a US bank to process transactions. The FCPA's remit is now broad, and, for many, there is a danger of overstretch. Indeed, a lively debate is currently taking place between what Matthew Stephenson describes as "FCPA scaremongers", who stress what they believe is the FCPA's overreach, and those who have a more sanguine attitude to the increased enforcement efforts of recent years.[6]

---

6. For a particularly good example of this, see (including the comments posted below) Stephenson (2016).

One piece of national legislation has gone beyond even that of the FCPA: the UK's Bribery Act 2010 (UKBA). This was drafted on the back of both the UK signing the OECD's anti-bribery convention and a number of high-profile foreign bribery scandals involving UK firms. It does not just cover bribery abroad, but also looks expressly at bribery that takes place within the UK. Any sort of bribery could potentially be prosecuted. Furthermore, it is also an offence under the UKBA to receive a bribe; the FCPA, on the other hand, simply criminalizes the act of giving the bribe. The UKBA does not allow so-called facilitation payments (sometimes termed "speed money"), while the FCPA *does* allow a defence of these if the payments are made to make an official do something more quickly (but not differently from what he or she would have done anyway). Most notably, the UKBA makes failing to prevent a bribe an offence. Now, no company can hang an employee out to dry unless it can show that it had adequate procedures in place to train and educate the employee concerned about what was acceptable behaviour in that setting. The FCPA contains no such procedure.

The UKBA is still relatively new, and there have been few convictions (see Box 8.2). There is also a chance that as the UK leaves the EU there may be ever more persuasive lobbying to get these strong provisions watered down. Quantifying the impact of the UKBA is therefore difficult. It is hard to analyse things that do not exist, and it is entirely plausible that UK companies have anticipated the change and modified their behaviour accordingly. The relatively small number of convictions does not mean that the UKBA is not having an impact. For instance, the UKBA has prompted talk of previously alien concepts, such as deferred prosecution agreements (DPAs), the first of which, involving Standard Bank, occurred in November 2015.[7] Some think that DPAs are a necessary evil, which allow companies to avoid making formal admissions of guilt while still forcing them to pay significant fines. Plus, if it transpires that a company has misled the UK authorities, then the agreement will be rendered null and void, and legal proceedings may be commenced. Others argue that DPAs still enable companies to get off too lightly (see Vitou & Kovalevsky 2016). Sceptics also claim that it will not be long (if, indeed, it is not happening already) before companies are simply factoring these potential costs into their business plans.

Creating and nuancing laws is an ongoing process. It is, however, only one part of getting anti-corruption right. Over the years, Susan

---

7. For more on this, see Clare (2015).

Rose-Ackerman has put forward a whole host of eminently sensible and logical suggestions that well-governed states with effective institutional frameworks might want to think about (Rose-Ackerman 1978, 1999; Rose-Ackerman & Palifka 2016). Most recently, Rose-Ackerman (together with Bonnie Palifka) has been open about the value that adopting a principal–agent framework (see Chapter 5) can bring, stressing the importance of government aims to "increase both transparency and oversight". Any reforms that "limit the incentives for payoffs" are worth undertaking (Rose-Ackerman & Palifka 2016: 526). The list of potential reforms may seem impossibly long. For example, governments need to be open about how they award contracts, just as they need to empower

---

Box 8.2. The UK's Bribery Act 2010

The Bribery Act 2010 is the strongest piece of anti-bribery legislation in the world. However, the number of prosecutions secured since its introduction has been lower than many hoped. Furthermore, a significant number of these prosecutions have hardly been for high crimes of state; an administrative clerk (and employee of the Ministry of Justice) from Croydon was the first person to be convicted under the UKBA after claiming he could persuade a court to let another individual off a motoring offence for the sum of £500. The second conviction went to an aspiring self-employed taxi driver, who tried to bribe a minicab licensing officer, while the third involved a Chinese student who offered his tutor at the University of Bath £5,000 to change one of his marks. The fact that a pistol accidentally fell out of the student's pocket as he left the meeting further complicated matters. He was sentenced to a year in prison (see Vitou & Kovalevsky 2013). The Serious Fraud Office (SFO) achieved its first conviction in 2014 (with a £23 million biofuel scam involving AgroEnergy); more large-scale convictions have slowly begun to follow (Cohn & Ridley 2014).

The slow progress made in terms of convictions should not, therefore, be a surprise. The UKBA is not retrospective, so it only applies to misdemeanours that have occurred since it came into force (in the middle of 2011). Given how long they take to generate, a flood of significant convictions was not to be expected straight away. Furthermore, the UKBA has widely been touted as a piece of legislation with real teeth; companies are aware of it, and many will have taken suitable measures to ensure that they do not fall foul of it. The UKBA has certainly been a slow burner in terms of quantifiable impact, but the same can also be said of the FCPA. As time passes, we are likely to see more and more convictions passed down by the courts.

---

independent regulatory bodies to oversee all aspects of their work. Law enforcement agencies should be well resourced, and judicial bodies should be independent in their actions. Those in the public sector must be open about their assets and prepared to explain how they amassed any (apparently) unexplained wealth. The regulations that shape business activity need to be crisp, clear and concise, just as tax regimes need to be as simple and straightforward as practically possible. Service provision should be transparent and easily understandable. All of these ideas (and many more) lead to more efficient and effective governance, and that is the real purpose of any anti-corruption drive.

THE TRANSPARENCY CHALLENGE

The challenge of putting transparency at the heart of government thinking is now a fundamental part of the type of reform that Rose-Ackerman advocates. Indeed, the vast majority of governments laud the value of transparency in abstract terms, even if they are often reluctant to do justice to it in the real world of bureaucratic politics. Initiatives in this area come in a number of different guises; there are broad commitments to general goals, and there are specific schemes that look to persuade governments to sign up to and implement a given agenda.

Two of the most well known of these schemes are the drive to bring about more open government and the push to encourage the public release of all data related to governments' affairs ("open data"). These initiatives have both received plenty of attention in previous years, although it is not always clear precisely how they are going to do justice to their aims (Dávid-Barrett *et al.* 2017). Transparency, of course, has long been regarded as an effective anti-corruption tool, but it was only with the launch of the Open Government Partnership (OGP) by eight governments in 2011 that it became institutionalized. Improvements in the quality of data and the technology available to process and analyse it, along with the development of an increasingly vocal international pro-transparency movement, had, by Autumn 2016, led 70 governments to sign the OGP and make over 2,500 commitments (Open Government Partnership 2016). These involve developing action plans with specific commitments to enable citizens to learn more about what the government is doing.

The objective is a deceptively simple one, and quite how governments do this in practice varies considerably from state to state. In other words, this is an international initiative that is translated very differently from place to place. The broad goals may be regarded as universal, but the implementation is decidedly national. One of the challenges is that there is an implicit assumption that the process of developing an open data and, indeed, an open government agenda is a value-neutral one. In practice, there are disputes about precisely what data should be released, how it should be released and how we should be able to access it. The language used to defend and implement open data agendas is often thoroughly technocratic, but, as Dávid-Barrett *et al.* (2017) note, that "overlook[s] the highly political context in which rules for open data are set and implemented".

This has led to a series of challenges – teething problems, optimists would no doubt say – with regard to making the idea of open data a reality. The data is not always published in a format that is easily useable. What it needs to be is both machine readable and in line with an agreed set of international standards. Offering up reams of pdfs might enable someone to tick a box on a checklist, but it does nothing to help interested observers understand what is really going on. There also need to be clear procedures in place for reporting problems that come up in the data; as things stand, no such procedures exist, even in states that are leading the way in terms of the transparency agenda (*ibid.*).

Some states have, however, made impressive progress in developing tools that enable citizens to find out more about how those in power spend their time and citizens' money as well as earn money through other sources. In the UK, for example, websites such as www.theyworkforyou. com (TWFY) allow citizens (from the UK and beyond) to see not just what their parliamentarians say and do in parliament, but also where they travel for work purposes. These websites also reveal the payments over and beyond their salary that parliamentarians receive for public appearances, speeches and other activities.

Just a few seconds of clicking on TWFY allows one to uncover, for example, that on 16 January 2016, Diane Abbott (Labour), the UK's Shadow Home Secretary, registered a £700 appearance fee for copresenting the BBC's *This Week* television show.[8] David Davis, the (Conservative) Secretary of State for Exiting the European Union, revealed on 1 July 2016 that he received approximately £34,000 per annum for the six days of work a year he does for Mansfelder Kupfer und Messing GMBH, a German

---

8. TheyWorkForYou (2016a), "Register of members' interests; Diane Abbott MP".

manufacturing company based in Hettstedt.[9] TWFY also produces an array of left-field facts and figures, presumably just to keep readers entertained; Daniel Kawczynski, the Conservative MP for Shrewsbury and Atcham, for example, has "used three-word alliterative phrases (e.g., 'she sells seashells') 371 times in debates". This, according to TWFY at least, is "above average amongst MPs".[10] So, now you know.

The drive to push enhanced processes of accountability and transparency has generated a fair amount of traction. This is the case in many parts of the globe, but it is most prominent in the developed world, where there is now more openness in government than there ever has been before. Indeed, some argue that there is now too much openness. Former UK Prime Minister Tony Blair, who held this post when the UK Freedom of Information Act 2000 was enacted, once described himself as an "idiot … [a] naive, foolish, irresponsible nincompoop" for passing such a law.[11] Others would undoubtedly disagree.

EMULATION AND INSPIRATION

States that experience more significant governance challenges nonetheless face more widespread and, in many ways, more fundamental sets of problems. These are not problems of tweaking systems of governance that generally work well but of developing reform agendas that involve significant and deep-seated change. Coming up with nationally tailored recipes for reform that (i) talk to existing power-holders, (ii) can mobilize broad coalitions of support and (iii) are intellectually well thought through is no small task.

Many of these reforms are unique creations, bespoke answers to bespoke problems, but many are not. As a start, developing a clear anti-corruption plan makes sense. However, it needs to avoid being a simple wishlist. There should be clearly defined aims and a clearly defined path explaining how such aims will be realized. Those aims will, by definition, talk to the unique context in which every state finds itself. The UK's anti-corruption plan of 2014 has, for example, 66 specific "actions", and it publishes updates on how many of those it achieves.[12] Furthermore, organizations such as TI UK

---

9. TheyWorkForYou (2016b), "Register of members' interests; David Davis MP".
10. TheyWorkForYou (2016c), "Register of members' interests; Daniel Kawczynski MP".
11. Quoted by Rosenbaum (2010).
12. See UK Government (2014), "United Kingdom anti-corruption plan"; UK Government (2015), "UK anti-corruption plan: progress update".

are making a point of holding the UK government to account by publishing their own evaluations of how well (or not, as the case may be) the UK government is doing. If nothing else, the UK government deserves credit for outlining what it wants to do and giving the wider world the ammunition to shoot it down if it fails.

Yet, when reform happens, it often involves national actors taking inspiration from elsewhere. There can, in other words, be more or less obvious processes of emulation at work. These processes tend to take place in line with one of what Wade Jacoby calls four modes. First, power-holders can faithfully and voluntarily emulate policies that they simply like the look of. In effect, their anti-corruption policies will be copied from elsewhere. Second, rather than being directly copied, a given policy may be "translated" into the local context. The emulation is still clearly voluntary, but the external policy is used more as a template than something to be directly dropped in. Third, governments may feel under a degree of pressure to introduce certain reforms. This might still involve the faithful execution of a given policy, but it is likely to be done in a patchy way, mainly to tick all the relevant boxes needed to, say, do justice to an international treaty. Finally, Jacoby argues that international organizations can set thresholds that national governments know they need to meet if they want something at the end. In Jacoby's (non-corruption) work, that means membership of the North Atlantic Treaty Organization (NATO) or the EU (Jacoby 2004: 6).

The latter two of these drivers of reform do not start out in the national arena, but the first two certainly do. Indeed, there is plenty of evidence to show that copying and the use of templates is quite commonplace. However, that does not mean the process or the outcome is the same everywhere. Far from it. There is a dynamism about the reform process that is different from place to place; but it is notable that many states emulate what is done in the Western world. There is a clear assumption that if it works in, say, Denmark, then it will work in other states as well ... eventually. For instance, the idea of introducing an ombudsman, an independent official to investigate complaints of maladministration, was seen until quite recently as quirkily Scandinavian. By 2008, 135 states had introduced the role into their domestic systems (Mungiu-Pippidi 2013: 1259).

Another higher-profile example of emulation comes in the form of anti-corruption commissions. Over the past 25 years, upwards of 50 states have created bespoke institutions that are tasked with tackling corruption. Their specific remits often differ considerably, but more or less all draw inspiration from the work of the ICAC and, to a lesser extent, the Corrupt Practices Investigation Bureau (CPIB) in Singapore (Quah 1994). Bertrand de Speville, a former commissioner of the ICAC, remains firmly of the belief that the "Hong Kong model" works, and that if states really did faithfully copy it then they would reap the benefits. He argues that, ultimately, the coffee is often too hot for many reformers to drink, and this limits (in some way) the remit, the independence or the resources of commissions that are created. De Speville claims this is the first step on the road to failure (see de Speville 2010).

Many anti-corruption agencies (ACAs) thus use the ICAC as a template. They understand the contribution it has made in Hong Kong, but they think that their particular settings require the model to be "translated". Sometimes this is successful; the ACAs in Croatia, Indonesia and Latvia, for example, are regarded as significant contributors to the anti-corruption fight (see Box 8.3; Kuris (2014)). The vast majority of others, however, have experienced failures. De Speville (2010) is clear as to why that is: such places diverted from what is known to work. Many critics are less strident, however, noting that just because the ICAC model has worked well in Hong Kong does not mean it will necessarily work everywhere else.

ANTI-CORRUPTION IN HIGH-CORRUPTION CONTEXTS

Emulating successful anti-corruption policies or institutions is still an impossible approach in countries where the basic tenets of a functioning state are not in place. In contexts like this, anti-corruption thinkers must conceptualize how to produce the very institutions needed to govern a modern state. A basic requirement is the establishment of a government with both legitimacy and a broad mandate to rule. In post-conflict settings in particular, this is often very difficult, and the more external forces get involved, the more problematic the process often seems to become. Policies that help states move towards developing a legitimate government that can execute policy; sets of institutions that allow citizens to defend and articulate their interests peacefully; and a judiciary that can uphold the rule of law are paramount. Any and every policy that pushes a state in that direction should be taken seriously.

One of the most pressing problems governments face in these situations is that of momentum. They often have so many issues to address that tackling corruption may be very low down on their to-do lists. Indeed, as

---

Box 8.3. Anti-corruption agencies (ACAs)

The debate about whether stand-alone ACAs are a good way to tackle corruption is a long-standing and ongoing one. Many ACAs have certainly been ineffectual and arguably counterproductive, largely as they can become politicized. Gabriel Kuris (2014) has nonetheless pointed out four key lessons that ACAs need to learn if they are going to sail through stormy seas when the weather turns.

First, ACAs need to be internally beyond reproach. They need to have good, clear integrity-enhancing procedures built into the way they work. Second, they need to build alliances with other interested parties. That includes civil society groups, the media and state institutions. They cannot exist aloof from everyday life. Third, they need to think about how best to launch preventative measures: developing the tools to educate people about the ills of corruption is important. Finally, Kuris claims that ACAs must think strategically, managing how they use their resources and wells of support to – when the time comes – help them outflank their opponents (Kuris 2014: 3).

The story of ACAs is not a particularly happy one, but, given that they are now recommended by UNCAC, it is unlikely that they will drop out of fashion any time soon.

---

noted on pages 98ff, corruption may help engender a degree of stability in settings where instability was previously rife. Rose-Ackerman and Palifka go further, arguing that in post-conflict settings the influx of relief and rebuilding funds can often weaken already wobbly institutions and offer ample opportunities for corruption. They note that emergency situations often "require a quick response by international donors", which can often be "a further excuse for ignoring financial integrity" (Rose-Ackerman & Palifka 2016: 320). A willingness to help can often be the catalyst for ingraining corruption into the way of doing things.

So, how have states with deeply ingrained corruption problems made progress? Two of the most recent superstars in this regard, Estonia and Uruguay, offer encouragement in that they show progress is possible, but discouragement in that it is difficult to emulate what they have done. Both states are small in size, relatively cohesive and elected very clean politicians, who built coalitions around which they could advance their reform agendas. Indeed, size appears to make a real difference. As Alina Mungiu-Pippidi notes, "it is far easier to build control of corruption if the body politic is limited, clearly bounded, and internally well organized in cohesive groups" (Mungiu-Pippidi 2013: 1282). Not many of the world's most corrupt countries fit that description.

Mungiu-Pippidi and Rothstein have developed persuasive arguments which illustrate that it makes little sense to look at what low-corruption countries are doing now; instead, we should be looking at what they did to become that way. It is not so much that western Europe was once a place where corruption was rife (although it certainly was); it is more that, somehow, many states have managed to pull themselves out of this swamp. The question is, how much can countries where corruption is currently systematic learn from these cases?

Mungiu-Pippidi addresses this by asking not so much how corruption was tackled, but how institutions that can resist the selfish urges of citizens were built (Mungiu-Pippidi 2013, 2015). The bad news is that the Danish route is not really open to many other states. Denmark went through what Mungiu-Pippidi describes as a period of enlightened despotism before constitutionalism developed. In other words, the Danish route involves a traditional monarchy taking the view that good governance is – broadly speaking – a worthwhile endeavour, even if notions of democracy were not (at the time) central to it. That leads, slowly but surely, to the rule of law and institutions with enough independence to uphold both that and the interests of the broader citizenry. Mungiu-Pippidi sees this route as only really being open to a small number of Middle-Eastern and Asian monarchies (Mungiu-Pippidi 2013: 1279).

Bo Rothstein looks at Denmark's neighbour, Sweden. He argues that the aim should not be to change corrupt norms: people do not need telling what corruption is and that is has a detrimental effect on society, they are already well aware of that. They engage in corrupt acts simply because, as noted in Chapter 5, they are stuck in a collective-action dilemma. The challenge is to "change agents' beliefs about what 'all' the other agents are likely to do". In terms of policy, Rothstein argues that there is not, and cannot be, one set of perfect institutions that are most important in catalyzing processes of change. Targeting an informal institution such as corruption while neglecting the way that formal ones work also makes little sense; all institutions in society need to move from "adhering to particularistic practices to universalism and impartiality". In the Swedish case, Rothstein argues that the whole idea of what it means to be a civil servant changed in the 1860s as the country underwent what he terms an indirect big bang. Sweden moved from a country where corruption was endemic to one where universalistic norms took root, and corruption became an anomaly rather than the norm (Rothstein 2011a: 246).

Both Mungiu-Pippidi and Rothstein make a point of saying that there is no right way of prompting this change. There is no clever set of tricks that can nudge people away from particularistic tendencies towards more universalist thinking. Rothstein lists 20 specific reforms that took place in Sweden in little more than a decade, all of which contributed to moving the country away from the corrupt place it used to be. The full set of institutions were targeted, and the aim was to shift Swedish culture away from its particularistic starting point to a more effective and efficient universalist position. Tackling corruption was one, but by no means the only, aim.

Some contemporary states have opted for a more direct big bang approach than that which Rothstein describes. In these scenarios, however, cultural change tends to be neglected. The focus is very much on sweeping away what is widely regarded as a corrupt political class. These "good governance coups" generally fail, and fail badly (Robinson & Sattar 2012). Robinson and Sattar flag both Pakistan and Thailand as places where this type of coup has taken place, although in many ways the most explicit example is Bangladesh in 2007. Corruption in Bangladesh "reaches far, wide and deep" and has long since become "institutionalized in the public service" (Zakiuddin n.d.; Quah 1999: 76). Indeed, it is a country where particularistic tendencies are very much the norm. Since formal independence in 1971, successive national governments have recognized these corruption problems and claimed to want to do something about them, more or less universally without success.

In 2007, a military-backed caretaker government, headed by former World Bank official Fakhruddin Ahmed, took over the reins of power. It claimed, with much tacit Western support, that it was suspending democracy to attack corruption head on. Only when the actors that used the system for their own interests were removed (and ideally imprisoned) would the country be returned to democratic rule. Ahmed's administration passed a wide array of new anti-corruption legislation; the Criminal Procedure Code Ordinance, for example, was amended in February 2007 – something that had been postponed more than 20 times since 1999 – to institutionalize the separation of powers between the judiciary and executive. A Bangladesh Financial Intelligence Unit (BFIU) was also set up in March 2007 with the aim of "combat[ting] financial crimes" and "retrieving assets and money laundered overseas", while the Electoral Commission's remit was rewritten in February 2007 to "creat[e] a more equal playing field free from corruption" (Iftekharuzzaman & Mahmud 2008: 184). For good measure, Bangladesh also acceded to UNCAC.[13]

Many Bangladeshis initially welcomed this dramatic turn of events. As 2007 drew to a close, however, more and more discontent emerged. Claims of the torture and ill-treatment of prisoners and suspects became more widespread, and the military-backed government soon ran into trouble when it tried to legally justify its behaviour. Indeed, the unwillingness of some judges to help was one of the most significant catalysts for the reinstatement of civilian rule in December 2008. The military's attempt to tackle corruption ultimately failed, not just on account of the resistance of those with plenty to lose, but also as it actively tried to undercut the institutions of Bangladeshi society. While clearly not perfect themselves, the courts in particular were not keen to be the poodles of the generals. The anti-corruption drive did little to change the fundamentals of Bangladesh's particularistic political culture.

CONCLUSION

Governments are frequently under significant pressure to move against corruption. The expectation is that they will be able to enact policies and "do something" that makes a visible difference. The bad news is that there are no short-term fixes available. In states where the institutional framework is robust and universalistic cultures are pervasive, governments still have options. Laws such as the FCPA and UKBA certainly have their critics, but they make it clear that bribery is – in a growing number of places – less likely to be tolerated than it once was. The development of an international transparency norm has led governments to begin implementing parts of an ambitious transparency agenda; there are teething problems, but the direction of travel is surely correct.

The effects will not, however, be immediately visible in the short term, and governments need to be aware that anti-corruption is most certainly a long-term project. Even in states such as Sweden and Denmark it took time to get anti-corruption right. In states where particularistic norms prevail, the challenge is more fundamental: how do you get around longstanding collective dilemmas and persuade people to have faith in others not

---

13. For more on the Bangladeshi case, see Hough (2013, Chapter 3).

indulging in corruption? Governance coups certainly are not the answer. Neither are calls to simply "become like the West". Potential reformers need to think carefully about how they bring other power-holders with them, and how they slowly but surely develop spaces where citizens can ask questions and defend their own interests. It took the UK the best part of 300 years to make clear progress in that regard; quite why we should expect other states to take one electoral cycle to achieve the same is not at all clear.

9.
People power: citizens, civil society and corruption

As the previous chapters have illustrated, in recent times we have seen policy-makers adopt a wide array of anti-corruption policies. While some have had limited success in achieving their aims, many have outright failed. Indeed, corruption remains every bit as challenging today as it was when it was first catapulted into the international policy arena in the 1990s. This final substantive chapter looks in detail at one of the responses to the apparent "failure" of the more traditional approaches to tackling corruption. It assesses the role that individual citizens can and do play in both highlighting corrupt practice and trying to do something about it. The rise of "citizen-centred approaches" has taken different forms in different places, and the scope and scale of their aims is broad. In plain English, some have much more potential to effect change than others. But, as a whole, they represent a new, interesting and potentially important set of anti-corruption ideas and opportunities.

THE ANTI-CORRUPTION INDUSTRY

Why have citizen-centred approaches recently taken on more prominent roles? One reason is the apparent failure of so-called top-down approaches to make much genuine headway. Indeed, the exponential rise in the salience of corruption as a public policy issue has gone hand-in-hand with criticism regarding what those active in the anti-corruption world have actually achieved. Such criticism is not (usually) directed at the authenticity of these activists' aims, but rather at some of the unintended outcomes of their work or, indeed, the way that many have become part of an "anti-corruption industry" (see, e.g., Michael 2004).

In terms of unintended outcomes, some have argued that noble anti-corruption aims simply lead to more bureaucracy, more red tape and very little ostensible and verifiable change in the extent or type of corruption that actually exists. Anechiarico and Jacobs, for example, use anti-corruption reform in New York to provocatively claim that such reforms not only often lead to "no change", but also contribute to "proliferating regulations and oversight mechanisms" that can "seriously undermine our ability to govern" (Anechiarico & Jacobs 1996). Anti-corruption sounds good, but in effect it means more hurdles for the good guys while the not-so-good guys simply find other ways of achieving their aims. It is, as Anechiarico and Jacobs state, "corruption control – no less than corruption itself – that has contributed to the contemporary crisis in public administration" (*ibid.*).

This is high-octane stuff. Indeed, it is not just in the US that these voices have been heard. As Chapter 7 illustrated, businesses have not always welcomed pieces of legislation such as the UKBA. UK companies might have to be cleaner when doing business outside British territory, but there are – so the critics argue – plenty of others who will step in to fill the breach. TI, a fierce defender of the UKBA, might claim that the UK is making a stand for global integrity, but some would argue that, in the cold light of day, British business is missing out to unscrupulous counterparts elsewhere.

While critics of a so-called anti-corruption industry agree that many anti-corruption reforms do not work, the focus of their criticism is nonetheless slightly broader. Instead of having their roots in the world of business, these criticisms tend to stem from the work of political anthropologists. The terminology can differ: Ed Brown and Jonathan Cloke, for example, talk of an "international crusade against corruption", while Steve Sampson prefers the notion of "anti-corruptionism". Luis de Sousa and his colleagues talk of a group of "integrity warriors" who zealously pursue their own aims. Whatever the terminology, they are directing their criticisms at the same basic sets of ideas.[1] For many critics of the "industry" of consultants, advisors and think-tanks that has arisen to help deal with the corruption challenge, anti-corruption has become a good way of generating the next contract or the next set of fees, and, subsequently, of securing their own existence. That is a bold claim to make. If it really is the case that the global fight against corruption is as much about bottom lines as it is about tackling corruption, then it is not at all clear where we should be

---

1. See, for example, Brown and Cloke (2004), Sampson (2008) and de Sousa *et al.* (2008).

going next. However, before buying into such dramatic claims, it is worth unpacking them just a little bit more.

Bryane Michael, arguably the most authoritative documenter of the development of the anti-corruption industry, claims that this industry has been developing since the early 1990s via a number of distinct, although frequently overlapping, waves (Michael & Bowser 2009). More specifically, in the immediate post-Cold War era there was a wave of anti-corruption activity. With the immediate threat of the Soviet Union dissipating, the US government (and its allies) became less happy to tolerate the behaviour of "corrupt" friends in the name of anti-communism. Globalization was developing rapidly, new democracies were being born and there was a(n ultimately mistaken) feeling that the "end of history" was nigh. Corruption rose up the political pecking order, even though it was still generally understood as a developing-world problem. The first challenge was subsequently to raise awareness about what corruption was, where it was flourishing and why tackling it made sense. Organizations such as TI were formed, and a wide range of politicians and other influential figures in public life began discussing the challenges that corruption posed. It was not so much about suggesting solutions as simply getting the problem recognized in the first place. The key institutional backers remained US based, with the World Bank and the United States Agency for International Development (USAID) being the most notable supporters of this agenda change.

This awareness raising carried on into the first decade of the twenty-first century, but as the 1990s came to an end, they were accompanied by a move towards action. This action varied in nature and type, but there were certainly distinct patterns. USAID and the World Bank were still the main institutional supporters, and it was not long before they were offering resources to help interested parties capacity-build and think about adopting apparent best practice in the fight against corruption. These organizations were also not scared to put their money where their respective mouths were: conservative estimates value the size of the industry as being around $100 million in 2003 and $5 billion in 2009 (Michael 2004; Michael & Bowser 2009).

Whether the "best practice" propagated by those involved in this process was anything of the kind remained a moot point, and more critical thinkers soon rose to question it. The consensus about the role of the state and the power of the market (see pages 78–9) prevailed. The sets of policy prescriptions tended to be remarkably similar, no matter what the specific problems were. Michael (2004) subsequently argues that the second wave can in fact be characterized by an increased willingness to help governments (as well as other organizations) expand their anti-corruption capabilities. A secondary market of anti-corruption service providers soon developed to help them do so. These individuals were often civil servants from Western countries, who moved from being "expert advisors" on good practice to being "contract managers and intermediaries for an army of 'expert' consultants" (Michael & Bowser 2009: 3). They were also sometimes, as the authors sniffily describe them, "Beltway Bandits", who dished out advice even though there was little evidence that their advice helped change very much at all.

Later, a third, slightly different, phase developed, centering largely on pragmatic, bilateral relationships. Michael (2004) argues that this era is characterized by the development of the EU into a key player in the anti-corruption industry, "with work done by actual boot-wearing law enforcement officials instead of eye-glass wearing graduate students and social science professors". Michael points to the launch of a plethora of EU special missions with specific anti-corruption mandates, alongside US policy moving "away from policy-by-proxy funding mechanisms (using USAID, OECD and World Bank 'partnership') in favour of pragmatic, targeted programmes" through agencies such as the US Department of Justice, Homeland Security and even the FBI (*ibid.*: 4). Furthermore, Michael argues that this third wave is characterized by a shift from "(often large-scale) procurements awarded to large consulting companies" towards direct cooperation between specific agencies. He claims that "the superstar consultants of the late 1990s" are now much fewer and farther between, and we now "see many Swedish and British police and customs officers roaming around eastern European capitals flogging their anti-corruption ware" (*ibid.*: 5–6).

Proponents of the anti-corruption industry thesis argue that the global fight against corruption is not only one in which a lot of money is spent, but also one that employs a considerable number of people to come up with implementation strategies, think pieces, policy papers and review documents with an aim to help specific actors reduce corruption levels. The cynics may argue that it is, at times, "difficult to tell whether activists … are motivated by conviction, material benefits or both"; but this would seem – as cynicism often does – to miss the point (Moroff & Schmidt-Pfister 2010: 92). Many of the actors involved (including self-declared grass-roots-orientated NGOs) are perfectly at home at the top tables of high politics. That, however, is not the problem. The real issue is the lack of impact, and the painful reality is that, for all the funding, all the planning and all the organizing, there is precious little evidence that moves to tackle corruption have systematically helped to mitigate the effect (let alone weed out the root causes) of corruption on everyday life. As Steve Sampson has astutely observed, "despite hundreds of millions of dollars, and hundreds of programmes, projects, and campaigns, conducted by an army of anti-corruption specialists, experts, and trainers, we have very little evidence of any decline in corrupt behaviour" (Sampson 2008; see also Mungiu-Pippidi 2006). Daniel Kaufmann has gone even further, claiming that there is a "silent crisis", as the anti-corruption movement appears unable to "make the transition from the awareness-raising stage" to what he describes as the "concrete action-orientated stage" (Kaufmann 2009: 27). The anti-corruption movement has subsequently found itself forced to reassess much of what it treated, throughout the 1990s, as self-evident common sense, questioning its own assumptions, ideological underpinnings and methods and strategies. Put another way, where breakthroughs have happened and where progress in specific country settings has been made, it appears more often than not that coincidence and place-specific influences have been every bit as important as anti-corruption strategies mandated by external bodies.

BRINGING THE CITIZENS BACK IN

No matter whether one buys into the narrative outlined by critics of the anti-corruption industry or not, it is clear that there is plenty of scope for alternative approaches. If the definition of madness is doing the same thing over and over again and expecting different outcomes, then many (inherently sane) people in the world of anti-corruption have realized that a different approach (or set of approaches) is needed. One of those strategies involves thinking less about top-down approaches that centre on governments and more about bottom-up approaches that empower civil society. After all, those who feel the direct effects of corruption the most have been and still are people on the ground. They are the ones who have to deal with petty bribery or the myriad corruption challenges that billions of citizens around the world face every day.

This has led to the rise of an increasingly well-developed set of civil society organizations that put corruption at the centre of their work. The first and most well-known of these is TI, but others, such as Global

Witness and Integrity Action, have all begun to think about new and innovative ways that they could use to fight corruption. These organizations are now professional actors that have become skilled at influencing both national governments and international organizations, but they also pride themselves on having their ears close to the ground. That can mean they take quite different forms in different places; TI in the UK, for example, existed for many years with little more than a dozen staff, focusing largely on exposing – and coming up with ideas to tackle – high-level corruption in the UK's finance and trade sectors. TI in Bangladesh, meanwhile, has upwards of 250 employees and focuses much more on the challenges of gaining access to basic services, which many Bangladeshis struggle with on account of corruption.

These organizations can and do disagree on both the mechanics of policy and political strategy, and the sector as a whole has its critics. Nevertheless, they have done an impressive job of both raising awareness and coming up with ideas and initiatives. A significant number of these initiatives involve actively empowering citizens to engage with anti-corruption activity.

POWER TO THE PEOPLE

For those sceptics who are unsure whether citizens can make a difference, the case of Mohamed Bouazizi should dispel any lingering doubts. Before the middle of December 2010, Bouazizi (or "Basboosa" as he was known locally) was an unremarkable street vendor in Sidi Bouzid, a city in Tunisia. However, on 17 December 2010, he shot to local, then national and, very soon after, international prominence after setting himself alight. He did this to protest against what he regarded as the corruption that was endemic in the Tunisian system. His protest centred on the regular bribes he needed to pay to be allowed to set up his stall as well as the ritual humiliation that he and others like him regularly suffered at the hands of local government officials. On this occasion, officials had confiscated the fruit that he sold, claiming that he had not paid the taxes demanded of him as a vendor. Bouazizi's interpretation of the situation would no doubt have been different; the bribes that he needed to pay and the arbitrariness of the local regime were deeply unfair. Ultimately, it was that unfairness that drove him to despair, and to make his dramatic protest, paying with his life. He died in hospital on 4 January 2011, at the age of 26.[2]

---

2. For more on this case, see Beaumont (2011).

Bouazizi's act of protest was the catalyst for the first of the revolutions that became known as the Arab Spring. Zine El Abidine Ben Ali, after 23 years in power in Tunisia, resigned in the face of widespread protests just ten days after Bouazizi died. He stepped down largely because of the actions that Bouazizi's behaviour unleashed. Yet, Bouazizi is perhaps an unlikely revolutionary role model. He was not known to be a particularly political man, and he had no previous political attachments. His act of self-immolation was not inspired by any particular faith or set of beliefs, but simply by his ongoing and ever-increasing powerlessness at the hands of the authorities. It is likely that it was precisely these characteristics that made others across the region recognize something of themselves in him. By all accounts, Bouazizi was hard working, family focused and optimistic. He wanted to do well for himself and his family, but he could not: the corrupt system would not let him.

Bouazizi's death is an extreme example of how citizens can make a difference. Thankfully, not everyone needs to be as desperate as he was to make their point. Indeed, there is plenty of diversity in the way that citizens have made anti-corruption contributions. This diversity can nonetheless be summarized by putting the various movements and initiatives into four broad categories (see Table 9.1).

AWARENESS RAISING

First, no matter what the setting, awareness raising has a role to play. In countries with systemic corruption challenges, the point is not to raise awareness that corruption exists: that is widely taken as a given. The awareness angle comes from finding new and innovative ways of either getting the public to think about corruption or making people more conscious of their rights. That may sound like a straightforward aim, but in many polities citizens simply are not aware that the extra payments they are making for their healthcare are not mandated, or that the extra costs added to the

Table 9.1 Citizen involvement and anti-corruption.

	High-corruption countries	Low-corruption countries
Awareness raising	Integrity Idol	Wikileaks
Empowerment	IPAB.com	Armchair Auditors

bill for a new permit are illegitimate. It may also be that corruption seems so pervasive that it is simply not worth questioning.

The forms that this awareness raising takes can subsequently vary widely. Jeunesses Musicales International (JMI), an international network of NGOs that uses music to help young people come together, for example, teamed up with TI to launch a singing competition for young bands that centred on the theme of anti-corruption.[3] The bands who took part in "FAIR PLAY: Anti-Corruption Youth Voices" were, so JMI and TI claimed, "raising awareness within their communities whil[e] contributing to the global call for accountability".[4] Text message campaigns are now reasonably commonplace, too. For example, in 2008, around 730,000 users in two areas of the Chinese city of Chongqing received SMSs offering them rewards if they provided tip-offs to the authorities about corrupt practice. These rewards ranged from ¥3,000 ($450) to ¥500,000 ($75,000). As a local official in Chongqing noted at the time, "using SMS is a more direct way to transmit information, and it has a broader audience".[5]

In deeply corrupt settings, the emphasis can also be turned on its head. In Nepal, for example, Accountability Lab, an NGO that tries to create new and innovate ways of encouraging more accountability across the public sector, has turned anti-corruption into entertainment.[6] Bribery is depressingly commonplace in Nepal, and civil servants are generally not trusted to act in the public interest; so, Accountability Lab helped to introduce a competition to find Nepal's most inspirational civil servant. That "inspiration" could come in any form, as long as notions of integrity were at its core. The winner was then given the title of Nepal's *Integrity Idol*.

The initiative culminated in a television show: a sort of *The X Factor* meets anti-corruption. Contestants were nominated – and over 300 were put forward in 2014 – on the basis of the integrity-enhancing work that they did in their local communities (Pattisson 2014). Five were then selected to go through to the final, where their work was highlighted on prime-time television. The Nepalese public voted for whomever they thought

---

3. See http://anticorruptionmusic.org/ and http://jmi.net/. Both viewed on 16 October 2016.

4. See Jeunesses Musicales International and Transparency International (2016), "Relaunch of fairplay anti-corruption youth voices". Available at http://bit.ly/2lSJJNU, viewed on 16 October 2016.

5. *People's Daily Online* (2008), "Govt uses SMS to battle corruption", 15 July. See http://bit.ly/2mARSqo, viewed on 16 October 2016.

6. For more on Accountability Lab, see www.accountabilitylab.org/, viewed on 10 October 2016.

Leela Mani Paudyal, chief secretary of the Government of Nepal, honouring the district education officer, Gyan Mani Nepal, who became the first winner of Nepal's *Integrity Idol* in 2014 (reproduced with kind permission of Accountability Lab, 2016).

should be crowned the winner. The idea behind *Integrity Idol* was not so much to "'name and shame' the lawbreakers, but to 'name and fame' those officials who were doing the right thing" (Glencorse & Parajuli 2015). As many as three million people are believed to have watched the first series of *Integrity Idol*, and over 10,000 texted their votes in or liked particular nominees on Facebook and YouTube. During the second series, that number leapt to more than 50,000.[7] Furthermore, according to Accountability Lab, all of this cost as little as $4,000 to put together (*ibid.* 2015).

The work that Nepalese civil servants do is often small scale, but this television show is an attempt to highlight that good guys exist and can flourish. It is those good guys (see Box 9.1) that the anti-corruption movement in Nepal wants to see the Nepalese people emulate. The idea has been so successful that it has also spread to other countries, with Liberia, Pakistan, Afghanistan, Mali and Indonesia also launching similar competitions.

No one is claiming that *Integrity Idol* will enable Nepal to rid itself of corruption. Indeed, even the show's makers claim that it is not really about the specific anti-corruption work that is being done; it is more about the

---

7. *The Himalayan* (2016), "Kandel wins *Integrity Idol* award", 11 January. Available at http://bit.ly/2lPS6LG, viewed on 10 October 2016.

Box 9.1. Pradip Raj Kandel: Nepal's *Integrity Idol*

Nepal's 2015 winner of *Integrity Idol* was Pradip Raj Kandel. Kandel came out on top because of his willingness to both make the general public aware of their rights and help them get involved in shaping their communities. His aim was to challenge the corrupt networks and relationships that shaped public life in the districts where he worked. In Kandel's mind, too many people had no idea what their rights were, and he felt that only through public hearings and more transparency could they become aware of all the corruption that existed around them.*

Kandel's work was often decidedly down to earth in nature. When he worked in Solukhumbu District (the district where Mount Everest is located), Kandel patiently set up processes that enabled management to get hold of citizens' documents more efficiently. While in Panchthar District (in eastern Nepal), he put a stress on education as being the core of citizen empowerment. He therefore led a drive to improve literacy rates.

Pradip Raj Kandel is not your archetypal anti-corruption campaigner. He stressed basic ideas that would help citizens develop skills so that they could hold power-holders to account. His vision was long-term, and it was more than enough to convince the Nepalese to vote him their 2015 *Integrity Idol* winner.

---

* For more on Pradip Raj Kandel's background, see http://bit.ly/2i1EA6T, viewed on 10 October 2016.

---

fact that such work is being done at all. *Integrity Idol*, as its website claims, simply "generates debate around the idea of integrity".[8] The show is meant to plant the seed of anti-corruption in the minds of those watching. It is also meant to prompt discussion about how to make those in the Nepalese public service behave more like *Integrity Idol* winners and less like the rent-seekers that so many, almost inevitably, seem to become.

WHISTLE BLOWING

Even in societies where corruption is not perceived as systemic, awareness raising still plays a role in helping citizens and policy-makers alike become aware of corrupt practices. This is particularly true when the type

---

8. See www.integrityidol.org/, viewed on 10 October 2016.

The winner of Nepal's 2015 *Integrity Idol* being presented with his award at the ceremony (reproduced with kind permission of Accountability Lab, 2016).

of corruption is not the petty bribery so often obvious in developing countries but white-collar crimes that happen behind closed doors. One of the most prominent ways that this happens in the developed world is through the process of whistle blowing.

Whistle blowing, however, is a classic example of something that sounds good in theory but is usually problematic in practice. Whistle-blowers are (former) employees or (former) members of an organization who report misconduct to those in positions that allow them to take corrective action. The majority of states now have what look like strong, clear whistle-blowing laws, and many organizations are very open in stating that thoughtful, critical employees who raise awareness of misconduct are most welcome. These laws and procedures appear to offer employees who see corruption taking place an array of legal protections and safeguards to ensure that they do not suffer on account of raising a dissenting voice. In practice, many whistle-blowers find that the moment they express scepticism about the behaviour of those in power, everything changes: normally for the worse.

In theory, "blowing the whistle" – language borrowed from early twentieth-century Britain, where policemen blew whistles to attract attention when they saw something untoward – should be very beneficial for organizations. An employee who sees something wrong and wants to put it right should be an asset to their organization; whistle blowing should, in other words, be a way for organizations to ensure that their processes, procedures and practical behaviour meet appropriate moral, ethical and legal norms.

In terms of the public sector, whistle-blowers are entitled to ask questions when they see behaviour that poses a direct threat to the public interest. This may include corruption, but it also covers activities such as health and safety practices. It can also include deliberate acts just as much as

The 2015 finalists of Liberia's *Integrity Idol* (reproduced with kind permission of Accountability Lab, 2016).

negligence. Although whistle-blower legislation around the world aims to address the same sets of issues, in practice there is quite a range of laws in place. In the US, for example, whistle-blowing procedures vary depending on the subject matter of the misconduct as well as the state in which it is taking place. Tellingly, you do not get any protection if you are an employee of a state government, or, indeed, if the subject is defined as being about national security.[9] In some states, whistle blowing is encouraged by the prospect of the whistle-blower receiving a portion of any loot returned

---

9. Supreme Court of the United States (2005), "Garcetti *et al.* v. Ceballos", Washington, DC: Certiorari to the United States Court of Appeals for the Ninth Circuit, No. 04-473.

on account of the whistle-blower's actions. In Nigeria, for example, you receive up to 5 per cent, while in the US the figure can range from 15 to 30 per cent (Tukur 2016; Curry 2010: 205).

Across the Atlantic in Europe, the European Convention on Human Rights (ECHR) has a detailed explanation of how it believes whistle-blowing rules and regulations should be developed (Frings *et al.* 2012). In the UK, meanwhile, the Public Interest Disclosure Act (PIDA) of 1998 tries to strike a balance between protecting the whistle-blower and protecting the organization from malicious behaviour. Concerns must first be raised internally by the potential whistle-blower, and only if they are not addressed can they be revealed to a relevant external regulator. If there is still no action, then the whistle-blower is entitled by law to go public (under the guise of anonymity). As Lord Nolan, the inaugural chair of the UK's Committee on Standards in Public Life (CSPL), has observed, PIDA "skilfully achiev[es] the essential but delicate balance between the public interest and the interest of the employers".[10]

That may well have been the case in 2002 (when Lord Nolan made that observation), but by the middle of the next decade there were some who felt that PIDA had not kept pace with the times. For example, a 2016 analysis of whistle blowing in the UK argued that in many important aspects PIDA was out of date. Among other things, the "Blueprint for Free Speech" report noted that more short-term help should be provided to whistle-blowers by courts before cases came to a full trial, in order to prevent retaliation against them. The report also made a case for "stigma compensation" for the damage done to a whistle-blower's professional reputation (see Farrington 2016). The report bluntly concluded that PIDA "is inadequate" and, furthermore, "does not meet most international standards" (Blueprint for Free Speech 2016).

Some of the inadequacies of PIDA were shown up in cases that involved a number of National Health Service (NHS) whistle-blowers (Sawer & Donnelly 2015). Maha Yassaie, a chief pharmacist, became a whistle-blower due to concerns she had about a colleague who was taking money from a drug company to prescribe that company's product. Yassaie's employer, the Berkshire West Primary Care Trust, dismissed her. She appealed against what she argued was unfair dismissal. She won,

---

10. Quoted in Select Committee on Home Affairs (2002), "Memorandum submitted by Public Concern at Work", Appendix 8. Available at http://bit.ly/2mdktV2, viewed on 7 December 2016.

ultimately receiving £375,000 in compensation from the UK's Department of Health, as "the investigation and disciplinary processes ... were, in some respects, flawed" (Turner 2016). Yet, try as she might over the next four years, Yassaie could not get another job. The reason for this only became clear when she obtained her staff records from the primary care trust. The records (wrongly) stated that she had been dismissed from her job, with no qualification as to the nature of her story. With that on her record, it is no surprise that finding another position was proving difficult.

Maha Yassaie's experience is by no means a one-off. Employers and those in power have lots of reasons to resent the courageous actions of whistle-blowers in exposing their misdemeanours. And whistle-blowers have not just lost their jobs; at times they have been forced to flee their homes, and sometimes they do not even manage that. The number of whistle-blowers who do not live to tell the tale is depressingly large.

FROM AWARENESS RAISING TO ACTION

The line between awareness raising and action is often a fuzzy one. The very act of highlighting corruption can by definition help in doing something about it. However, there is also plenty of room for broader citizen empowerment. In the developing world in particular, citizens are increasingly being given the opportunity to do something about the corruption that they witness on a day-to-day basis. Two such ways that this can happen are via the use of mobile phone technology and via online corruption reporting tools.

In terms of mobile phone technology, what has come to be known as the Citizen Feedback Model (CFM) in Pakistan is a good example.[11] This approach stems from the efforts of Zubair Bhatti, the former district coordination officer (DCO) of Jhang District, a part of Lahore. He was keen to find ways of dealing with the widespread bribery that he knew was plaguing transactions between local civil servants and the public. Bhatti was well aware that neither his office nor those of other DCOs across Pakistan had the resources to investigate all of the allegations of bribery that came their way. He also knew that the current system of citizen reporting was both long winded and bureaucratic as well as open to malicious accusations that often had more to do with disgruntled revenge attacks than genuine

---

11. See http://www.punjabmodel.gov.pk/, viewed on 16 October 2016.

incidences of corrupt practice. Bhatti decided that he needed help, and that the good citizens of Jhang District were best placed to provide it (Masud 2015a).

He resolved to find a way for citizens to report their experiences. The ideal way to do this, Bhatti reasoned, was by encouraging them to talk to him. He did this by persuading officers in one particular office (which registered property) to note down the mobile phone numbers of citizens who they served. Bhatti himself then rang some of the numbers to find out about citizens' experiences. He was not impressed with what he heard; many had never been told the price of the services they were making use of, and there was plenty of evidence of collusion between officials to charge excess fees, which were clearly ending up in their own pockets.[12] By calling citizens directly, Bhatti wanted to show that he cared and that he wanted to learn from their experiences. Anti-corruption suddenly had something of a personal touch, and that personal touch made it seem much more credible than many of the failed initiatives that had gone before.

Bhatti's efforts caught the eye of Shahbaz Sharif, the chief minister of Punjab (the province where Lahore is situated). He wanted Bhatti's ideas to be scaled up and institutionalized across all 36 districts in the province. The process of individually calling people could not work on a large scale, so in 2010 Sharif set up the Punjab Information Technology Board. This was designed to both process the numbers of people who were interacting with public officials and send them text messages. The development of the project was not always plain sailing, but a $100,000 grant from the World Bank's innovation fund for technical assistance ultimately helped to iron out many of the logistical creases.

Given that mobile phones are as ubiquitous in Pakistan as they are everywhere else, this proved to be an ideal way of getting a feel for where bribery appeared to be most endemic as well as which individuals seemed to be at the centre of these transactions. The crucial parts of the CFM are the guaranteed anonymity it provides to those reporting bribery and the checks that are put in place to ensure the model does not turn into a glorified witch-hunt. It also looks broadly politically neutral, something that is important in states where clientelistic structures and patronage have deep roots. No one is sacked on account of reports that come via the CFM. However, offices and individuals are put under closer scrutiny to see if the reports match reality. If they do, and if public officials continue to demand

---

12. For a full analysis of the development of the CFM, see Masud (2015b).

bribes, then they leave themselves wide open to prosecution. By 2015, over eight million citizens had been contacted via SMS, and over a million had provided feedback. Over 3,000 "corrective actions" have also been taken (Indrawati 2015). The CFM is viewed as so useful that it has been replicated in other places such as Albania and Romania.

Pakistan's neighbour, India, has also developed models that use citizen feedback to improve the delivery of public services. The most well known of these does not use text messages to generate feedback. Instead, it actively encourages citizens to fill in a report online. Again, the system is anonymized, and, again, there is a degree of technological sophistication involved. But it is the simplicity of the reporting mechanism that has made the website – www.ipaidabribe.com (IPAB) – so attractive.

IPAB started out in 2010, in the southern city of Bangalore, when Janaagraha (literally "People Power"), a non-profit organization, began to develop the idea of a portal where citizens could record their experiences of bribery. Here, citizens report whether they have been asked to pay a bribe, where the official who made the request worked, how much he or she wanted and whether they ultimately ended up paying. It did not take long for IPAB to become something of an international sensation, and within a matter of months the website was getting coverage in news outlets such as *The New York Times*, *The Economist* and the BBC (Messick 2015).

But IPAB (like other similar sites) was not a problem-free enterprise. After an initial period of enthusiasm, the number of reports dipped. Indeed, by 2012 there were real worries about whether the site had a future. While there was evidence that public officials were becoming increasingly aware that soliciting bribes might leave them more open to criticism than was once the case, the real challenge was persuading governments to make substantive changes to governance structures on the basis of the feedback that came in. Indeed, and as Rick Messick notes in an interesting blog post on IPAB, there are only two clear cases of such change happening on account of IPAB's work. The Department of Stamps and Registration in Bangalore changed the way that property was registered, while the Transport Department in the same city altered the way that driving licences were obtained (see Box 9.2; Messick (2015)). Messick further argues that the IPAB experience highlights that "it takes an enormous amount of publicity to generate the pressure needed to force authorities to act". Indeed, even in IPAB's "home" of Bangalore – a tech-savvy city with a vibrant media, fiercely contested elections and a middle class that has plenty of reasons to want corruption faced down – genuine anti-corruption progress has been painfully slow. As Messick again notes, "if it takes this much to produce reform in Bangalore, the chances that similar efforts will produce results in less hospitable settings are surely slight" (*ibid.*).

Box 9.2. IPAB, corruption and driving licences

The Indian website www.ipaidabribe.com prides itself on using crowdsourcing techniques to come up with new anti-corruption ideas. One such idea centred around the problem of getting a driving licence in the southern city of Bangalore.

State transport commissioner Bhaskar Rao made the decision to embrace IPAB's data, with the aim of "cleans[ing] my department".* Indeed, Rao's technology team helped pinpoint areas where there seemed to be particular problems. Traffic police was one problem area, as was the acquisition of a driving licence. Rao realized that institutionalized relationships between the driving-test schools and examiners often resulted in extra "fees" being charged over and above the prescribed rate. This money was then pocketed by the officials involved.

Rao tackled this issue by working with a local IT company to come up with a completely automated test centre. No need for driving-test examiners; everyone would automatically know at the end of the test how they had done. How? Drivers had to negotiate a particular route in the test centre, and their progress was tracked by a series of sensors. If they crossed too many sensors (i.e., made too many mistakes), then they failed. They would also know exactly where those mistakes were made, as the whole test had an electronic footprint.

Options for bribery in the automated system were non-existent, and decisions on whether driving tests had been passed or not were now based on evidence rather than ability to pay. As Rao put it, "the whims and fancies" of testers now no longer played a role, and India slowly began to get a few better-qualified drivers on its roads.**

---

* Quoted in Campion (2011), "Bribery in India: a website for whistleblowers", *BBC News*, 6 June. Available at http://www.bbc.com/news/world-south-asia-13616123, viewed on 16 October 2016.

** Stom (2012), "Websites shine light on petty bribery worldwide", *The New York Times*, 6 March.

Like the CFM, IPAB has nonetheless caught the admiring eye of administrations elsewhere, and websites based on the IPAB model have sprung up in over a dozen countries. Some manifestations, such as those in China, have not been particularly successful, but others continue to flag bribery as and when it is reported. The Chinese experience is, in many ways, indicative of why getting the institutional infrastructure right matters so much if citizen-centred approaches are to have a chance of succeeding. The Chinese government shut down all IPAB sites within a matter of months (and often weeks) in 2011, as they developed into tools via which people could vent their frustrations. The Chinese sites just were not professional enough to deal with the challenges they faced, and without the explicit support of the Chinese regime they were seen as too lawless and too disruptive. So, the Chinese government forced them all offline.[13]

Indeed, one of the Chinese government's responses was to create its own crowdsourcing website (in 2013) and latterly a specific crowdsourcing app (in 2015) to facilitate corruption reporting (Florcruz 2013). With the app in particular, China's anti-corruption agency, the Central Commission for Discipline Inspection (CCDI), wants "to encourage members of the public to pass on evidence of officials' misconduct" (Yi & Yan 2015). Apps aimed at helping citizens report corruption allegations in provinces such as Guangxi, Shandong, Guangdong and Henan, as well as cities such as Chongqing, Xi'an, Nanjing and Ningbo, have also popped up. If citizens are quick enough with their phones, they can even send in pictures and short videos of the alleged corrupt acts taking place.

If one looks a little deeper at how the Chinese authorities want the app to be used, and the context within which that use is to be set, then more than a little scepticism is in order. First, the Communist Party keeps a tight control over how alleged corrupt acts are reported. Any attempts to report corruption through other channels or, indeed, to highlight possible indiscretions on social media are often clamped down on. As Cindy Guan notes, it is discussions about corruption held via the ubiquitous WeChat messaging service (a cross between Twitter and Facebook) that are most extensively censored (Guan 2015). This may even be the case when the corruption reported leads to criminal convictions; corrupt officials may well be punished, but if whistle-blowers report them outside of official channels, then the whistle-blowers themselves can often find themselves in serious trouble.[14]

Cindy Guan also highlights two further problems with the Chinese approach. On the one hand, it is not clear what happens to all of this data.

---

13. For an excellent comparison of the Indian and Chinese experiences, see Ang (2014).
14. For an example of this, see Chiu (2013).

We know little about how the government investigates allegations, and we know even less about what type of investigations it prioritizes. The CCDI does publish lists of miscreants, but no one besides those in positions of power in China knows much about who they are or the contexts of their stories. On the other hand, and in contrast to IPAB and CFM, the CCDI app actively encourages third-party reporting. So, reports come not just from citizens who have experienced corruption, but also from those who (think they) have witnessed it. The problem with this is that the door is being opened to vagueness and inaccuracy, and the chances of events and processes being misconstrued will increase. The number of reports submitted is also likely to rise significantly (Guan 2015).

In terms of the impact of these citizen-centred approaches, there will always be bumps in the road. Many will fail, but there will be some clever, well-thought out strategies that will have an effect. The context within which they are set is important, and they are most likely to work when they are well organized, have the tacit (or open) support of those in power and form part of a coherent move to tackle corruption more broadly.

CITIZEN-EMPOWERMENT IN LOW-CORRUPTION COUNTRIES

Getting citizens involved in anti-corruption in countries that theoretically have fewer corruption problems is a slightly different task. That is because the nature of the corruption challenge is different. More specifically, the need to indulge in bribery to obtain day-to-day public services is not nearly as widespread, and corruption tends to be something that is perceived as happening in faraway places, behind closed doors. To be clear, there is certainly a perception that corruption exists. TI's 2013 GCB, for example, showed that 27 per cent of Danes, 44 per cent of Finns and (as was noted on page 62) a particularly emphatic 65 per cent of New Zealanders thought that the level of corruption in their respective countries had increased over the last two years.[15] These high numbers emanate from the three states that came first, second and third in TI's CPI of the same year.[16] Such beliefs are frequently held on the basis of perception rather than experience.

---

15. Transparency International (2013b), "Global Corruption Barometer". Available at www. transparency.org/gcb2013/, viewed on 16 October 2016.
16. Transparency International (2013a), "Corruption Perceptions Index". Available at www. transparency.org/cpi2013/results, viewed on 15 October 2016.

It is this perception that has prompted some nominally low-corruption states to try to channel citizens' disgruntlement with perceived corruption into the anti-corruption process. One country that has tried to do this is the UK. Despite the fact that Britain has long been perceived as a country where corruption is largely in check, British citizens remain convinced that corruption is a significant problem. According to the 2013 GCB, 86 per cent of British people thought that "corruption is a problem" that needs to be addressed, while 65 per cent of people thought that over the last two years the level of corruption in the UK had increased.[17] Given that the state in the UK, like states everywhere, is overburdened with claims on its time and resources, various UK politicians have sought to use the UK's commitment to transparent governance (see Chapter 8) to enable citizens to pinpoint where precisely this corruption is taking place. In the words of the then communities and local government secretary, and latterly anti-corruption champion, Eric Pickles, the UK needed to empower "an army of armchair auditors" to scrutinize the work of government.[18] For Pickles's department at least, this move would signal the beginning of a new era of government transparency and accountability, with any outgoings of £500 or more being publicly revealed online. The wider world was subsequently going to have access to the nuts and bolts of how in excess of £300 million (the departmental budget in 2010) was being spent.

Pickles was talking about his own department, but this was clearly only meant to be the start of things. David Cameron's Conservative/Liberal Democratic government embraced this new world of openness and accountability, opening up information on a whole range of topics, from crime statistics to spending commitments, contract awarding to hospital waiting lists. This new openness would not only help to clamp down on waste, but also drive both efficiency and responsiveness.[19] Citizens would be able to see where money was spent, and they would be able to pass judgement on whether they felt it was being spent appropriately. Indeed, Cameron used the same terminology as Pickles in explaining what was going to happen: a "whole army of effective armchair auditors" was going to help clean up British government.[20]

---

17. Transparency International (2013c), "Global Corruption Barometer (United Kingdom)". Available at http://bit.ly/1eRDkWu, viewed on 16 October 2016.

18. UK Government (2010), "Eric Pickles 'shows us the money'", 12 August. Available at http://bit.ly/2lqLj7M, viewed on 16 October 2016.

19. Cameron (2010), "PM's podcast on transparency". Available at http://bit.ly/2mtjYHa, viewed on 16 October 2016.

20. Quoted in Worthy (2013), "Where are the armchair auditors?", *Open Data Institute*, 1 June. Available at http://bit.ly/2mF6pRH, viewed on 16 October 2016.

Furthermore, the government promised to develop a system of performance management based around a range of performance indicators. The 200 plus indicators would be an ideal tool for the public to hold those with entrusted power to account. This was, or so it seemed, bordering on the revolutionary. Engaged citizens would be able to unpack and dissect the minutiae of government performance, and the age of faceless bureaucrats pulling the strings from behind a cloak of anonymity would be behind us.

Impressive though the brave new world sounded, the outcomes have been disappointing. The army has not so much organized a mutiny as never really enlisted in the first place. There are one or two notable, and quite specific, exceptions (see Box 9.3), but they are few and far between. This, however, is not necessarily the fault of the prospective armchair auditors. There are a number of good reasons why in practice there are far too many hurdles in the way for them to really do any decent auditing work.

The UK's Institute for Government (IfG) explains that there are (at least) three reasons why initiatives like this run into problems. The IfG boils it down to (i) poor-quality data, (ii) poor communication (understood as inadequate explanations of what the data means) and (iii) very little evidence that there was any great public willingness to use the system in the first place (Freeguard *et al.* 2015). While (iii) is something that should probably not be too much of a surprise – minus the pay of a fully trained auditor, it cannot be that big of a shock that people are not queuing up to be amateur forensic accountants – the existence of (i) and (ii) is disappointing.

The IfG, to be fair, was quick to recognize that some government departments (and service providers more broadly) were doing their best to be open with both data and explanations of it; however, some appeared to take their obligations anything but seriously. Data were often simply not available, and when they were available, they were in a format that was unsearchable or very hard to actually use in any straightforward sense. A pile of pdf documents the size (if printed out) of a hefty doorstop might well fulfil transparency obligations, but it is hard to imagine that anyone but the unhealthily obsessed could do anything with it.

Over the course of the last few months, a number of websites and apps have been developed to help make data sifting easier and, more specifically, to enable the interested external observer to uncover potential malpractice. In the area of public procurement data, for example, the website www.spendnetwork.com is a useful starting point, while openspending. org claims to "track and analyse public financial information globally".[21]

---

21. See https://openspending.org/, viewed on 16 October 2016.

The development of tools such as these notwithstanding, the data still remain patchy and largely impenetrable. The numbers mean little to those who do not understand the context, and there is effectively nothing out there explaining why decisions were made and specific contracts awarded. However, unless an armchair auditor possesses the talents of Sherlock Holmes, the patience of a saint and, perhaps most importantly, some sort of tip-off or piece of inside information to help them head in the right direction, then they are very likely to quickly lose enthusiasm.

Box 9.3. Mrs Angry: the Barnet Blogger who uncovered a £1.3 million audit scandal

Theresa Musgrove is just the type of armchair auditor that governments claim to love. In practice, however, one suspects that bloggers with her tenacity are just the type of people that they have probably come to fear.

In 2011, and under the pseudonym of "Mrs Angry", Musgrove worked alongside a group of other committed citizens to keep an eye on the outgoings of Barnet council in North West London. Their work attracted public attention when they looked into a contract that was awarded to MetPro Rapid Response, a security firm that had been employed by the council to (among other things) prevent potentially critical voices from entering a public meeting.

Musgrove and the Barnet Bloggers discovered that MetPro Rapid Response had been hired "without any tendering procedure, had no contract, no supervision, no system of regulated payment, and was unlicensed". Furthermore, MetPro Rapid Response's staff frequently worked with children, yet no vetting had been done to check that those employees were suitable for the role (Butler 2011).

The poking and prodding of the Barnet Bloggers led Barnet council not just to break ties with MetPro Rapid Response, but also to produce a report on how they came to get a contract in the first place. The report pulled no punches, revealing systematic neglect of normal procedure.*

Musgrove's approach reveals what armchair auditors can achieve. Indeed, she and others in Barnet have had other successes. If governments are genuine about embracing openness and transparency, they are going to have to get used to seeing more of people like Mrs Angry in future.

---

* For more on the report, see Broken Barnet Blog (2011), "Easycouncil: the stinking truth exposed by the MetPro report". Available at http://bit.ly/2mLjNTF, viewed on 16 October 2016.

Perhaps it is nonetheless too soon to be so downbeat about people-power in this area. The rise of the open data agenda and the existence of a number of initiatives to both broaden its scope and streamline the processes that underpin it mean that things may look very different in the near(ish) future. Governments are slowly, and often patchily, embracing this agenda, but the devil remains in the detail. Unless the IT infra-structure of the public sector can be improved and data accessibility is enhanced, then armchair auditing will remain the privilege of the (very) few.

CONCLUSION

There are plenty of reasons to be hopeful that new and innovative ideas have a real contribution to make. Citizens can now sidestep the mediatory role that institutions often play and become anti-corruption activists themselves. Crowdsourcing helps provide up-to-date data on what is actually happening, giving interested parties detailed pictures of where the key problems appear to lie. Pinpointing a given office or group of officials as being particularly corruption prone means that the state at least understands where specific problems reside.

It would, however, be disingenuous to expect too much of these new initiatives. In states where corruption is the norm, awareness raising is one thing, but it is asking a lot of people to act in a way that could either lead to negative consequences for themselves or that involves lots of time and effort with little obvious expectation that things will change. Putting that more bluntly, a citizen may not want to pay a bribe to a doctor, but it is likely that they will if not doing so leaves them unable to access the treatment they need. The initiatives highlighted here are, as Rebecca Cress has noted, "only effective in combating bribery where an adequate educational, social, and political framework exists to support [their] use" (Cress 2014).

Furthermore, making the data produced through citizen-centred ini-tiatives work remains a challenge to which the broader anti-corruption community needs to rise. Indeed, citizen-centred initiatives will not in and of themselves change much at all. The wider anti-corruption com-munity needs to make use of the new information that is out there. This involves thinking about how all the different parts of the anti-corruption world might speak a language that everyone understands. These data sets will mean little if the gap between those who can make anti-corruption work and those who are reporting their experiences remains as it is now. All that being said, these approaches nonetheless have potential. That it will take time to make them work is obvious, and there will be problems along the way. But, it is likely to be this area where we see some of the most innovative new anti-corruption ideas develop.

10.
Conclusion

I started this book with three specific aims. I wanted to say something about what corruption is, what causes it and what we might want to think about when trying to tackle it. Perhaps unsurprisingly, finding consensus in doing justice to those aims is a task fraught with pitfalls. Corruption remains very difficult to accurately define (and every bit as hard to measure); there are a number of different ways of explaining the reasons for its existence; and, although there are a multitude of anti-corruption options out there, success stories are depressingly thin on the ground. If corruption was not such a serious problem, causing so much pain and distress to so many, then it might be tempting to follow the logic of Homer Simpson and turn our attentions elsewhere. As Springfield's finest once said, "if something's hard to do, then it's not worth doing". For good measure, he followed that with "if at first you don't succeed, give up". However, given that corruption has become one of the most prominent global public policy challenges of the twenty-first century, these simply are not options.

Before we can begin to rise to the challenge of tackling corruption, we have to do quite a lot of groundwork. It is clearly not possible to pick anti-corruption policies from a catalogue: anti-corruption is not like mail-order shopping. It is, however, certainly worth studying the experiences of states that have made the transition from high-corruption countries to nominally low-corruption settings. We nonetheless need to be clear that it will never be possible to replicate the Swedish or Danish experiences (to take just two of the most frequently lauded) elsewhere. Indeed, if the Swedish model was dropped onto a territory where systematic corruption was the norm, then you would not suddenly have outbreaks of interpersonal trust everywhere and the rapid development of an expansive, high-quality welfare state. If the Swedish model were placed into a developing state, you would be much more likely to inadvertently encourage even more rampant rent-seeking. It would not and could not work. As and when states do try to take a short cut to tackling corruption, they quickly run into problems. Bo Rothstein may argue that it took little more than a decade for Sweden's indirect big bang to begin to pay off, but it took the UK around 300 years to develop the relatively corruption-free institutions that we see today. Quite why, for example, anyone would have thought that Bangladesh could do it in 18 months (as was the case in 2007 and 2008 – see pages 146–48) is something of a mystery.

That rather sombre conclusion need not, however, lead us to be all doom and gloom. Progress has been made, both in the developed and the developing world. That progress is certainly patchy, and there are often backward steps as well as forward ones, but that is the way progress generally works. The efforts of Indonesia's anti-corruption commission, for example, have certainly made room for just a little more optimism, as have at least some of the developments in states such as Georgia and Liberia.[1] Indeed, optimism might not seem like a sensible starting point, but it should be: corruption is a deep-rooted problem, but never has the issue been more discussed, more debated and more thought about than it is now. That does at least mean that thoughtful souls will, sooner or later, hopefully be able to make progress.

This book began by illustrating that corruption is something that has been discussed for a very long time. It is a concept with a long and colourful history. For much of that history, corruption was understood very differently to how it is now. Corruption was something that happened when moral standards slipped and when states and communities moved away from pursuing the upstanding values that kept them strong. Corruption was only rarely understood as being about individual indiscretions. To be clear, if a leader fell prey to the twin vices of power and prestige then they could be and often were described as corrupt. The term was nonetheless much more frequently used to describe larger, often more abstract, processes. This understanding of corruption often slips into the background in contemporary debates, particularly when they involve national and international policy-makers. For one thing, morals and values are deeply contested, and drafting successful policy responses is hard enough without

---

1. For more on Indonesia's Corruption Eradication Commission (KPK), see Bolongaita (2010). For more on Georgia, see World Bank (2012). For more on Liberia, see Salihu (2012).

having to think explicitly about what can quickly become deeply normative questions. Plus, Western policy-makers in particular are now well aware that pushing the developing world to implement behaviours that fit in with Western normative understandings of what is right and wrong can lead to biting criticism. Western leaders are acutely conscious that many of their own (colonial) pasts mean that they need to be more culturally sensitive than they perhaps used to be.

Morals and ethics nonetheless still play only a limited role in shaping our understandings of corruption. As Chapter 3 illustrated, the core tenets of a corruption definition exist, but that does not stop those tenets from being criticized. Corruption is widely understood as a deliberate act in which someone with entrusted power abuses their public role for some sort of private gain. However, if one were so inclined, one could criticize more or less every part (with the possible exception of corruption being deliberate) of that definition as being insufficient. Coming to a conclusion about what exactly "abuse" is requires a subjective judgement by the analyst, while the increased emphasis on bringing the private sector back into corruption discussions means that those in public roles are now not the only ones who can be described as behaving in a corrupt manner. In fact, there are now plenty of occasions when it is not altogether clear where the boundary between public and private begins and ends. Furthermore, even the notion of private gain is also harder to pin down than it might initially seem.

These definitional debates are important, and corruption analysts need to be aware of them. Getting bogged down in them, however, makes little sense. The fact that it has been so difficult to come up with a universal definition of corruption is one of the main reasons the subject received so little academic attention until relatively recently (defined as the 1990s). That is not an excuse to avoid thinking about these questions, but it is a good reason not to obsess about them. If one is thinking about doing any empirical work in this area, or, indeed, tackling corruption in the real world, then it makes sense to be specific about the corruption problem one is addressing by defining the terms that are relevant to it. There will never be a catch-all definition that suits everyone, but there have to be key pillars on which the majority of people can agree. As the American Justice Potter Stewart once said back in 1964 regarding pornography (while presiding over the case of Jacobellis v. Ohio), he could not come up with a watertight definition of it, but he knew it when he saw it (Lattman 2007). The same can easily be read across to corruption analysis.

The fact that corruption is so difficult to define inevitably makes measuring it a real challenge. That, however, should be no surprise; scholars have found it every bit as difficult to measure other contested concepts, such as democracy and freedom. The Homer Simpson strategy of giving up and going home might be particularly appealing here, but that would once again get us nowhere constructive in trying to work out the impact that anti-corruption initiatives are actually having. Broad-based aggregate indicators of corruption have their uses as awareness-raising tools, but they are of little practical value in working out how to take the anti-corruption fight forward. China's apparently impressive rise from 100th to 83rd in the 2015 CPI, for example, means precisely nothing in substantive terms, as we have no idea what a move from 36 points out of 100 to 37 actually means.

However, more focused indicators of corruption experiences and proxies of corruption do offer some promise. Knowing how much "leakage" there might be in a government budget will not tell you precisely how much corruption there is, but it will give you a reliable indicator of something that is clearly going wrong. Corruption may well be one of the causes of that. If a government can then craft policies to deal with leakage and the misallocation of resources, then their impact can indeed – in theory, at least – be measured over time. That will be useful for policy-makers on the ground improving public services and for donors explaining to (perhaps sceptical) audiences that their efforts are bearing fruit. Measuring corruption should never be an end in itself, and newer initiatives in this area are making genuine contributions to helping policy-makers work out whether their efforts really are worthwhile.

This book spent a considerable amount of time trying to unpack the causes of corruption. Given that working out what causes any social phenomenon (and why and how it does so) is fearsomely difficult at the best of times, it should be obvious that this particular debate is still evolving. There is no real prospect of a consensus in sight. For many, the most logical starting point is to expect the worst. Humans are seen as being inherently self-interested and, indeed, selfish. They look to defend their interests and to make sure that they and their families and friends are able to survive and, if possible, flourish. If that leads to positive outcomes for others, so be it, but the gut instinct and the initial thought is always one of self-preservation. That does not mean that everyone will use every opportunity to inappropriately look after their own interests, but it does mean that, over time, we should expect individuals to take advantage of the opportunities that come their way. Corruption is, for these analysts, an inherent part of the human condition.

You do not have to embrace such a negative understanding of human nature to agree that even citizens who really would like to do something about corruption often find themselves with little opportunity to do so. The collective-action problems that individuals face can be significant. It makes little sense for someone to refuse to pay a bribe only to then be prevented from accessing the health care they desperately need. Corruption sometimes takes place because it is the only option available, no matter how much a given individual may hate the fact that they need to partake in it. There is, however, evidence that in states where trust in the institutions of governance, and, indeed, trust at a person-to-person level, can be generated, people can be coaxed and cajoled into overlooking corrupt opportunities if they come along. Not completely and not forever, but cultures of "acting appropriately" mean that, for example, when looking for a parking space in New York, the most appropriate response for a UN diplomat from Scandinavia is to keep driving around until they find a suitable spot. It is not to abandon their car next to a fire hydrant, safe in the knowledge that no one can force them to pay a parking fine (see page 82ff).

While arguments about the causes of corruption rage on, there is rather more consensus on the impact that corruption has on economic development. One certainly needs to keep a keen eye on the data used and the way econometric analysis in particular is conducted, but even then it is still clear that corruption has a range of negative effects on economic activity. Those effects are, however, not the same everywhere. Sometimes corruption can crush productive economic activity and become the main hindrance to development. Sometimes, however, corruption can have a much less spectacular impact, making it unclear whether corruption is having any influence at all. There are even times when a case can be made for corruption as a stabilizing force, which helps a state to avoid becoming totally ungovernable.

The nuanced relationship between corruption and economic development should not lead anyone to think that corruption is an attractive policy choice. China, for example, is now as rich as it has ever been, but that does not mean that other prospective developing nations should want to hardwire corruption into their systems' DNA in the way that China has done. Sooner or later, the Chinese economy will stop growing, and the Chinese will have to look for ways to effectively deal with the underlying corruption on which their system is based. President Xi may talk a good anti-corruption game, but there is still plenty of work to do. As the work of Mushtaq Khan has shown, there are reasons why corruption can be a stabilizing force and may lead to resources being allocated to sectors that can push an economy along. But none of these reasons makes corruption the optimal choice.

An altogether different sort of economic challenge is faced not so much by developing countries but by those in the Western world, where "enablers of corruption" are at home. Enablers will do jobs that are perfectly above board, such as offering legal advice; advising on investment options; and helping interested parties to acquire nice properties, fast cars and other high-value items. Their profiles will be completely above board, and they will make important contributions to economic development in some of the world's most well-off places. However, there remains far too little willingness, and, indeed, far too little compulsion, to really think about where some of the assets that are being invested come from. It can be rather more or rather less obvious that particular types of investments represent laundered money from elsewhere, but the onus clearly needs to be on enablers to ask about and report back on where this money is coming from. The international community is making progress in this regard, and the push towards more open beneficial ownership regulations and following guidelines developed by organizations such as FATF is encouraging. But there is still much work to do. Beneficial ownership might well have been the anti-corruption term of the year in 2016, but an awful lot of countries are wary of embracing the spirit as well as the letter of the agreements to which they have signed up. Plenty of states would be much happier if registers of beneficial owners were not available to the public at large, for example, and many anti-corruption campaigners were disappointed when, in 2016, David Cameron made it clear that the UK's overseas territories were going to be exempt from the UK's (otherwise impressive) new legislation in this area (Wintour 2016).

FATF may have plenty of work ahead of it, but it is still one of the more successful international anti-corruption agreements. As Chapter 7 illustrated, UNCAC remains the most lauded international initiative, but its effect has been patchy at best. States may pass legislation that meets with UNCAC requirements, but UNCAC has little power to compel signatories to actively enforce these rules. The same applies to the OECD's anti-bribery treaty, with little more than a handful of states falling into TI's category of "active enforcers". International law is inevitably "softer" than national law, but the outputs from these initiatives are regarded as disappointing by many. However critical one might be of what these agreements have achieved, they remain the only credible attempts to date. In the international arena, there really is no current alternative. That having been said, new evidence (see pages 112–13) illustrates that the OECD treaty in particular may need to keep evolving. It is not progress if firms from signatory states are now less likely to offer bribes (as is, indeed, the case) but firms from non-signatory states then move in to pick up the slack. Either the OECD treaty needs to find a way of getting non-signatories involved, or it risks simply diverting corrupt transactions to firms based in states that have little interest in abiding by its principles.

If one were to ask business about international attempts to regulate corrupt practice, chances are it would talk more about national pieces of legislation than about international law. Despite being largely dormant for a quarter of a century, the US FCPA has now become something which firms from all countries that operate in the global economy have to be aware of. The fact that the FCPA can now be seen to apply to companies that only have a minimal presence in the US is, for many, evidence that the FCPA is overstretching. For others, it is simply a clear, powerful statement against a deep-rooted norm that traditionally saw foreign bribery as part of the game. Throw in the even more powerful UKBA, and it is clear that national anti-corruption regimes are having an impact on how firms think about bribery as a business tool. Quite how these thoughts are evolving remains a moot point; the UKBA in particular is still new, and convictions under it have been few in number and often small in scope, but these laws send a clear statement that things in the bribery world are changing. There is also evidence that states where firms have been prosecuted under the FCPA are more likely to beef up and enforce their own domestic bribery laws. Again, this is certainly progress.

Governments intent on tackling corruption nonetheless face a real challenge in demonstrating that their efforts are having an impact. High-profile attempts to imprison big names might look good, but they can often have the feel of tokenism. Changing the norms of behaviour is a long-term game and, indeed, it is not one that national governments can realistically play. They have neither the time nor the tools to take on such challenges. In this regard, it is an impressive government that embraces agendas for reform over the medium, let alone the long, term. Successful reform requires the identification of specific goals and a clear explanation of how these reforms are going to be achieved. Any government that claims it will adopt a zero-tolerance approach or that it will sweep away corruption should be treated with some caution. In a world of ever more populist rhetoric, it is much better to under-promise and over-deliver than the other way around.

Many anti-corruption reforms ultimately prove underwhelming. This can be because they were never properly thought through in the first place, or because political headwinds simply diverted them from their aims. It can, of course, simply be that, from the outset, they were never earnestly meant. The best reforms are those that bring a broad range of actors together to pursue sets of agreed aims. Sometimes this involves talking to power-holders or power-brokers who have interests that need to be respected. This may involve talking to people who ideally would be avoided. But in many states there is no way around the fact that those in power could potentially have much to lose if genuine reforms were to be enacted. Expecting them to give up what they have and even agree to things that could lead them or their allies into conflict with the law is simply unrealistic. Turkeys do not vote for Christmas, after all. The real challenge is working out what progress is possible where. Policies that help citizens find out just a little more about how decisions are made and how they can legitimately defend their own interests as well as hold those in power responsible for their actions are likely to be steps forward. However, do not expect them to be simple steps or ones that those with something to lose will take lying down. The road to reform is incremental and confusing, and it often involves spending considerable time lost down culs-de-sac.

The advent of modern technology has undoubtedly added a new dimension to anti-corruption thinking. This has led to the development of a panapoly of innovative anti-corruption tools. These range from apps that allow corruption to be instantaneously reported to websites enabling people to see how much parliamentarians earn over and above their salary. In the best cases, new technologies allow researchers to create, for example, data sets that can flag potentially corrupt tendering processes and prevent micro-level state capture from taking place. Organizations such as the World Bank are also able to use GPS technology and Google Earth to monitor projects, with the specific aim of ensuring that money really is going where it is supposed to. Crowdsourcing helps provide up-to-date data on what is going on where; if used carefully, it should help states with an integrated anti-corruption framework move just a little quicker than they have traditionally. That, however, is an important caveat. Anti-corruption is not an island in the sea. It makes little sense to create institutions that do not talk or work with each other and with broader society at large. Successful anti-corruption needs an educational element, just as it needs an institutional and a social element. Only when all these things interact and work together is serious progress likely to be made.

The fact that an international transparency norm now exists will not ensure that corruption becomes a thing of the past, but it certainly does make keeping corruption under wraps more difficult. We now know more about which individuals and companies get which contracts, how much they pay for them and what they agree to provide than we ever have before. We could, however, still know a whole lot more. It would be good if data were more complete and user-friendly. It would also be good if we knew more about the murky world of offshore finance. Careful steps to help us learn more about which companies belong to which people, who takes companies' profits home, how wealth is generated and what the interests of power-brokers are will help keep those in positions of power and influence just a little more accountable.

It makes little sense to proclaim any of these things as the start of a new era, mainly as those looking to indulge in corruption will no doubt see opportunities here, too. Assets can be transferred around the world at breakneck speed, and they can easily end up in jurisdictions where the outside world has no access to information about them. The Panama Papers may well have caused plenty of journalistic excitement, but in truth no one is going to be able to sweep away these jurisdictions any time soon. The advent of ever more nuanced and focused technology offers both challenges and opportunities alike to those involved in corrupt activities as well as those looking to root it out.

"Trying", to quote Homer Simpson one final time, "is the first step toward failure". As is often the way, there is a little truth in what Homer says. Tackling corruption is not like cramming for a test. It does not, and cannot, involve simply studying the material, learning the answers and then reaping the rewards. The real world just does not work like that. In reality, those who look to tackle corruption will nearly always fail at some point. Too many people have too much at stake for it to be any other way. However, failure is part of the process of learning. In the world of corruption and anti-corruption, we are slowly but surely learning more about what might be productive ways forward. Policy-makers have long since learnt that you live, you learn, you try, you fail, and then you try again. And, as a quip attributed to golfer Gary Player states, "it's funny that the harder I practice, the luckier I get". Politicians do not get to practice much. Theirs is a real world that moves quickly and often breathlessly. But no matter what corruption challenges they face, someone, somewhere is likely to have faced something similar from which they can draw (either positive or negative) inspiration. You cannot read across answers in a simple fashion, but, as this book has hopefully shown, there are often examples and cases that can help inform the judgements you make. If you take that approach, then all need not necessarily be doom and gloom.

Bibliography

Abdelal, R. E., R. Di Tella & J. Schlefer 2008. *Corruption in Germany: Managing Germany's Largest Corruption Scandal*. Boston, MA: Harvard Business School.

Ablo, E. & R. Reinikka 1998. "Do budgets really matter? Evidence from public spending on education and health in Uganda". Policy Research Working Paper 1926. Washington, DC: World Bank.

Abramo, C. W. 2008. "How much do perceptions of corruption really tell us?" *Economics: The Open-Access, Open-Assessment E Journal* 2(2008-3): 1–56.

Aidt, T. S. 2003. "Economic analysis of corruption: a survey". *Economic Journal* 113(491): F632–F652.

Alesina, A. & G.-M. Angeletos 2005. "Corruption, inequality and fairness". *Journal of Monetary Economics* 52(7): 1227–44.

Amsden, A. 1989. *Asia's Next Giant: South Korea and Late Industrialization*. Oxford: Oxford University Press.

Andersson, S. & P. M. Heywood 2009. "The politics of perception: use and abuse of Transparency International's approach to measuring corruption". *Political Studies* 57(4): 746–67.

Anechiarico, F. & J. B. Jacobs 1996. *The Pursuit of Absolute Integrity: How Corruption Control Makes Government Ineffective*. Chicago, IL: University of Chicago Press.

Ang, Y. Y. 2014. "Authoritarian restraints on online activism revisited: why 'I-Paid-A-Bribe' worked in India but failed in China". *Comparative Politics* 47(1): 21–40.

Aoki, M. *et al.* (eds) 1997. *The Role of Government in East Asian Economic Development: Comparative Institutional Analysis*. Oxford: Clarendon Press.

Ardigo, I. & D. Hough 2017. "Bishops that live like princes; Bishop Tebartz-van Elst and the challenge of defining corruption". *Public Integrity*. Forthcoming.

Argandoña, A. 2006. "The United Nations Convention Against Corruption and its impact on international companies". Working Paper 656. Barcelona: IESE Business School.

Aristotle (ed. 1946). *The Politics of Aristotle*. Oxford: Clarendon Press.

Arndt, C. & C. Oman 2006. *Uses and Abuses of Governance Indicators*. Paris: OECD Development Centre Study.

Asiedu, E. & J. Freeman 2009. "The effect of corruption on investment growth: evidence from firms in Latin America, Sub-Saharan Africa, and transition countries". *Review of Development Economics* 13(2): 200–14.

Bailey, D. H. 1966. "The effects of corruption in a developing nation". *Western Political Quarterly* 19: 719–32.

Banuri, S. & C. Eckel 2012. "Experiments in culture and corruption: a review". In *New Advances in Experimental Research on Corruption*, D. Serra & L. Wantchekon (eds). Bradford: Emerald.

Batra, G., D. Kaufmann & A. Stone 2003. *Investment Climate around the World: Voices of the Firms from the World Business Environment Survey*. Washington, DC: World Bank.

BBC News 2014. "GlaxoSmithKline fined $490m by China for bribery". Available at www.bbc.co.uk/news/business-29274822, viewed on 3 December 2016.

BBC News 2015a. "Switzerland to return Sani Abacha 'loot' to Nigeria", 17 March. Available at www.bbc.com/news/world-africa-31933083, viewed on 7 December 2016.

BBC News 2015b. "LIBOR: what is it and why does it matter?" 3 August. Available at www.bbc.co.uk/news/business-19199683, viewed on 16 October 2016.

BBC News 2016. "Apple tax: Irish cabinet to appeal against EU ruling", 2 September. Available at www.bbc.com/news/world-europe-37251084, viewed on 7 December 2016.

Beaumont, P. 2011. "Mohammed Bouazizi: the dutiful son whose death changed Tunisia's fate", *The Guardian*, 20 January. Available at http://bit.ly/2m5ZrEJ, viewed on 9 October 2016.

Biron, C. 2014. "In accepting Ethiopia, transparency group 'sacrifices credibility'", *Inter Press Service*, 20 March. Available at http://bit.ly/2n2EM8w, viewed on 24 November 2016.

Blueprint for Free Speech 2016. "UK law fails to adequately protect whistleblowers". Report. London: BfFS. Available at http://bit.ly/2no9vNJ, viewed on 17 January 2017.

Bolongaita, E. P. 2010. "An exception to the rule? Why Indonesia's anti-corruption succeeds where others don't: a comparison with the Philippines' ombudsman". *U4* 4. Bergen, Norway: Chr. Michelsen Institute. Available at http://bit.ly/2mmonZz, viewed on 8 December 2016.

Bonner, R. 2009. "The stink of corruption", *The Guardian*, 14 March. Available at www.theguardian.com/books/2009/mar/14/politics, viewed on 21 May 2016.

Brinkerhoff, D. W. 2000. "Assessing political will for anti-corruption efforts: an analytic framework". *Public Administration and Development* 20(3): 239–53.

Brinkerhoff, D. W. 2010. "Unpacking the concept of political will to confront corruption". *U4* Brief. Bergen, Norway: Chr. Michelsen Institute.

Broken Barnet Blog 2011. "Easycouncil: the stinking truth exposed by the MetPro report". Available at http://bit.ly/2mLjNTF, viewed on 16 October 2016.

Brown, E. & J. Cloke 2004. "Neoliberal reform, governance and corruption in the south: assessing the international anti-corruption crusade". *Antipode* 36(2): 272–94.

Brown, G. 2007. "Prevention of corruption – UK legislation and enforcement". *Journal of Financial Regulation and Compliance* 15(2): 180–85.

Brown, M. 2015. "The EITI and the challenge of transparency", *Sussex Centre for the Study of Corruption Blog*. Available at http://bit.ly/2mEAl2R, viewed on 25 November 2016.

Buchan, B. & L. Hill 2014. *An Intellectual History of Political Corruption*. London: Palgrave Macmillan.

Bukovansky, M. 2002. "Corruption is bad: normative dimensions of the anti-corruption movement". Working Paper 2002/5. Available at http://bit.ly/2niHR0f, viewed on 3 December 2016.

Bukovansky, M. 2006. "The hollowness of anti-corruption discourse". *Review of International Political Economy*, 13(2): 181–209.

Butler, P. 2011. "Mrs Angry: how to be an armchair auditor", *The Guardian*, 8 July. Available at http://bit.ly/2n9E6eG, viewed on 16 October 2016.

Cameron, D. 2010. "PM's podcast on transparency". Available at http://bit.ly/2m2D2Yc, viewed on 16 October 2016.

Campion, M. 2011. "Bribery in India: a website for whistleblowers", *BBC News*, 6 June. Available at www.bbc.com/news/world-south-asia-13616123, viewed on 16 October 2016.

Cassin, R. 2016. "Och-Ziff takes fourth spot on our new top ten list", *FCPA Blog*. Available at http://bit.ly/2cPYUkP, viewed on 28 November 2016.

Chadbourne, M. & P. Washington 2012. "Beyond transparency: EITI stretches 'civil society' role". *Oil and Gas Journal*, 2 April. Available at http://bit.ly/2n2NHHi, viewed on 24 November 2016.

Chapman, T. *et al.* 2016. "International bribery laws and firm strategic behavior: did the OECD anti-bribery convention increase bribery?" IPES Working Paper, Princeton University. Available at http://bit.ly/2lHT2Ds, viewed on 21 November 2016.

Chêne, M. 2009. "Update on UNCAC implementation in Africa". *U4* Expert Answer. Bergen: U4 Anti-Corruption Resource Centre, Chr. Michelsen Institute.

Chiu, J. 2013. "Chinese censors silence corruption blogger", *Committee to Protect Journalists*, 25 July. Available at http://bit.ly/2n9EXfo, viewed on 15 October 2016.

Cillizza, C. 2016. "The Bob McDonnell Supreme Court ruling makes convicting politicians of corruption almost impossible", *Washington Post*, 27 June.

Clare, L. 2015. "Deferred prosecution agreement: the sign of things to come?" *Anticorruption Blog*. Available at http://bit.ly/2lGVD0E, viewed on 28 November 2016.

Cohn, C. & K. Ridley 2014. "SFO nails its first convictions under new bribery laws", *Reuters*, 8 December. Available at http://reut.rs/2mF7QlC, viewed on 28 November 2016.

Conference of the States Parties to the United Nations Convention against Corruption 2009. "Report of the Conference of the States Parties to the United Nations Convention against Corruption on its third session, held in Doha from 9 to 13 November 2009". Vienna: UNODC.

Council of Europe 2014. "Group of States against Corruption (GRECO)". Available at http://bit.ly/2iiMvNL, viewed on 23 November 2016.

Cress, R. 2014. "Social media and anticorruption reform: when does crowdsourcing work?" GAB: The Global Anticorruption Blog. Available at http://bit.ly/2mpGu2n, viewed on 16 October 2016.

Crick, B. 1959. *The American Science of Politics: Its Origins and Conditions*. Berkeley, CA: University of California Press.

Curry, W. S. 2010. *Government Contracting: Promises and Perils*. New York: Routledge.

Cvetanoska, L. 2017. "The European Union's anti-corruption enlargement conditionality: comparing the Czech Republic, Romania and Macedonia". PhD Thesis. Brighton: University of Sussex.

Dahl, R. A. 1961. "The behavioral approach in political science: epitaph for a monument to a successful protest". *American Political Science Review* 55(4): 763–72.

Dahlgreen, W. 2016. "Chinese people are most likely to feel the world is getting better", *YouGov*. Available at http://bit.ly/2c9YPgn, viewed on 5 December 2016.

Daily Telegraph 2011. "Ipsa: the MPs' criticisms", 5 January. Available at http://bit.ly/2kKNTpY, viewed on 5 December 2016.

Dávid-Barrett, E. & K. Okamura 2016. "Norm diffusion and reputation: the rise of the extractive industries transparency initiative". *Governance* 29(2): 227–46.

Dávid-Barrett, E. & M. Fazekas 2016. "Corrupt contracting: partisan favouritism in public procurement: Hungary and the United Kingdom compared". Working Paper 49. Budapest: ERCAS.

Dávid-Barrett, E., P. M. Heywood & N. Theodorakis 2017. "Open data as an anti-corruption tool: theory and UK practice". *Public Administration Review*. Forthcoming.

Davies, R. 2015. "Starbucks pays UK corporation tax of £8.1m", *The Guardian*, 15 December. Available at http://bit.ly/22g4geV, viewed on 7 December 2016.

Day, M. 2015. "Vatican to put on trial reporters who exposed shameful corruption", *The Independent*, 24 November.

de Graaf, G., P. von Maravic & P. Wagenaar (eds) 2010. *The Good Cause: Theoretical Perspectives on Corruption*. Leverkusen: Barbara Budrich.

de Maria, B. 2008. "Neo-colonialism through measurement: a critique of the corruption perception index". *Critical Perspectives on International Business* 4(2/3): 184–202.

de Sardan, J.-P. O. 1999. "A moral economy of corruption in Africa?" *The Journal of Modern African Studies* 37(1): 25–52.

de Sousa, L., P. Larmour & B. Hindess (eds) 2008. *Governments, NGOs and Anti-Corruption: The New Integrity Warriors*. London: Routledge.

de Speville, B. 2010. "Anticorruption commissions: the 'Hong Kong model' revisited". *Asia-Pacific Review* 17(1): 47–71.

de Tocqueville, A. 1961. *Democracy in America*, vols 1 and 2. New York: Schocken.

Dougherty, C. 2007. "Germany battling rising tide of corporate corruption", *The New York Times*, 15 February. Available at http://nyti.ms/2mL7iLo, viewed on 10 November 2015.

Downs, A. 1957. *An Economic Theory of Democracy*. New York: Harper and Row.

Economist, The 2015. "NGOs and governments grapple over ownership of mining and energy firms", 24 October. Available at http://econ.st/1W35AMl, viewed on 24 November 2016.

Edwards, B. 2009. "World Bank corruption", *Foreign Policy in Focus*, 21 May. Available at http://fpif.org/world_bank_corruption/, viewed on 22 November 2016.

Elgot, J. 2016. "World leaders pledge to tackle corruption at London summit – as it happened", *The Guardian*, 12 May. Available at http://bit.ly/2njdqqV, viewed on 7 December 2016.

European Bank for Reconstruction and Development (EBRD) 2014. "Business and Environment And Enterprise Survey, 2012–2014". Available at http://ebrd-beeps.com/data/2012-2013/, viewed on 6 November 2016.

European Council 1997. "Convention against corruption involving officials", 26 May. Available at http://bit.ly/2lnlidi, viewed on 23 November 2016.

Extractive Industries Transparency Initiative 2016. "Human rights groups call to suspend Azerbaijan from participation in EITI", *Netherlands Helsinki Committee*, 21 October. Available at http://bit.ly/2lW6Mq6, viewed on 24 November 2016.

Farrington, R. 2016. "UK needs radical reform of protection for whistleblowers, says report", *People Management*, 1 August. Available at http://bit.ly/2nnUnQq, viewed on 17 January 2017.

Fazekas, M. & G. Kocsis 2015. "Uncovering high-level corruption: cross-national corruption proxies using government contracting data". Working Paper GTI-WP/2015:02. Budapest: ERCAS.

Fazekas, M. & I. J. Toth 2016. "From corruption to state capture". *Political Research Quarterly* 69(2): 320–34.

Ferraz, C., F. Finan & D. Moreira 2012. "Corrupting learning: evidence from missing federal education funds in Brazil". Discussion Paper 6634. Bonn: Forschungs institut zur Zukunft der Arbeit.

Financial Action Task Force 2016a. http://www.fatf-gafi.org, viewed on 16 August.

Financial Action Task Force 2016b. "Who we are". Available at http://www.fatf-gafi.org/about/, viewed on 23 November 2016.

Financial Action Task Force 2016c. "Public statement", 21 October. Available at http://bit.ly/2ezwEoS, viewed on 24 November 2016.

Fisman, R. & E. Miguel 2006. "Cultures of corruption: evidence from diplomatic parking tickets". Working Paper 12312. Cambridge, MA: NBER. Available at www.nber.org/papers/w12312, viewed on 12 November 2016.

Fisman, R. & J. Svensson 2007. "Are corruption and taxation really harmful to growth? Firm level evidence". *Journal of Development Economics* 83(1): 63–75.

Florcruz, M. 2013. "Chinese government launches anti-corruption site for netizens to submit tips", *International Business Times*, 9 April. Available at http://bit.ly/2mFkIs3, viewed on 16 October 2016.

Freeguard, G., R. Munro & E. Andrews 2015. *Whitehall Monitor: Deep Impact?* London: Institute for Government. Available at http://bit.ly/2mFupXs, viewed on 16 October 2016.

Friedrich, C. J. 1967. *Introduction to Political Theory: Twelve Lectures at Harvard*. New York: Harper.

Friedrich, C. J. 2002. "Corruption concepts in historical perspective". In *Political Corruption: Concepts and Contexts*, A. J. Heidenheimer & M. Johnston (eds). New Brunswick, NJ: Transaction.

Frings, A. *et al.* 2012. "European Court of Human Rights protects whistleblowers from dismissal – right to blame the employer against better knowledge?" *Lexicology*, 2 October. Available at http://bit.ly/2nau1xY, viewed on 7 December 2016.

Gambino, L. 2016. "Trump: Hillary Clinton may be 'most corrupt person ever' to run for president", *The Guardian*, 22 June. Available at http://bit.ly/2mFl6Xx, viewed on 5 December 2016.

Garrard, J. & J. Newell 2006. *Scandals in Past and Contemporary Politics*. Manchester: Manchester University Press.

Gaviria, A. G. 2002. "Assessing the effects of corruption and crime on firm performance: evidence from Latin America". *Emerging Markets Review* 3: 245–68.

Genaux, M. 2004. "Social sciences and the evolving concept of corruption". *Crime, Law and Social Change*, 42(1): 13–24.

Gibson, O. 2015. "Sepp Blatter facing life ban from football for Platini payment", *The Guardian*, 24 November.

Glencorse, B. & S. Parajuli 2015. "Integrity gets great ratings", *Foreign Policy*. Available on http://atfp.co/1gDpsrS, viewed on 10 October 2016.

Global Competitiveness Report 2015. "Competitiveness rankings: ethics and corruption". Available at http://bit.ly/1vKWWJu, viewed on 6 November 2016.

Guan, C. 2015. "Take two: will a second attempt at hacking corruption in China work?" *GAB: The Global Anticorruption Blog*, 28 December. Available at http://bit.ly/2nj4Pom, viewed on 16 October 2016.

Hafner, M. *et al.* 2016. "The cost of non-Europe in the area of organised crime and corruption". Study, Annex II: Corruption. Brussels: European Parliament. Available at http://bit.ly/1Sgcfmy, viewed on 14 August 2016.

Hallisey, C. 2015. "Ethics and the subject of corruption". *Contributions to Indian Sociology* 49(3): 305–21.

Harling, P. 1996. *The Waning of "Old Corruption": The Politics of Economical Reform in Britain, 1779–1846.* Oxford: Clarendon Press.

Harrison, E. 2007. "Corruption". *Development in Practice* 17(4/5): 672–78.

Heidenheimer, A. J. (ed.) 1970. *Political Corruption: Readings in Comparative Analysis.* New York: Holt, Rinehart & Winston.

Heidenheimer, A. J. 1989. "Introduction". In *Political Corruption: A Handbook*, A. Heidenheimer, M. Johnston & V. T. LeVine (eds). New Brunswick, NJ: Transaction.

Heidenheimer, A. J. & M. Johnston 2002. "Introduction". In *Political Corruption: Concepts and Contexts*, A. J. Heidenheimer & M. Johnston (eds). New Brunswick, NJ: Transaction.

Hellman, J. S. & D. Kaufmann 2001. "Confronting the challenge of state capture in transition economies". *Finance and Development* 38(3). Available at www.imf.org/external/pubs/ft/fandd/2001/09/hellman.htm, viewed on 6 December 2016.

Hellman, J. S., G. Jones & D. Kaufmann 2003. "Seize the state, seize the day: state capture and influence in transition economies". *Journal of Comparative Economics* 31(4): 751–73.

Hellman, J. S. *et al.* 2000. *Measuring Governance, Corruption and State Capture.* Washington, DC: World Bank.

Hellmann, O. 2017. "The historical origins of corruption in the developing world: a comparative analysis of East Asia". *Crime, Law and Social Change.* Forthcoming.

Heywood, P. M. 2012. "Integrity management and the public service ethos in the UK: patchwork quilt or threadbare blanket?" *International Review of Administrative Sciences* 78(3): 474–93.

Heywood, P. M. 2015. "Measuring corruption: perspectives, critiques, and limits". In *Routledge Handbook of Political Corruption*, P. Heywood (ed.). London: Routledge.

Heywood, P. M. & J. Rose 2015. "The limits of rule governance". In *Ethics in Public Policy and Management: A Global Research Companion*, A. Lawton, Z. van der Wal & L. Huberts (eds), pp. 181–96. London: Routledge.

Himalayan, The 2016. "Kandel wins *Integrity Idol* award", 11 January. Available at http://bit.ly/2lPS6LG, viewed on 10 October 2016.

Hodgson, G. M. & S. Jiang 2007. "The economics of corruption and the corruption of economics: an institutionalist perspective". *Journal of Economic Issues* XLI(4): 1043–61.

Holmberg, S. & B. Rothstein 2014. "Correlates of quality of government". Working Paper 21. Gothenburg: Quality of Government Institute. Available at http://qog.pol.gu.se/Publications/workingpapers, viewed on 4 December 2016.

Hood, C. 2011. "A public management for all seasons? Afterword: bringing back agents". In *Public Administration: 25 Years of Analysis and Debate*, R. A. W. Rhodes (ed.), pp. 199–214. Oxford: Wiley-Blackwell.

Hopkin, J. 2002. "States, markets and corruption: a review of some recent literature". *Review of International Political Economy* 9(3): 574–90.

Hough, D. 2013. *Corruption, Anti-Corruption and Governance*. London: Palgrave Macmillan.

Hough, D. 2016. "Here's this year's (flawed) Corruption Perception Index. Those flaws are useful", *Washington Post*, 27 January. Available at http://wapo.st/20sdq6f, viewed on 16 October 2016.

Hough, D. 2017. "Corruption and anti-corruption in Germany; a case of 'good, but could do better'". *German Politics and Society* 35(1): 63–82.

Huntington, S. 1968. *Political Order in Changing Societies*. New Haven, CT: Yale University Press.

Huther, J. & A. Shah 2000. "Anti-corruption policies and programmes: a framework for evaluation". Policy Research Working Paper 2501. Washington, DC: World Bank.

Iftekharuzzaman & T. Mahmud 2008. "Bangladesh". In *Transparency International, Global Corruption Report 2008*. Cambridge: Cambridge University Press.

International Monetary Fund 1996. "Partnership for Sustainable Global Growth". Interim Committee Declaration. Washington DC: IMF.

International Monetary Fund 1997. "The role of the IMF in governance issues". Guidance Note. Washington, DC: IMF. Available at http://bit.ly/2lSipyK, accessed on 22 November 2016.

International Monetary Fund 2016a. "IMF and good governance". Factsheet. Washington, DC: IMF. Available at http://bit.ly/ZeJiBo, accessed on 22 November 2016.

International Monetary Fund 2016b. "IMF surveillance". Factsheet. Washington, DC: IMF. Available at http://bit.ly/2naCPUB, viewed on 22 November 2016.

Index of Economic Freedom 2016. Data available at www.heritage.org/index/explore?view=by-variables, viewed on 11 November 2016.

Indrawati, S. M. 2015. "What will it take to realize Pakistan's potential?" Speech. Washington, DC: World Bank. Available at http://bit.ly/2n4fsPy, viewed on 16 October 2016.

Innes, A. 2014. "The political economy of state capture in central Europe". *Journal of Common Market Studies* 52(1): 88–104.

Jacoby, W. 2004. *The Enlargement of the European Union and NATO: Ordering from the Menu in Central Europe*. Cambridge: Cambridge University Press.

Jain, A. K. 2001. "Corruption: a review". *Journal of Economic Surveys* 15(1): 71–121.

Jensen, N. & E. Malesky 2016. "Does the OECD Convention affect bribery? Investment liberalization and corruption in Vietnam". Unpublished manuscript.

Johnson, J. & P. Mason 2013. "The proxy challenge: why bespoke proxy indicators can help solve the anti-corruption measurement problem". *U4* Brief, July (2). Bergen, Norway: Chr. Michelsen Institute.

Johnston, M. 2005a. *Syndromes of Corruption*. Cambridge: Cambridge University Press.

Johnston, M. 2005b. "Measuring the new corruption rankings: implications for analysis and reform". In *Political Corruption: Concepts and Contexts*, A. J. Heidenheimer & M. Johnston (eds). New Brunswick, NJ: Transaction.

Johnston, M. 2006. "From Thucydides to Mayor Daley: bad politics, and a culture of corruption?" *P.S. Political Science and Politics* 39(4): 809–12.

Johnston, M. 2013. *Corruption, Contention, and Reform: The Power of Deep Democratization*. Cambridge: Cambridge University Press.

Johnston, M. 2016. "Political will or political won't". *International Affairs Forum* 7(2): 13–17.

Johnston, M. & S. Kpundeh 2002. "Building a clean machine: anti-corruption coalitions and sustainable reform". Working Paper. Washington, DC: World Bank Institute.

Kaczmarek, S. & A. Newman 2011. "The long arm of the law: extraterritoriality and the national implementation of foreign bribery". *International Organization* 65(4): 745–70.

Kar, D. & J. Spankers 2015. "Illicit financial flows from developing countries: 2004-2013". Report. Washington, DC: Global Financial Intergrity. Available at http://bit.ly/1Vlbw83, viewed on 14 August 2016.

Kaufmann, D. 2005. "Myths and realities of governance and corruption: the global competitiveness report, 2005– 2006". New York: World Economic Forum.

Kaufmann, D. 2009. "Aid effectiveness and governance: the good, the bad and the ugly". Special Report. Washington, DC: Development Outreach, World Bank Institute.

Kaufmann, D. & A. Gillies 2016. "From Panama to London: legal and illegal corruption require action at the UK anti-corruption summit". Article. Washington, DC: Brookings. Available at http://brook.gs/1T7JCbQ, viewed on 13 July 2016.

Kaufmann, D., A. Kraay & M. Mastruzzi 2007. "The Worldwide Governance Indicators project: answering the critics". Working Paper. Washington, DC: World Bank.

Kaufmann, D., A. Kraay & M. Mastruzzi 2009. "Governance matters VIII". Policy Research Paper 4978. Washington, DC: World Bank Development Research Group.

Kaufmann, D., A. Kray & M. Mastruzzi 2010. "The Worldwide Governance Indicators: methodology and analytical issues". Policy Research Working Paper 5430. Washington, DC: World Bank.

Kaufmann, D., A. Kraay and P. Zoido-Lobatón 1999. "Aggregating governance indicators". Policy Research Working Paper 2195. Washington, DC: World Bank.

Kaufmann, D. & P. Siegelbaum 2006. *Privatization and Corruption in the Transition*. Washington, DC: World Bank.

Kaufmann, D. & P. C. Vicente 2005. "Legal corruption". *Economics and Politics* 23(2): 195–219.

Khan, M. 1996. "Patron–client networks and the economic effects of corruption". *The European Journal of Development Research* 10(1): 15–39.

Khan, M. 2004. "State failure in developing countries and strategies of institutional reform". In *Toward Pro-Poor Policies: Aid Institutions and Globalization*, B. Tungodden, N. Stern and I. Kolstad (eds). Oxford: Oxford University Press.

Khan, M. 2006a. "Corruption and governance". In *The New Development Economics: after the Washington Consensus*, K. S. Jomo and B. Fine (eds), pp. 200–21. London: Zed Press.

Khan, M. 2006b. "Determinants of corruption in developing countries: the limits of conventional economic analysis". In *International Handbook on the Economics of Corruption*, S. Rose-Ackerman (ed.). Cheltenham: Elgar.

Khan, M. & K. S. Jomo (eds) 2000. *Rents, Rent-Seeking and Economic Development: Theory and Evidence in Asia*. Cambridge: Cambridge University Press.

Kirton, H. 2016. "Four ex-Barclays bankers sentenced for roles in LIBOR rate-rigging scandal", *City A.M.* Available at http://bit.ly/29t6lQM, viewed on 5 December 2016.

Klitgaard, R. 1988. *Controlling Corruption*. Berkeley, CA: University of California Press.

Knack, S. 2007. "Measuring corruption: a critique of indicators in Eastern Europe and Central Asia". *Journal of Public Policy* 27(3): 255–91.

Knack, S. & P. Keefer 1995. "Institutions and economic performance: cross-country tests using alternative institutional measures". *Economics and Politics* 7(3): 207–27.

Knights, M. 2016. "Old corruption: what British history can tell us about corruption today". Report. London: Transparency International.

Koehler, M. 2013. *The Foreign Corrupt Practices Act in a New Era*. Cheltenham: Elgar.

Kook, S. 2013. "Financial Action Task Force (FATF). Evolving in its effort to combat money laundering and terrorist finance". Treasury Notes, 27 March. Washington, DC: US Department of the Treasury. Available at http://bit.ly/2lKd1RU, viewed on 24 November 2016.

Koziol, M. & C. Tolmie 2010. *Using Public Expenditure Tracking Surveys to Monitor Projects and Small-Scale Programs: A Guidebook*. Washington, DC: World Bank.

Kuris, G. 2014. *From Underdogs to Watchdogs: How Anti-Corruption Agencies Can Hold Off Potent Adversaries*. Princeton, NJ: Princeton University Press.

Lambsdorff, J. G. 2005a. "The methodology of the 2005 corruption perceptions index". Report. Passau: Internet Center for Corruption Research. Available at www.icgg.org/downloads/CPI_Methodology.pdf, accessed 28 October 2016.

Lambsdorff, J. G. 2005b. "Determining trends for perceived levels of corruption". Discussion Paper V-38-05. Passau: University of Passau.

Lambsdorff, J. G. 2006. "Causes and consequences of corruption: what do we know from a cross-section of countries?" In *International Handbook on the Economics of Corruption*, S. Rose-Ackerman (ed.). Cheltenham: Elgar.

Lattman, P. 2007. "The origins of Justice Stewart's 'I know it when I see it'", *The Wall Street Journal*, 27 September. Available at http://on.wsj.com/1zQpDl6, viewed on 8 December 2016.

Lee, D. 2007. "Hyundai boss too important to be jailed, judges decide", *Los Angeles Times*, 7 September. Available at http://articles.latimes.com/2007/sep/07/business/fi-hyundai7, viewed on 5 December 2016.

Leff, N. 1964. "Economic development through bureaucratic corruption". *American Behavioral Scientist* 8(3): 8–14.

Leys, C. 1965. "What is the problem about corruption?" *The Journal of Modern African Studies* 3(2): 215–30.

Locke, J. 2005. "The second treatise of government. an essay concerning the true original, extent, and end of civil government". In *The Selected Political Writings of John Locke*, P. E. Sigmind (ed.), pp. 17–125. New York: Norton.

Lucas, L. 2013. "Pernod Ricard whisky sales fall in China", *The Financial Times*. Available at https://www.ft.com/content/01aaa4d2-931f-11e2-b3be-00144feabdc0, viewed on 6 December 2016.

Macalister, T. 2013. "Starbucks pays corporation tax in UK for first time in five years", *The Guardian*, 23 June. Available at http://bit.ly/2ncXZRS, viewed on 13 July 2016.

MacMullen, R. 1988. *Corruption and the Decline of Rome*. New Haven, CT: Yale University Press.

Maleske, M. 2013. "The impact and continuing evolution of the FCPA", *Inside Counsel*, 22 May. Available at http://bit.ly/2lKl1Cs, viewed on 28 November 2016.

Maritime Anti-Corruption Network 2016. Available at www.maritime-acn.org, viewed on 16 August.

Marquette, H. 2003. *Corruption, Development and Politics: The Role of the World Bank*. Basingstoke: Palgrave Macmillan.

Marquette, H. 2004. "The creeping politicisation of the World Bank: the case of corruption". *Political Studies* 52(3): 413–30.

Marquette, H. 2012. "'Finding God' or 'moral disengagement' in the fight against corruption in developing countries? Evidence from India and Nigeria". *Public Administration and Development* 32(1): 11–26.

Marquette, H. & C. Peiffer 2015. "Corruption and collective action". Research Paper 32. Birmingham: Development Leadership Programme.

Masud, M. O. 2015a. "Calling in against corruption", *Foreign Policy*, 30 June. Available at http://atfp.co/1FUkEmd, viewed on 14 October 2016.

Masud, M. O. 2015b. "Calling citizens, improving the state: Pakistan's citizen feedback monitoring programme, 2008–2014". Case Study. Princeton, NJ: Innovations for Successful Societies, Princeton University. Available at http://bit.ly/29he02d, viewed on 16 October 2016.

Mauro, P. 1995. "Corruption and growth". *Quarterly Journal of Economics* 110(3): 681–712.

Mauro, P. 1997. "Why worry about corruption?". *Economic Issues* 6. Washington, DC: IMF.

Mauro, P. 1997. "The effects of corruption on growth, investment and government expenditure: a cross-country analysis". In *Corruption and the Global Economy*, K. A. Elliott (ed.). Washington, DC: Institute for International Economics.

Maza, S. C. 1993. *Private Lives and Public Affairs: The Causes Célèbres of Prerevolutionary France*. Berkeley, CA: University of California Press.

McKinstry, L. 2010. "Brown is the worst Prime Minister in Britain's history", *The Express*, 1 February. Available at http://bit.ly/2nlZeNQ, viewed on 6 December 2016.

McKitrick, E. L. 1957. "The study of corruption". *Political Science Quarterly* 72(4): 502–14.

McMahon, R. 2006. "The World Bank and corruption". CFR Backgrounder, 21 April. New York: Council on Foreign Relations. Available at http://on.cfr.org/2ncR7E5, viewed on 22 November 2016.

Messick, R. 2015. "The use of social media to combat corruption: the 'I Paid a Bribe' website in India", *GAB: The Global Anticorruption Blog*, 13 May. Available at http://bit.ly/2lKtdme, viewed on 16 October 2016.

Michael, B. 2004. "The rapid rise of the anti-corruption industry". Local Governance Brief. Budapest: Open Society Institute.

Michael, B. & D. Bowser 2009. "The evolution of the anti-corruption industry in the third wave of anti-corruption work". Working Paper. Hong Kong University. Available at http://bit.ly/2mqq9Jg, viewed on 23 May 2016.

Mintz Group 2016. "Where the bribes are". Data available at http://fcpamap.com/, viewed on 28 November 2016.

Mitnick, B. M. 1975. "The theory of agency: the policing 'paradox' and regulatory behavior". *Public Choice* 24: 27–42.

Montesquieu, C.-L. de S. 1999. *Considerations on the Causes of the Greatness of the Romans and the Decline*, trans. D. Lowenthal. Indianapolis, IN: Hackett.

Monyake, M. 2016. "Understanding the 'incorruptible' Jonas; the curious case of South Africa's Deputy Minister of Finance", Sussex Centre for the Study of Corruption Blog. Available at http://bit.ly/2n6Crtp, viewed on 6 December 2016.

Moroff, H. & D. Schmidt-Pfister, 2010. "Anti-corruption movements, mechanisms and machines – an introduction". *Global Crime* 11(2): 89–98.

Mungiu-Pippidi, A. 2006. "Corruption: diagnosis and treatment". *Journal of Democracy* 17(3): 86–99.

Mungiu-Pippidi, A. 2013. "Controlling corruption through collective action". *Journal of Democracy* 24(1): 101–15.

Mungiu-Pippidi, A. 2014. "Becoming Denmark: historical designs of corruption control". *Social Research* 80(4): 1259–86.

Mungiu-Pippidi, A. 2015. *The Quest for Good Governance: How Societies Develop Control of Corruption*. Cambridge: Cambridge University Press.

Napal, G. 2006. "An assessment of the ethical dimensions of corruption". *Electronic Journal of Business Ethics and Organization Studies* 11(1): 5–9.

Nie, D. & A.-M. Lamsa 2015. "The leader–member exchange theory in the Chinese Context and the ethical challenge of Guanxi". *Journal of Business Ethics* 128: 851–61.

Noonan, J. T. 1986. "Bribery". *Notre Dame Journal of Law, Ethics and Public Policy* 2: 741–72.

Norris, P. 2010. "Measuring governance". In *Sage Handbook of Governance*, M. Bevir (ed.), pp. 411–57. London: Sage.

Norton, R. F. 2012. "OECD Anti-Bribery Convention: a review of global enforcement". London: Norton Rose Fulbright. Available at http://bit.ly/2m7b79k, viewed on 22 November 2016.

Nye, J. S. 1967. "Corruption and political development: a cost-benefit analysis". *American Political Science Review* 61(2): 417–27.

OECD 1997. "OECD Convention on Combating Bribery of Foreign Public Officials in International Business Transactions". Paris: OECD.

OECD 2013. "Glossary of statistical terms". Available at http://bit.ly/2mqs7t8, viewed on 5 December 2016.

OECD 2014. "The rationale for fighting corruption". Report. Paris: CleanGovBiz Initiative. Available at http://bit.ly/2nscP9p, viewed on 14 August 2016.

OECD 2016a. "OECD Convention on Combating Bribery of Foreign Public Officials in International Business Transactions". Paris: OECD. Available at www.oecd.org/corruption/oecdantibriberyconvention.htm, viewed on 21 November 2016.

OECD 2016b. "Country monitoring of the OECD Anti-Bribery Convention". Paris: OECD. Available at http://bit.ly/2m9T9E2, viewed on 22 November 2016.

Olson, M. 1965. *The Logic of Collective Action: Public Goods and the Theory of Groups*. Cambridge, MA: Harvard University Press.

Open Contracting 2016. "About the Open Contracting Partnership". Available at http://www.open-contracting.org/about/, viewed on 29 November 2016.

Open Government Partnership 2016. "What is the Open Government Partnership?" Available at http://www.opengovpartnership.org/about, viewed on 25 November 2016.

Osajda, M. 2012. *The UK Bribery Act of 2010: Whiter the FCPA*. London: Thomson Reuters.

Osborne, H. 2015. "Outright owners of homes outstrip mortgage holders for first time since 80s", *The Guardian*, 25 February. Available at http://bit.ly/2lKe84a, viewed on 6 December 2016.

Overseas Development Institute 2007. "World Governance assessment". Available at http://bit.ly/2mqkdjt, viewed on 6 November 2016.

Pattisson, P. 2014. "Nepal's *Integrity Idol* seeks civil servants with the X factor", *The Guardian*, 11 December. Available on http://bit.ly/2m6WK5a, last viewed on 10 October 2016.

People's Daily Online 2008. "Govt uses SMS to battle corruption", 15 July. Available at http://en.people.cn/90001/6449995.html, viewed on 16 October 2016.

Perry, P. 1997. *Political Corruption and Political Geography*. Aldershot: Ashgate.

Persson, A., B. Rothstein & J. Teorell 2010. "The failure of anti-corruption policies: a theoretical mischaracterization of the problem". Working Paper 19. Gothenburg: Quality of Government Institute.

Persson, A., B. Rothstein & J. Teorell 2013. "Why anticorruption reforms fail-systemic corruption as a collective action problem". *Governance* 26(3): 449–71.

Peters, J. G. & S. Welch 1978. "Political corruption in America: a search for definitions and a theory, or if political corruption is in the mainstream of American politics why is it not in the mainstream of American politics research?" *The American Political Science Review* 72(3): 974–84.

Philp, M. 1997. "Defining political corruption". *Political Studies* 45(3): 436–62.

Philp, M. 2006. "Modelling political corruption in transition". In *Dimensionen politischer Korruption: Beiträge zum Stand der internationalen Forschung*, U. Alemann (ed.), pp. 91–108. Wiesbaden: VS Verlag für Sozialwissenschaften.

Philp, M. & E. Dávid-Barrett 2015. "Realism about political corruption". *Annual Review of Political Science* 18: 387–402.

Pieth, M. 1997. "Contributions of industrialised countries in the prevention of corruption: the example of the OECD". Speech given at the 8th IACC, 7–11 September. Available at http://bit.ly/2magy8z, viewed on 21 November 2016.

Pieth, M. (ed.) 2012. *Collective Action: Innovative Strategies to Prevent Corruption*. St Gallen: Dike Verlag.

PRS Group 2016. "International country risk guide". Available at http://bit.ly/2j8MLy0, viewed on 6 November 2016.

Public Protector of South Africa (PPSA) 2016. "State capture". Report 6. Pretoria: Public Protector of South Africa.

Putnam, R. 1993. *Making Democracy Work: Civic Traditions in Modern Italy*. Princeton, NJ: Princeton University Press.

Putnam, R. 2000. *Bowling Alone: The Collapse and Revival of American Community*. New York: Simon & Schuster.

Quah, J. S. T. 1994. "Controlling corruption in city-states: a comparative study of Hong Kong and Singapore". *Crime, Law and Social Change* 22(4): 391–414.

Quah, J. S. T. 1999. "Comparing anti-corruption measures in Asian countries: lessons to be learnt". *Asian Review of Public Administration* 11(2), July–December: 71–90.

Reinikka, R. & J. Svensson 2003a. "Survey techniques to measure and explain corruption". Report. Washington, DC: World Bank.

Reinikka, R. & J. Svensson 2003b. "The power of information: evidence from a newspaper campaign to reduce capture of public funds". Working Paper. Washington, DC: World Bank, Development Research Group.

Reinikka, R. & J. Svensson 2006. "Using micro-surveys to measure and explain corruption". *World Development* 34(2): 359–70.

Riley, S. 1998. "The political economy of anti-corruption strategies in Africa". In *Corruption and Development*, M. Robinson (ed.). London: Cass.

Robinson, N. & N. Sattar 2012. "When corruption is an emergency: 'good governance' coups and Bangladesh". *Fordham International Law Journal* 35: 737–79.

Rodrik, D. 1995. "Getting interventions right: how South Korea and Taiwan grew rich". *Economic Policy* 20: 53–101.

Rose-Ackerman, S. 1978. *Corruption: A Study in Political Economy*. New York: Academic Press.

Rose-Ackerman, S. 1999. *Corruption and Government: Causes, Consequences and Reform*. Cambridge: Cambridge University Press.

Rose-Ackerman, S. & B. J. Palifka 2016. *Corruption and Government: Causes, Consequences and Reform*, 2nd edn. Cambridge: Cambridge University Press.

Rosenbaum, M. 2010. "Why Tony Blair thinks he was an idiot", *BBC News*. Available at http://bbc.in/2mqBWae, viewed on 1 December 2016.

Ross, S. A. 1973. "The economic theory of agency: the principal's problem". *American Economic Review* 62(2): 134–39.

Rothstein, B. 2011a. "Anti-corruption: the indirect 'big bang' approach". *Review of International Political Economy* 18(2): 228–50.

Rothstein, B. 2011b. *The Quality of Government: Corruption, Social Trust, Inequality in International Perspective*. Chicago, IL: University of Chicago Press.

Rothstein, B. 2014. "What is the opposite of corruption?" *Third World Quarterly* 35(5): 737–52.

Rothstein, B. & J. Teorell 2008. "What is quality of government? A theory of impartial political institutions". *Governance* 21(2): 165–90.

Rowley, C., R. Tollison & G. Tullock (eds) 1989. *The Political Economy of Rent-Seeking*. Boston: Kluwer.

Rubenfeld, S. 2011. "Germany's anti-bribery efforts get high marks from OECD", *The Wall Street Journal*, 23 March. Available at http://on.wsj.com/2m7gipK, viewed on 15 November 2015.

Rucker, P. 2015. "Exxon blocking US progress on energy transparency; watchdog chief", *Business Insider*, 7 December. Available on http://read.bi/2mOEFNj, viewed on 25 November 2016.

Rundquist, B. S., G. S. Strom & J. G. Peters 1977. "Corrupt politicians and their electoral support: some theoretical and empirical observations". *American Political Science Review* 71: 954–63.

Salihu, G. 2012. "Fighting corruption: effective examples from surprising places", OXPOL: The University of Oxford Politics Blog, 26 November. Available at http://bit.ly/2msPRP1, viewed on 8 December 2016.

Sampson, S. 2007. "Can the World Bank do the right thing? When anti-corruption movements become anti-corruption budget lines". Paper presented at the American Anthropological Association Annual Meeting, Washington DC, November 2007. Available at www.lunduniversity.lu.se/o.o.i.s?id=12683&postid=1146197, viewed on 5 November 2016.

Sampson, S. 2008. "Corruption and anti-corruption in South-East Europe: landscapes and sites". In *Governments, NGOs and Anti-Corruption: The New Integrity Warriors*, L. de Sousa, P. Larmour and B. Hindess (eds). London: Routledge.

Sampson, S. 2010. "Diagnostics: indicators and transparency in the anti-corruption industry". In *Transparenz: multidisziplinaere Durchsichten durch Phoenomene und Theorien des Undurchsichtigen*, S. Jansen, E. Schroeter and N. Stehr (eds), pp. 97–111. Wiesbaden: VS Verlag.

Sawer, P. & L. Donnelly 2015. "Meet the NHS whistle-blowers who exposed the truth", *Daily Telegraph*, 11 February. Available at http://bit.ly/16D7sbq, viewed on 17 January 2017.

Schiller, C. 2000. "Improving governance and fighting corruption: an IMF perspective". Report. Washington, DC: IMF. Available at http://bit.ly/2o1bvMj, accessed 22 November 2016.

Scott, I. 2011. "The Hong Kong ICAC's approach to corruption control". In *Handbook of Global Research and Practice in Corruption*, A. Graycar and R. Smith (eds). Cheltenham: Elgar.

Scott, J. C. 1969. "The analysis of corruption in developing nations". *Comparative Studies in Society and History* 11(3): 315–41.

Select Committee on Home Affairs 2002. "Memorandum submitted by Public Concern at Work". Appendix 8 (Appendices to the Minutes of Evidence), February. London: UK Parliament. Available at http://bit.ly/2n6vLLU, viewed on 7 December 2016.

Shleifer, A. & R. W. Vishny 1993. "Corruption". *Quarterly Journal of Economics* 108(3): 599–617.

Sidhu, K. 2009. "Anti-corruption compliance standards in the aftermath of the Siemens scandal". *German Law Journal* 10(8): 1343–54 .

Smarzynska, B. K. & S.-J. Wei 2002. "Corruption and cross-border investment: firm-level evidence". Working Paper W7969. Cambridge, MA: NBER.

Smart, A. 1993. "Gifts, bribes, and Guanxi: a reconsideration of Bourdieu's social capital". *Cultural Anthropology* 8(3): 388–408.

Smith, A. 1776. *An Inquiry into the Nature and Causes of the Wealth of Nations*. London: W. Strahan & T. Cadell.

Smith, G. 2015. "Kenyatta vows to act on corruption", *The Herald*, 24 November, p.12.

Smith, W. D. 2009. "Corruption and eighteenth-century social science: mapping the space of political economy". *Studies in Eighteenth-Century Culture* 38: 261–76.

Sparling, R. 2015. "Political corruption and the concept of dependence in Republican thought". *Political Theory* 41(4): 618–47.

Spence, P. 2015. "VW emissions scandal; what's it all about?" *Daily Telegraph*, 4 November. Available at http://bit.ly/1NHwTxa, viewed on 16 October 2016.

Spiegel, Der 2007. "Wolfowitz resigns", *Spiegel Online*, 18 May. Available at http://bit.ly/2mamq1x, viewed on 22 November 2016.

Stephenson, M. 2014a. "Mauro (1995) does NOT show that corruption slows growth", *GAB: The Global Anticorruption Blog*. Available at http://bit.ly/2m7cOUg, viewed on 4 December 2016.

Stephenson, M. 2014b. "A regional anti-corruption convention in the Asia-Pacific?" GAB: The Global Anti-Corruption Blog. Available at http://bit.ly/2mas6Zd, viewed on 23 November 2016.

Stephenson, M. 2014c. "Klitgaard's misleading 'corruption formula'", GAB: The Global Anticorruption Blog, 27 May. Available at http://bit.ly/2n6EzBe, viewed on 13 November 2016.

Stephenson, M. 2015. "Some slightly sarcastic, semi-serious suggestions for improving anticorruption conferences", GAB: The Global Anticorruption Blog, 8 September. Available at http://bit.ly/2mP1As3, viewed on 16 November 2016.

Stephenson, M. 2016. "Does an FCPA violation require a quid pro quo? Further developments in the JP Morgan 'Sons & Daughters' case", GAB: The Global Anticorruption Blog. Available at http://bit.ly/2m7pAlT, viewed on 28 November 2016.

Stom, S. 2012. "Websites shine light on petty bribery worldwide", *The New York Times*, 6 March.

Stromseth, J. R., E. J. Malesky & D. Gueorguiev 2017. *China's Governance Puzzle*. Cambridge: Cambridge University Press.

Supreme Court of the United States 2005. Garcetti *et al.* v. Ceballos. Washington, DC: Certiorari to the United States Court of Appeals for the Ninth Circuit, No 04-473.

Svensson, J. 2005. "Eight questions about corruption". *Journal of Economic Perspectives* 19(3), 19–42.

Swaleheen, M. 2011. "Economic growth and endogenous corruption: an empirical study". *Public Choice* 146: 23–41.

Tanzi, V. 1994. "Corruption, government activities and markets". Working Paper 94/99. Washington, DC: IMF.

Tanzi, V. 1998. "Corruption around the world: causes, consequences, scope and cures". Working Paper 98/63. Washington, DC: IMF.

Tanzi, V. 2000. *Policies, Institutions and the Dark Side of Economics*. Cheltenham: Elgar.

TheyWorkForYou 2016a. "Register of members' interests: Diane Abbott MP". Available at http://bit.ly/2nmvCjn, viewed on 26 November 2016.

TheyWorkForYou 2016b. "Register of members' interests: David Davis MP". Available at http://bit.ly/2mIHVK2, viewed on 25 November 2016.

TheyWorkForYou 2016c. "Register of members' interests: Daniel Kawczynski MP". Available at http://bit.ly/2n6MaQh, viewed on 25 November 2016.

Thomas, M. 2010. "What do the Worldwide Governance Indicators measure". *European Journal of Development of Research* 22(1): 31–54.

Thompson, J. 2000. *Political Scandal: Power and Visibility in the Media Age*. Cambridge: Polity.

Thompson, T. & A. Shah 2005. "Transparency International's corruption perceptions index: whose perceptions are they anyway". Report. Washington, DC: World Bank.

Toobin, J. 2016. "The supreme court gets ready to legalize corruption", *The New Yorker*, 4 May. Available at http://bit.ly/1TKJ2Rp, viewed on 3 December 2016.

Trace International 2016. "Shipping and maritime initiative". Available at www.traceinternational.org/shipping/, viewed on 25 November 2016.

Transparency International 2011. "Bribe Payers Index". Available at www.transparency.org/bpi2011, viewed on 27 October 2016.

Transparency International 2013a. "Corruption Perceptions Index". Available at www.transparency.org/cpi2013/results, viewed on 15 October 2016.

Transparency International 2013b. "Global Corruption Barometer". Available at www.transparency.org/gcb2013/countries, viewed on 6 November 2016.

Transparency International 2013c. "Global Corruption Barometer (United Kingdom)". Available at http://bit.ly/1eRDkWu, viewed on 16 October 2016.

Transparency International 2013d. "UNCAC review mechanism: up and running but urgently needing improvement". Report. Available at http://bit.ly/2mIGhYw, viewed on 21 November 2016.

Transparency International 2015a. "Exporting corruption". Available at www.transparency.org/exporting_corruption/, viewed in 21 November 2016.

Transparency International 2015b. "Financial statements". Available at http://bit.ly/2nmg5Ai, viewed on 24 October 2016.

Transparency International 2016a. "Bribe Payers Index (overview)". Available at http://bit.ly/2mOPGhW, viewed on 27 October 2016.

Transparency International 2016b. "Corruption Perceptions Index 2015". Available at www.transparency.org/cpi2015/, viewed on 24 October 2016.

Transparency International 2016c. "FAQs on corruption". Available at http://bit.ly/2mJ1L7T, viewed on 16 September 2016.

Transparency International 2016d. "Global Corruption Barometer (overview)". Available at http://bit.ly/18SKsXh, viewed on 27 October 2016.

Transparency International 2016e. "What is corruption?" Available at http://bit. ly/2hk4wqT, viewed on 5 December 2016.

Transparency International 2016f. "Methodology". Available at http://bit.ly/1Sm3Yyj, viewed on 24 October 2016.

Transparency International 2016g. "People and corruption: Europe and Central Asia". Report. Berlin: Transparency International. Available at www.transparency.org/ whatwedo/publication/7493, viewed on 2 January 2017.

Transparency International 2017. "Corruption Perceptions Index 2016". Available at http://bit.ly/2jo7lKy, viewed on 12 February 2017

Treisman, D. 2007. "What have we learned about the causes of corruption from ten years of cross-national empirical research?" *Annual Review of Political Science* 10: 211–44.

Tukur, S. 2016. "How Nigerians can make money, be protected in new whistle blowing policy – Finance Minister", *Premium Times*, 21 December 2016. Available at http:// bit.ly/2nrqNIl, viewed on 25 March 2017.

Turner, C. 2016. "Whistleblowers being 'blacklisted by NHS' as staff records state they were 'dismissed' even after being cleared at tribunal", *Daily Telegraph*, 20 August. Available at http://bit.ly/2b9poAk, viewed on 17 January 2017.

Ugur, M. & N. Dasgupta 2011. "Evidence on the economic growth impacts of corruption in low-income countries and beyond: a systematic review". Systematic Review. London: EPPI-Centre, Social Science Research Unit, Institute of Education, University of London.

UK Government 2010. "Eric Pickles 'shows us the money'". News Story, 12 August. Available at http://bit.ly/2lKPm3Z, viewed on 16 October 2016.

UK Government 2014. "United Kingdom anti-corruption plan". Policy Paper. Available at http://bit.ly/1w2Zygy, viewed on 17 August 2016.

UK Government 2015. "UK anti-corruption plan: progress update". Policy Paper. Available at http://bit.ly/2mqVoE0, viewed on 29 November 2016.

United Nations 1996. "General Assembly Declaration against Corruption and Bribery in International Commercial Transactions". Document A/RES/51/191. New York: United Nations. Available at www.un.org/documents/ga/res/51/a51r191.htm, viewed on 20 November 2016.

Uslaner, E. 2008. *Corruption, Inequality and the Rule of Law*. Cambridge: Cambridge University Press.

Uslaner, E. 2013. "Trust and corruption revisited: how and why trust and corruption shape each other". *Quality and Quantity: International Journal of Methodology* 47(6): 3603–8.

van Heerde-Hudson, J. (ed.) 2014. *The Political Costs of the 2009 British MPs' Expenses Scandal*. London: Palgrave Macmillan.

Vigen, T. 2015. *Spurious Correlations*. New York: Hachette.

Vitou, B. & Kovalevsky, R. 2013. "Botched bribery attempt results in Bribery Act conviction no. 3 for son of Chinese foreign public official", *thebriberyact.com*. Available at http://bit.ly/2m3Y1hO, viewed on 28 November 2016.

Vitou, B. & Kovalevsky, R. 2016. "Opinion: DPAs must show greater benefits", *thebriberyact.com*. Available at http://bit.ly/1MhKP0N, viewed on 28 November 2016.

Wall Street Journal, The 2014. "'Rule of law' or 'rule by law'? In China, a preposition makes all the difference", 20 October.

Walton, G. 2013. "Is all corruption dysfunctional? Perceptions of corruption and its consequences in Papua New Guinea". *Public Administration and Development* 33(3): 175–190.

Walton, G. 2016. "A critic's guide to anti-corruption conferences", DevPolicy Blog, 11 August. Available at http://bit.ly/2mPngUZ, viewed on 17 November 2016.

Walton, G. W. & A. Jones 2016. "Subnational collective action in Papua New Guinea". Paper presented at the American Political Science Association Annual Meeting, Philadelphia, 1–4 September 2016.

Watson, B. 2013. "Siemens and the battle against bribery", *The Guardian*, 18 September. Available at http://bit.ly/2mPbzh0, viewed on 8 November 2015.

Wedeman, A. 2012. *Double Paradox: Rapid Growth and Rising Corruption in China.* Ithaca, NY: Cornell University Press.

Werlin, H. 1973. "The consequences of corruption: the Ghanaian experience". *Political Science Quarterly* 88(1): 71–85.

Wintour, P. 2016. "Overseas territories spared from UK law on company registers", *The Guardian*, 12 April. Available at http://bit.ly/25ZKjuI, viewed on 8 December 2016.

Wolfensohn, J. D. 1996. "Annual meeting address". Washington, DC: World Bank. Available at http://bit.ly/1JgWvyU, viewed on 22 November 2016.

Wolfowitz, P. 2005. "Good governance and development: a time for action". Speech in Jakarta, Indonesia, 11 April. Available at http://bit.ly/2mJaW87, viewed on 22 November 2016.

World Bank 1997. "Helping countries combat corruption: the role of the World Bank". Report. Washington, DC: World Bank. Available at http://bit.ly/2b4hOnV, viewed on 5 December 2016.

World Bank 2012. "Georgia's fight against corruption in public services wins praise". Press Release. Available at http://bit.ly/2o94dTm, viewed on 25 March, 2017.

World Bank 2013. "Investment project financing implementation support guidance note". Washington, DC: World Bank.

World Bank Independent Evaluation Group 2009. "Review of IDA internal controls: an evaluation of management's assessment and the IAD review". Washington, DC: World Bank.

Worldwide Governance Indicators 2016a. "What is governance?" Available at http://bit.ly/1rwwuAb, viewed on 4 November 2016.

Worldwide Governance Indicators 2016b. "WGI data sources". Available at http://bit.ly/2c7UrKf, viewed on 4 November 2016.

World Values Survey 2016. Available at www.worldvaluessurvey.org/, viewed on 6 November 2016.

Worthy, B. 2013. "Where are the armchair auditors?" *Open Data Institute*, 1 June. Available at https://theodi.org/blog/guest-blog-where-are-armchair-auditors, viewed on 16 October 2016.

Wraith, R. & E. Simpkins 1963. *Corruption in Developing Countries.* St Leonards, NSW: Allen & Unwin.

Wright, R. 2015. "Apprentice jockey Egan faces corruption ban", *The Times*, 24 November.

Wrong, M. 2010. *It's Our Turn to Eat.* London: Fourth Estate.

Xinsheng, Q. 2016. "China's hunting for corrupt fugitives is justifiable", *China Daily*. Available at http://bit.ly/2ndlf2b, viewed on 7 December 2016.

Yan, Z. 2016. "China, ASEAN to bring officials to justice", *China Daily*, 3 November. Available at http://bit.ly/2mINsjN, viewed on 23 November 2016.

Yi, Z. Yi & Z. Yan 2015. "Mobile app joins toolbox in anti-corruption effort", *China Watch*, 21 July. Available at http://bit.ly/2m7kbev, viewed on 16 October 2016.

Yinan, Z. 2012. "Xi pledges to implement rule of law", *China Daily*, 5 December. Available at http://bit.ly/2m7tYkC, viewed on 30 November 2016.

Zakiuddin, A. (n.d.). *Corruption in Bangladesh: An Analytical and Sociological Study*. Dhaka: TI Bangladesh.

Zapotosky, M., R. S. Helderman & L. Vozzella 2014. "Jonnie Williams had unusual influence over McDonnell's office, Cabinet member says", *Washington Post*, 7 August.

Zhong, N. 2010. "The causes, consequences and cures of corruption: a review of issues". Working Paper. Hong Kong: Chinese University of Hong Kong. Available at http://bit.ly/2naaeSg, accessed on 7 December 2011.

Index